James Candish

The Kingdom of God

Biblically and Historically Considered

James Candish

The Kingdom of God
Biblically and Historically Considered

ISBN/EAN: 9783743397545

Manufactured in Europe, USA, Canada, Australia, Japa

Cover: Foto ©Lupo / pixelio.de

Manufactured and distributed by brebook publishing software (www.brebook.com)

James Candish

The Kingdom of God

THE KINGDOM OF GOD

BIBLICALLY AND HISTORICALLY CONSIDERED.

The Tenth Series of the Cunningham Lectures.

BY

JAMES S. CANDLISH, D.D.,
PROFESSOR OF THEOLOGY, FREE CHURCH COLLEGE, GLASGOW.

EDINBURGH:
T. & T. CLARK, 38 GEORGE STREET.
1884.

EXTRACT DECLARATION OF TRUST.

MARCH 1, 1862.

I, WILLIAM BINNY WEBSTER, late Surgeon in the H.E.I.C.S., presently residing in Edinburgh,—Considering that I feel deeply interested in the success of the Free Church College, Edinburgh, and am desirous of advancing the Theological Literature of Scotland, and for this end to establish a Lectureship similar to those of a like kind connected with the Church of England and the Congregational body in England, and that I have made over to the General Trustees of the Free Church of Scotland the sum of £2000 sterling, in trust, for the purpose of founding a Lectureship in memory of the late Reverend William Cunningham, D.D., Principal of the Free Church College, Edinburgh, and Professor of Divinity and Church History therein, and under the following conditions, namely,—*First*, The Lectureship shall bear the name, and be called, 'The Cunningham Lectureship.' *Second*, The Lecturer shall be a Minister or Professor of the Free Church of Scotland, and shall hold the appointment for not less than two years, nor more than three years, and be entitled for the period of his holding the appointment to the income of the endowment as declared by the General Trustees, it being understood that the Council after referred to may occasionally appoint a Minister or Professor from other denominations, provided this be approved of by not fewer than Eight Members of the Council, and it being further understood that the Council are to regulate the terms of payment of the Lecturer. *Third*, The Lecturer shall be at liberty to choose his own subject within the range of Apologetical, Doctrinal, Controversial, Exegetical, Pastoral, or Historical Theology, including what bears on Missions, Home and Foreign, subject to the consent of the Council. *Fourth*, The Lecturer shall be bound to deliver publicly at Edinburgh a Course of Lectures on the subjects thus chosen at some time immediately preceding the expiry of his appointment, and during the Session of the New College, Edinburgh; the Lectures to be not fewer than six in number, and to be delivered in presence of the Professors and Students under such arrangements as the Council may appoint; the Lecturer shall be bound also to print and publish, at his own risk, not fewer than 750 copies of the Lectures within a year after their delivery, and to deposit three copies of the same in the Library of the New College; the form of the publication shall be regulated by the Council. *Fifth*, A Council shall be constituted, consisting of (first) Two Members of their own body, to be chosen annually in the month of March, by the Senatus of the New College, other than the Principal; (second) Five Members to be chosen annually by the General Assembly, in addition to the Moderator of the said Free Church of Scotland; together with (third) the Principal of the said New College for the time being, the Moderator of the said General Assembly for the time being, the Procurator or Law Adviser of the Church, and myself the said William Binny Webster, or such person as I may nominate to be my successor: the Principal of the said College to be Convener of the Council, and any Five Members duly convened to be entitled to act notwithstanding the non-election of others. *Sixth*, The duties of the Council shall be the following :—(first), To appoint the Lecturer and determine the period of his holding the appointment, the appointment to be made before the close of the Session of College immediately preceding the termination of the previous Lecturer's engagement; (second), To arrange details as to the delivery of the Lectures, and to take charge of any additional income and expenditure of an incidental kind that may be connected therewith, it being understood that the obligation upon the Lecturer is simply to deliver the Course of Lectures free of expense to himself. *Seventh*, The Council shall be at liberty, on the expiry of five years, to make any alteration that experience may suggest as desirable in the details of this plan, provided such alterations shall be approved of by not fewer than Eight Members of the Council.

CONTENTS.

LECTURE I.

THE KINGDOM OF GOD THE DESIRE OF ALL NATIONS.

	PAGE
Introductory,	1–14
Patriarchal Society,	14–19
Ancient Oriental Empires,	19–22
Greek Commonwealths,	22–29
Greek Philosophy,	29–33
The Roman Empire and Law,	33–36
Failure of all these efforts,	36–45

LECTURE II.

THE KINGDOM OF GOD IN THE OLD TESTAMENT.

Its Beginning at the Exodus,	49–52
Its real Nature,	53–57
How far realized in Israel,	58–63
Its apparent Failure but lasting Effects,	64–67
Prophecy of a better Kingdom of God,	67–78
Return from the Exile,	78–83
The Theocracy and the Law,	83–88

SUPPLEMENT TO LECTURE II.

POST-CANONICAL JEWISH LITERATURE.

Wisdom of Ben Sirach,	89–91
Baruch,	91, 92
1 Maccabees,	92–94
Pharisees and Sadducees,	95–97
Psalms of Solomon,	97–104
Wisdom of Solomon,	104, 105

CONTENTS.

	PAGE
Apocalyptic Literature,	106–110
Sibylline Oracles,	110–114
Book of Enoch,	114, 115
John the Baptist,	115–117

LECTURE III.

THE KINGDOM OF GOD IN THE TEACHING OF CHRIST.

His initial Proclamation,	121–123
Nature of the Kingdom He proclaimed,	123–142
Its Blessings spiritual,	121–134
To be enjoyed in Affliction,	131–134
Way of entering the Kingdom,	135–138
The Kingdom a Vital Power compared to Seed,	138–142
The Righteousness of the Kingdom of God,	143–154
Its Inwardness; Brotherly Love and Forgiveness,	144–148
Its Universality,	148–154
Jesus the King of God's Kingdom, Son of God, and Son of Man,	154–159
His present Rule,	159–164
His Coming again to Judgment,	164–167

SUPPLEMENT TO LECTURE III.

THE KINGDOM OF GOD IN THE TEACHING OF THE APOSTLES.

Epistle to the Hebrews,	168, 169
Peter,	170, 171
James,	171
Views of the original Apostles,	172–174
Views of Paul,	174–180
Why the Kingdom is less prominent in the Epistles than in Jesus' Teaching,	180–185
The Kingdom of God in the Apocalypse,	185–189

LECTURE IV.

DOCTRINAL IDEA OF THE KINGDOM OF GOD.

Distinctively and comprehensively Christian,	193–195
Leading Sayings of Christ,	195, 196
Definition proposed,	197
Really established by Christ,	198–200
Relation of the Kingdom of God to the Church,	200–208
A Fellowship of Men with God,	209–216
Its Motive Power that of a New Life,	216, 217

CONTENTS.

	PAGE
The Holy Spirit,	217–219
The Kingdom established by Redeeming Love,	219–224
Confirmation of this from Views of *Ecce Homo* and Ritschl,	224–231

LECTURE V.

ATTEMPTS TO REALIZE THE KINGDOM OF GOD IN THE PAST.

Views of the Early Fathers,	235–242
Rise of the Idea and Reality of the Catholic Church,	242–249
Conversion of the Empire and Constantine's Policy,	249–252
Rise of the Papacy,	252–258
The Holy Roman Empire,	259, 260
Imperial and Papal Theories,	260–267
Failure of these and Protests against them,	267–270
Forerunners of the Reformation,	270–274
The Humanists,	274–277
The Reformation,	277–279
The Anabaptists,	279–283
The Lutheran Church,	283–287
Views of Zwingli,	287–289
Calvin and the System of Alliance of Church and State,	287–293
Views of the English Puritans,	293–298

LECTURE VI.

THE KINGDOM OF GOD IN RELATION TO MODERN SOCIAL IDEALS.

Systems that rely on Human Power,	302–309
Democratic Socialism,	303–306
Its Relation to Christianity,	306–309
Systems that rely on Natural Laws,	309–320
Philosophy of the *Aufklärung*,	311–314
Philosophy of Kant,	314–318
Political Economy and its Hopes,	318–320
Systems that rely on Divine Grace,	321–343
Roman Catholic Doctrine,	321
Theory of Identity of Church and State,	321–326
Theory of Alliance of Church and State,	327–330
Theory of Absolute Separation of Church and State,	330–334
Millennialism,	335–339
Conclusion,	339–343

APPENDIX.

NOTES TO LECTURE I.

	PAGE
A. The Kingdom of God in Modern Theological Literature,	347–350
B. Theocratic Ideas in the Ancient Oriental Empires,	350, 351
C. Plato's Relation to the Athenian Democracy,	352, 353
D. Philosophical Basis of Roman Law,	353–355
E. Naturalism and Pessimism,	355–357

NOTES TO LECTURE II.

F. On the Phrase "Kingdom of Priests,"	357–360
G. On the Early Religion of Israel,	360–362
H. Views of the Kingdom of God in the Psalms,	362–365
I. The Doctrine of a Suffering Messiah in the Old Testament,	365–368
J. The Teaching of John the Baptist on the Kingdom of God,	368–371

NOTES TO LECTURE III.

K. On the Phrase "Kingdom of Heaven,"	371–375
L. The Kingdom in Jesus' Teaching a Present Reality,	376–380
M. Jesus' Last Controversy with the Jews,	380–385
N. Jesus' Teaching as to His Coming again,	385–387
O. The Notion of the City of God,	388–390

NOTES TO LECTURE IV.

P. On Luke xvii. 20, 21,	390–392
Q. Definitions of the Kingdom of God,	392–396
R. Views of the Relation of the Church to the Kingdom of God,	396–405
S. The Doctrine of Atonement implied in the Kingdom of God,	405, 406

NOTES TO LECTURE V.

T. The Kingdom of God in the Writings of the Early Fathers,	406–409
U. Augustine on the City of God,	409–415
V. Toleration in connection with Attempts to realize the Kingdom of God,	415–420

NOTE TO LECTURE VI.

W. On the System of Alliance of Church and State,	420–423

LECTURE I.

THE KINGDOM OF GOD THE DESIRE OF ALL NATIONS.

Acts xvii. 26.—" He made of one every nation of men for to dwell on all the face of the earth, having determined their appointed seasons and the bounds of their habitation ; that they should seek God, if haply they might feel after him, and find him, though he is not far from each one of us."

Daniel ii. 43, 44.—" And whereas thou sawest iron mixed with miry clay, they shall mingle themselves with the seed of men : but they shall not cleave one to another, even as iron is not mixed with clay. And in the days of these kings shall the God of heaven set up a kingdom, which shall never be destroyed : and the kingdom shall not be left to other people, but it shall break in pieces and consume all these kingdoms, and it shall stand for ever."

LECTURE I.

THE KINGDOM OF GOD THE DESIRE OF ALL NATIONS.

NO one can read attentively many modern theological works, without observing that the kingdom of God occupies a much more prominent place in them than it had in the writings of former times. This is partly due to the fact, that scholars of the present day are more careful to preserve the genuine historical ideas of other ages and peoples, instead of casting them into the forms or moulds of later thought. Hence, as the kingdom or reign of God was undoubtedly the leading idea of the prophets of Israel and of our Lord himself, the historical spirit of study leads men to consider their teaching as centring in that, rather than in the more modern ideas of religion, incarnation, atonement, the Church, or the like. But it is not only in treatises on the history of Israel, or on prophecy, or on the teaching and life of Jesus, that we find the kingdom of God made a leading subject of consideration; it plays as important a part in the best modern works on Christian doctrine and Christian ethics. This shows that the interest in the idea is not merely an historical one; but that it is felt by many to be of great importance, even in the present day, for the right understanding of Christian truth and Christian duty. It is not merely an old Jewish form of thought, which it is useful to study for the elucidation of the Biblical literature, but which as a form of conceiving Christianity may be superseded by more abstract or philosophical notions; it is regarded by many as the most natural and adequate conception that we can take to guide us in forming a system of Christian theology. Further, this notion of the kingdom of God has not merely a speculative but a practical bearing; it is an idea that craves to be realized in fact, or rather, it is not merely an idea, but a great reality, which has not yet fully attained its perfection, but in the perfecting of which men's help and labour may and should be employed.

Yet, though on these accounts the subject of the kingdom of God has deservedly gained a prominent place in modern theological thought, it has not to any great extent been made matter of express and systematic study for itself, and it is to be feared that to many minds the term conveys only a very indefinite meaning, or that it may not be always understood in the same sense. Though it has been habitually used by Christians in all ages, its occurrence in the Lord's Prayer of itself having assured that, it has not had its sense cleared and defined by theological discussion like so many other Christian phrases; and in its practical aspect, we need only recall in the most hasty manner the history of Christendom, to be aware in how many various forms the kingdom of God has been expected or attempted to be set up. Such phrases as, the Millennial Reign, the City of God, the Holy Catholic Church, the Holy Roman Empire, the Fifth Monarchy, Christ's Crown and Covenant, the Christian State, are some of the historical expressions that the idea has had, whether as devout imaginations or as stern practical applications. How these various forms of realizing the kingdom of God arose, how far each of them deviated from Christ's institution and design, and what is the true way in which that design is to be carried out, are questions that suggest inquiries full of interest and instruction.[1]

There seems, therefore, to be a need and prospect of usefulness in a discussion of the kingdom of God, which I propose to consider in these lectures in its Biblical and historical aspect. The central part of the whole inquiry must be the question, What was that kingdom that Jesus proclaimed and founded? but for the understanding of his teaching about it, it will be necessary first to consider what had been said and done in Old Testament times in regard to the kingdom of God, and what was the ideas of those to whom Jesus spoke; and it may also be useful to inquire what desires and longings for a perfect society had appeared in the heathen world as unsatisfied cravings that were to be satisfied in Christianity. Then the true meaning and bearing of our Lord's teaching may be more clearly brought out, if we follow the investigation of the kingdom of God in the New Testament with a historical survey of the different ways in which it has been understood, or misunderstood, and attempted to be realized, in after ages. This may enable us to see what practically the kingdom of God is now, and how it is to be promoted. For our inquiry cannot stop with the teaching of Christ. If we wish to under-

[1] See Appendix, Note A.

stand, not merely the truths he taught about the kingdom, but the kingdom itself which he founded, we must consider the historical results of his work.

The kingdom of God is, as I have already said, and as will appear more fully in the sequel, the name by which our Lord himself habitually spoke of his work. It is not, indeed, the only name he gave to that work; he spoke of it also as the saving that which was lost, the bearing witness to the truth, the giving eternal life; and some of these expressions have formed the basis of conceptions of Christianity that have been more systematically studied than that of the kingdom of God; but this last is that which he most frequently uses, and comprehends all the rest. It has this also to distinguish it from the others, that it describes an aim that is not yet fully realized. When we think of Christ's work as a salvation of the lost soul, we find that, in the case of multitudes, to be an accomplished fact; the believer in Jesus has received forgiveness, peace with God, and new spiritual and eternal life. So, when we think of it as a revelation of truth, or the introduction of a new and perfect religion, we see that already done by the work of Christ to which nothing remains to be added. On that very account these conceptions may be better fitted to be dogmas in a system of theology than the more comprehensive idea of the kingdom of God. For that describes a thing that in its perfection is not yet realized, and shall not be till the end of the world. It is an idea that brings in the social element of Christianity, and that can only be made a perfect reality when Christianity has been fully developed, *i.e.* when all the saved have been gathered out of the world and united to Christ. The other notions by which we think of Christ's work, as the salvation of the soul, the revealing the perfect religion, giving a new life, may be fully realized in the experience of any single soul already; but the kingdom of God is a world-historical thing, covering ages with its growth, and coming gradually in the course of these to perfection. It is a thing at the realization of which all Christians are called to labour, and it is important to understand its true form and nature; because many attempts have been made to realize it, which have been partial, mistaken, or premature.

Further, as expressed in this great idea, Christ's work is one of a series of efforts that have been made or designed by the greatest minds in many lands, for the elevation and amelioration of mankind. It is the idea of a commonwealth in which humanity is to attain its perfection; and this has been the aim of all the noblest legislators, statesmen, and philosophers. Many different schemes have been imagined in speculation, or proposed in practice, for this end; and these have been anticipations and unconscious prophecies, or competitors and rivals, of the real and perfect kingdom of God set up by Christ. The consideration of the more outstanding ideal states, that have been sketched by philosophers, or attempted to be realized by legislators, may be useful as indicating the reality and greatness of the need that is met by the proclamation of the kingdom of God, and also as bringing out by comparison and contrast its real nature. We may see how far those who aimed at such Utopias were working in the right line, and what led to the failure of their schemes; and thus we may learn what are the conditions of the problem to be solved, and the difficulties to be surmounted by any successful attempt to unite men in a right moral society, and to gather all men into one. We shall be able in the light of those things better to understand Christ's design and work; and we shall find that some of the ideals and actual attempts of men after a perfect state have exercised an influence on the way in which the Christian kingdom of God has been conceived and sought to be realized. Not only have Old Testament ideas often been carried over without due discrimination to New Testament times; but the principles of the Platonic Republic, and even of the Roman Empire, have more or less unconsciously been allowed to influence men's ideas of the Christian society, and their measures for its realization.

I shall endeavour therefore, treating the subject historically, to take into account, not only the preparation for the Christian idea of the kingdom of God in the line of God's special revelation to Israel, but also those aims and ideas of other nations that partially strove after the same end, and that came afterwards into contact, for good or evil, with the carrying out of Christ's ideal and aim.

There are further questions in regard to the kingdom of God that are both interesting and important, bearing on its relation to the doctrines of Christianity, what other truths it implies as its presuppositions and foundations on the one hand, and as its consequences or corollaries on the other; and how far it is fitted to be a central idea round which the various doctrines of the Christian system may be grouped, or to throw light on any of them. It is, we believe, capable of many such applications with great advantage; but these are all questions belonging to the province of dogmatic or systematic theology; and to enter on a discussion of them without a solid basis having been previously laid on Biblical investigation, would be to build without a foundation on what might prove to be mere shifting sand. If we are assured that the kingdom of God as Christ conceived it is a reality, and if we understand its nature aright; then, when we consider what other views as to God and man and the world are implied in it, we are pursuing an investigation of realities that are sure and firmly established, and so what we ascertain may be of great value: but if the idea of the kingdom be a mere temporary form in which Christ's work has been clothed; then in making it a basis for theological inference or construction we may be merely forming a logical system around an arbitrarily chosen notion. The Biblical study of the subject must therefore precede the dogmatic; though if the former be fruitful, it may and should be followed up by the latter, to gather and arrange its fruits. But the Biblical inquiry is itself so large and important as fully to occupy these lectures; and the theological working out of its results must be left unattempted here. This limitation of scope is all the more necessary, because the Biblical inquiry must be regarded, in the light of a true idea of Scripture, as essentially historical; and therefore including or requiring, for its full prosecution, a study of the history of the notion of the kingdom of

God before and since the coming of Christ. Biblical theology is, strictly speaking, a branch of historical theology, and to be successful must be historical in its nature and method. The aim, therefore, of these lectures will be to pursue a historical inquiry as to the origin, import, and practical use of the Christian idea of the kingdom of God.

As the investigation is historical and mainly Biblical, it is clearly impossible to give at the outset any full definition or description of the kingdom of God : that must be the result of inquiry, and cannot be assumed as its basis. Yet, in order to guide us in the general direction of our inquiry, we may fairly take for granted, what even a first view of the use of the term in Scripture shows, that it denotes in general the Christian ideal of human society. What is the precise nature of that ideal must be gathered from a study of the Christian records and institutions in the light of the historical causes that led to them. Now the preparation for Christianity was twofold, in heathendom and in Israel, the former being mainly, though not exclusively, negative, and the latter mainly, but not entirely, positive. In the Gentile world men and nations were suffered to walk in their own ways, that they might feel after God and find him, who is not far from any one of us, and has never left himself without a witness. Their preparation for a city or kingdom of God consisted mainly in the wants and longings awakened by the failure of earthly cities and kingdoms, making them ready to welcome one from above. But theirs was not entirely a negative preparation for Christianity: there were also elements, though comparatively few, of a more positive kind;

ideas and principles were reached by heathen thinkers, without which Christianity would have been defective or distorted. In Israel, again, there was a theistic and ethical religion, which gave men, by divine teaching, the main foundation-principles of Christianity, and a promise that gave firm and unquenchable hopes for the future. But the preparation for Christianity by Judaism was not all positive, since in a very important aspect of it the law was a schoolmaster to Christ, producing a sense of sin that men might be shut up to faith in the Saviour.

Both of these lines of preparation have therefore a right to be considered, with a view to understand the historical meaning and relations of the Christian kingdom of God. Had the relation of either been purely negative, it might have been left out of account without any positive loss, though even then it might have been considered with interest and advantage ; but if in any degree, however small, Gentile thought and experience contributed positive elements to Christianity, these cannot be neglected without the danger of an imperfect understanding of its history. It is certain that philosophical and political ideas derived from the Gentile world have largely influenced the theology and organization of the Christian Church ; so that however little a study of heathen thought on this subject may contribute positively to the comprehension of New Testament Christianity, it is a necessary preliminary to the appreciation of its later forms and development. Whether, for example, Platonism had any appreciable influence on the theology of the apostles, may be a fair question ; but we cannot understand that of the Fathers without taking into account its history and tendency. So too, as has been recently shown, the organization of the primitive Church has been formed partly after Gentile as well as Jewish types.[1] If thus we are entitled or even required to trace the efforts, ideas, and hopes of a perfect human society, without as well as within the bounds of the Hebrew race, which we believe to have been the object of a more direct divine training than any other; it will be natural and suitable to begin with the Gentile preparation for Christianity, and then proceed to the more special Jewish one.

I propose in the remaining part of this lecture to consider the efforts and longings in the Gentile world after a perfect society, which show the kingdom of God to be the desire of all nations.[2]

Then in the second lecture I will consider the preparation in Israel for the kingdom of God, or the national theocracy of the Old Testament and its prophecies of a universal kingdom of God.

The subject of the third will be the teaching of Jesus Christ as to the kingdom of God, which he came to proclaim and to found.

In the fourth it will be my endeavour to bring out as clearly as possible, in a doctrinal form, what the kingdom of God, thus prepared for and introduced into the world, really is.

In the fifth lecture I propose to take a survey of the history of the kingdom of God, so as to observe the

---

[1] See Hatch, *Organization of the Early Christian Church.* Rivingtons, 1881.

[2] I am aware that this is not a correct rendering of Hag. ii. 7, and I do not use it as such, but simply as a happy and appropriate expression for an idea that is true and scriptural.

chief forms in which it has been attempted to be realized.

Lastly, in the sixth lecture I shall consider the practical question how the kingdom of God is to be realized, and compare this as the Christian ideal with other social ideals of the present day.

Such is the general plan that I propose to follow in the discussion of this subject. It is one that embraces a very wide field, even though I leave out of view some aspects of it that are important and interesting. I cannot profess to deal thoroughly or at first hand with the materials of more than the Biblical, and particularly the New Testament inquiry, though I have thought it desirable for the right understanding of these to enter on more general fields of history, trusting to competent authorities.

I trust that the inquiry on which we are entering, by showing that Jesus Christ has really originated a kingdom of God which affords the only promise of a perfect human society that the world has ever seen, may be of use for confirming our faith in Christianity; and by showing what Christ's institution really was, may help to point out in what way we ought to work for the realization of the high ideal. An additional reason for taking up this subject is, that some of those who have in modern times most successfully and fruitfully brought out the notion of the kingdom of God in Scripture, as in this country F. D. Maurice and the author of *Ecce Homo*, and in Germany Dr. Albert Ritschl, have done this in connection with views of the work of Christ that are seriously defective, as compared with those which the great body of Christian scholars have drawn from Scripture. It is well to examine, whether a true apprehension of the kingdom of God, as Christ meant it, really supports their defective views, and is not rather a confirmation of the Church's faith in Christ as her Redeemer.

If the notion of a kingdom of God, or a perfect kingdom or state in general, presents itself to men as an ideal, a thing to be desired and longed for, this must be because man is by nature a social being, and finds his good and happiness, not by himself alone, but in union and combination with his fellows. The individual realizes his own end, only in so far as he lives in and for the entire community of which he is a part. This is a really moral society, one based on righteousness and mutual regard. Without this, man cannot really attain his end; but this has ever been only an ideal, longed and striven for but never reached, often, too, longed and sought for unconsciously and blindly by men impelled by an instinctive feeling of want, but not knowing distinctly what they wanted. In order then to see how the Gentile world has been seeking and feeling after that fulfilment of man's end as a social being which is given in the kingdom of God, we must look at the rise and progress of civil society among men, and trace the various forms it has been made to assume in the effort to make it as perfect and comprehensive as possible.

Probably the earliest form of human society was the family; and larger combinations of men grew from that and partook of its nature. The theory of a state of nature as one of individual independence or universal war, and of governments being formed by mutual contract for self-defence, has been useful as a hypothesis in political reasoning; and something like it would be the conclusion to which we should be led, if the scientific theory of man's evolution from a brute or savage state by natural selection and survival of the fittest was established as a fact. But this cannot be said to be so, and the historical evidence seems to point to the patriarchal or clan form of association as the most primitive. In the early state of society there were no nations, but men were united by kinship or religion, very often by both; and many remains of this sort of society are to be traced even yet in India and elsewhere.[1] The pure clan consists of the kindred of some hero who is eponymous, and not seldom is worshipped as divine. The tie that connects its members is the natural one of birth, and the authority that rules over them is that of the head of the family, who is not always the heir according to the modern principles of primogeniture, but the ablest man among the near kindred of the chief. The laws of such a society are family customs and traditions, and these limit the power of the chief. The whole clan is treated as a family, the members of which may not intermarry; but there is also, besides the narrower circle of affinity within which marriage is not allowed, reaching as far as kindred could be

[1] See *Asiatic Studies, Religious and Social*, by Sir Alfred C. Lyall, K.C.B., C.I.E. Murray, 1882.

traced, a wider circle of other clans outside of which they may not marry.[1] In many cases the connection by blood becomes in course of time fictitious, as members might be introduced by adoption or by means of imaginary genealogies, and in order to facilitate marriage a large clan might sometimes be subdivided. Thus the original family character of the unity might be obscured or variously modified; but in spite of all changes this general form of social organism has in some parts of the world lasted long as the means by which order and government are maintained. It is probably, of all forms of society, that which is most directly based on physical relations; yet even this form of a kingdom may be said to be of God, inasmuch as it rests on the divine institution of marriage as its indispensable foundation, and has also been generally associated with religion as its sanction. It need not be said that this form of social life cannot possibly be regarded as an ideal or ultimate one: it has in it no guarantee for the righteousness and beneficence of the governing power, and in so far as it limits mere arbitrary despotism, it does so merely by old custom, which may be unwise and unsuitable. It is also of a narrow and isolating character, tending to limit sympathy and regard to fellow-clansmen, and not to extend those benevolent feelings to others. It can create no large and comprehensive community; and has continued on an extensive scale only where, as in India, it has been worked into the religious

---

[1] Something like this seems to have been the case in Israel. Num. xxxvi. 3, and 1 Chron. xxiii. 22, seem to presume that marriage was usually to another tribe, but it must be within the twelve tribes of Israel.

system of Brahmanism, with its elaborate arrangement of castes, which has formed such an obstacle to the moral progress of that great country; or when it was similarly embodied in the feudal system of the Middle Ages, which proved also a hindrance to human progress.[1]

The patriarchal clans of an early age, when they became united in larger bodies, gave to the entire communities thus formed the element of race or caste distinctions, producing an aristocracy or oligarchy of blood; as is seen most clearly in the distinction of patricians and plebeians in Rome. The evil of this form of aristocracy is, that it interposes insuperable barriers between the different strata of society. Each man must continue in the rank, or it may be the very employment, in which he was born, however well fitted and desirous he may be for another; and more particularly all power and rule is inalienably confined to the members of certain families, or of a certain race. This exclusiveness inevitably creates separate interests, and by degrees comes to be felt as repugnant to justice. Hence, in the history of most peoples, at a certain stage a struggle arises betwen the unprivileged and the privileged ranks, a rising of the lower races or castes against the system by which they are hopelessly debarred from the powers and advantages enjoyed by those above them. This struggle, in the case of peoples that had a future before them, ended in the long run, sometimes after many vicissitudes, in the overthrow of the old aris-

---

[1] Sir Alfred Lyall, in the work quoted above, points out the analogy between the state of India and that of mediæval Europe.

tocracy of blood, and the substitution of either a democracy or an aristocracy of wealth and ability, in which there were no impassable barriers or immovable lines of separation between classes. But sometimes in the course of the struggle men of power and ambition arose as leaders of the people against the nobles, and established themselves, and in some cases their families, as tyrants, exercising an absolute sway over all the community alike. In this way the normal development of peoples from clans or aggregations of clans into free commonwealths was in many cases interrupted or entirely broken off, and despotism became a temporary or a lasting form of government in many nations.

In India, where the system of caste distinctions was more thoroughly interwoven with religion than anywhere else, the revolt against it took the form, not as in other countries, of a political movement, but of a rebellion against the Brahmanic religion, in the appearance of Buddhism, which embodied a special protest against the principle of caste in the older system. But this religion, though it had an extraordinary amount of success among the Turanian peoples, and has become the faith of a great part of the human race, was in its native land overcome and expelled by the older Brahmanism. Thus in India the ancient patriarchal system, with its rigid distinctions petrified by caste and consecrated by religion, has weighed upon the people down to the present day; while Buddhism itself, though in its original form showing some wonderful resemblance to Christian principles, in its universal scope and its substitution of the ethical for the ceremonial in religion, yet from its atheistic and pessimistic character, never could be the foundation of a good or hopeful social state. This, however, belongs to a later age, and to that movement of the race in which the human side of the perfect society was most thought of, while its divine sanction and head was overlooked. In the earlier stages of history the tendency was the other way, to neglect the rights and interests of men, and to look to a supposed divine authority in some absolute sovereign.

In the plains of Mesopotamia, there early began that series of great empires which played so important a part in the history of the ancient world. The earliest of these seem to have been mere works of brute force, successful warriors using their power, at first for plunder, and then for enslaving and dominating over their weaker neighbours. Such ambition and greed, being in their own nature insatiable, led to the thought and desire of universal conquest. At first the conquerors aimed only at accumulating tributary provinces, and this clearly would not lead to the formation of an empire, though the wave of conquest sweeping over foreign lands would destroy the old clan system, and sweep the ground clear for new forms of society. Later, however, the kings of the East sought to make their conquests permanent, by bringing the subjugated peoples into some sort of order of government, and transforming them from mere tributaries into subjects. Then arose the idea of a universal empire, which had that element of world-wide extension that the patriarchal or clan system lacked. But this could hardly be called a form of society, as the other was, since it was a mere despotism, having for its law the arbitrary will of one man imposed by force of arms. His rule might be stern and cruel, like that of Sennacherib or Nebuchadnezzar, or mild and fatherly as that of Cyrus was said to be, or wise and calculating as that of Darius Hystaspis;[1] but its character depended entirely on what his might be. He might be regarded as sent by Heaven, or himself worshipped as a deity; but the god who so manifested his will could only be conceived as a god of mere almighty power, not as an essentially holy and just and good being.

The Bible very suggestively describes these ancient Oriental empires as taking their origin from Nimrod, who was a mighty hunter before the Lord (Gen. x. 8-11), and the beginning of whose kingdom was Babel, where the sons of men attempted to build a tower up to heaven that they might not be scattered abroad on the earth. What they called "the gate of God," the Hebrew writer calls "confusion;" and through all the records of revelation Babel, or Babylon, the great ungodly city, founded on mere might in disregard of the natural ordinances of God, by which mankind are divided into families and nations, that they might seek him, is the type of every such ungodly world power, opposed to the true city of God.

Most of the Oriental empires had a religious character, and might be regarded as in some sense kingdoms of the gods. The monarchs of Assyria and Babylon, who in their long buried and recently recovered inscriptions narrate with boastful and tiresome iteration their campaigns and conquests, habitually speak of themselves as appointed and raised to their thrones by

---

[1] See Herodotus, iii. 89.

the gods, sometimes as sons of gods, a title which seems often to be used in a figurative or conventional sense; they describe the deities as arming them, helping them, and fighting for them; and sometimes they describe themselves as enforcing the will of the gods, and imposing their laws, institutions, and ordinances on the peoples they conquer. Nay, they speak of being guided by seers and dreams, and receiving answers to prayer in token of the favour of the gods.[1] In all these things there is a striking resemblance to the theocratic kingship in Israel; which shows that the notion of the king being the son of God, the viceroy of heaven, and carrying out in his dominion the will of God, is not altogether peculiar to the people who enjoyed a special revelation from God; but is rather one of those religious ideas that are anterior to the special dealing by which God separated the seed of Abraham to himself, a part of the primitive patriarchal religion, only distorted by polytheism. But while we find in these ancient records the idea of the king being the servant and vicegerent of the deity, we do not observe in them any trace of the people being regarded as standing in a direct relation to the gods whose will and law their kings enforced. The king might be regarded as divine, and his rule as the rule of heaven, and it might be said in that sense that the government was a theocracy; but this sort of theocracy, if it may be called so, is the very opposite of the old ideas of the Semitic clans, that the deity is essentially and naturally connected with the tribe or people of his worshippers, that he is lord and father not of the king alone and as distinct from the other

[1] See Appendix, Note B.

members of the clan, but of them all, and that his rule is exercised, not through the arbitrary will of the king, but through the old customs or the magical divinations that bind both the king and all the people. The theocracy of Israel is of this latter kind, only more pure in the moral character of its rule, and possessing a living power of advance and growth, because there was in it a true fellowship with the living and holy God. The extended conquests of the ancient Oriental empires, while they destroyed the old patriarchal governments in the clans and tribes, each reverencing a tutelary deity as their lord and father, substituted no general government or religion for the people; but made religion and a relation to heaven a concern of the king alone directly, and of his subjects only through him. The ideal and perfection as it was of this tendency, which appears in the records of the ancient Assyrian and Babylonian kings, may be seen in the Chinese Empire, with its paternal despotism and official State religion, resulting in this, that for the mass of the people practically there is no religion at all.[1] It is not in this direction that any fruitful progress towards a kingdom of God could be made.

It was in Greece that the idea of a free commonwealth was first conceived and attempted to be carried out. That is a society of men in which order, and right, and the general good should be secured, not by the will of a despot enforcing, it may be a divine command, or it may be his own pleasure, on subjects, but by a power working from within through the voluntary recognition of the members of the State.

[1] See Hegel, *Philosophy of History*, p. 137.

The tribes of Greece early passed through that critical stage of progress which, according to Dr. Arnold,[1] marks the transition of a state from childhood to manhood; when the ascendency enjoyed by a nobility of blood or a conquering race gives place to an ascendency of wealth, that is, to a state in which political power and influence are at least open to all the citizens without distinction of blood, or in other words, in which all are citizens. Such a constitution may indeed be more or less popular, and there may be violent conflicts and changes in it; but it has left behind the state of things in which birth is the essential political distinction, and the commonwealth is not really one nationality. The Hellenic States attained their political manhood comparatively early; and the danger to which the transition is exposed of a despotism being established by some king or military leader was happily and quickly escaped, so that before the power of the Persian Empire began to loom in the eastern horizon the tribes of Greece had so far advanced in the ideas of liberty as to make it their boast that they were not slaves or subjects of any man.[2]

They were not, however, lawless anarchists, but well-ordered polities, held together by laws and principles that were understood and prized by the people. Of these polities there were two main types, different in spirit and character, which in the Peloponnesian war came into fatal internecine conflict, though they stood together in their successful opposition to the

---

[1] Arnold's *Thucydides*, vol. i. Appendix I.
[2] Οὔτινος δοῦλοι κέκληνται φωτὸς οὐδ' ὑπήκοοι. Æsch. *Persæ*, 242.

Persian invasion. These were Sparta and Athens, and the great historian of their war enables us to understand their respective ideals and principles.

The Spartans boasted at the beginning of the Peloponnesian war, that they had long inhabited a city at once free and crowned with glory, and that this was due to their being trained in habits of order and obedience, so that they had acquired a wise self-command ($\sigma\omega\phi\rho\sigma\sigma\acute{\nu}\nu\eta$ $\emph{ἔ}\mu\phi\rho\omega\nu$), of which a sense of shame and a manly spirit formed the main ingredients. They had been taught what was most necessary for the defence of their freedom, and did not trouble themselves with superfluous accomplishments. In a word, it was discipline, the maintenance of wise order and established custom, to which they looked to maintain their polity and freedom. Hence may be explained their conservative and military character, and their comparative simplicity of life, and indifference to the cultivation of literature, philosophy, and arts, which flourished at Athens. These features and principles of the Spartan character are brought out in the speech which Thucydides puts into the mouth of Archidamus, dissuading his countrymen from rashly engaging in war with Athens (i. 84); and the spirit of them appears on the epitaph on the 300 at Thermopylæ: "O stranger, tell the Lacedæmonians that we lie here in obedience to their laws" (Herodotus, vii. 228).

On the other hand, the principles and spirit of the Athenian polity are indicated in Pericles' funeral oration over those who fell in the first year of the war (Thuc. ii. 35–46), and these differ in some important points from the Spartan ideal. Their constitution was a democracy, in which all citizens are admitted to a share in the government, under the conviction that all can contribute something to the common cause. All had liberty in regard to their manner of life, without interference or molestation from those who might differ from them; it was not thought necessary to impose a rigid discipline on all, like that to which the Spartans were subject, for the sake of maintaining order and military defence. Yet the Athenians held themselves no less safe with their public spirit and general resources, and were ruled by a respect for the laws, and for those unwritten principles of justice and generosity whose only sanction was the shame attached to their violation. They cultivated the arts and enjoyments of life, and made their existence joyful with feasts and exhibitions, yet without extravagant expense; and they pursued the study of philosophy and literature without being thereby made effeminate. This is an ideal very different from that of Sparta, and it is in its own way a very beautiful one. Its fundamental principle would seem to be the fullest liberty in the State, and the freest use of all the faculties and means of developing and enriching their nature, while for the right and safe guidance of these liberal and unrestrained tendencies reliance was placed on the spirit of patriotism, the enlightenment of wisdom, and the love of esteem and praise. Public spirit, liberality, culture, fame, were the motives trusted to, as conserving and directing agencies in the Athenian republic.

We find an echo of Pericles' description in the Athenian poets of that day, especially the three great tragedians; and the way in which they celebrate the praises of their city shows that the spirit of its polity was indeed that of freedom and spontaneity, not seeking to maintain order and right by mere force, but trusting to the character of the citizens, their reverence for law, their public spirit, their culture and wisdom. By Æschylus their freedom is set in contrast with the despotisms of the East; the host of Xerxes is described as consisting of kings subject to the great king, and following at his awful command (*Pers.* 24, 58); while the Greeks call no man master (*ib.* 241, 242), and are united by common interests and patriotism (*ib.* 402–405). On the other hand, in a passage in the *Eumenides*, he brings out the more conservative elements in the Athenian polity which he was anxious to maintain and strengthen. There Athene says, in reference to the Areopagus—

>   "Here, Athenians
> Shall reverence of the gods and holy fear
> That shrinks from wrong, both night and day possess
> A place apart, so long as fickle change
> Your ancient laws disturb not; but if this
> Pure fount with muddy streams ye trouble, ye
> Shall draw the draught in vain. From anarchy
> And slavish masterdom alike my ordinance
> Preserve my people! Cast not from your walls
> All high authority; for where no fear
> Awful remains, what mortal will be just?
> The holy reverence use, and ye possess
> A bulwark and a safeguard of the land
> Such as no race of mortals vaunteth."
>   (*Eum.* 690–702, Blackie's translation.)

Sophocles does not so directly picture the Athenian polity, and his famous chorus in praise of Colonus (*Œd. Col.* 663–719) dwells entirely on the natural beauty and mythological glories of his native land.

But the thought of the blessings of free and good government in general is frequent with him, and his conception of it is thoroughly Athenian. The dispositions of city life (ἀστυνόμους ὀργάς) are mentioned, along with speech and lofty thought, among the highest achievements of man (*Antig.* 355), and at the same time the sacred eternal unwritten laws of the gods are recognised as inviolable and paramount to all human ordinances (*Antig.* 450-7 ; *Œd. Tyr.* 865-71).

In Euripides we begin to hear the echoes of philosophy ; and wisdom becomes more prominent as the pillar of the State than the reverence or law celebrated by the older poets. He paints Athens as the home of the Muses, where happy people, children of the blessed gods, draw from the land itself glorious wisdom with all delight, and to whom the Goddess of Beauty sends loves that dwell with wisdom as helpers to all kinds of virtue (*Medea*, 824-45).

All these are but the poetical and imaginative reproduction of the picture which Thucydides represents Pericles as drawing in the language of thought and reflection ; and they show that the conception really was one generally entertained.

This bright picture is presented by the great Athenian statesman as not a mere ideal, but a reality ; and so perhaps it was for a season. But hardly had the city attained that full bloom of liberty and culture, when it began to degenerate ; and though Athenian literature and art for ages continued, and indeed still continues, to be a power in the world, the ideal democracy of Pericles was irretrievably lost, and Athens was no longer what he had declared her to be, a model in political institutions to other States. This was due in part not to any defect in the principles of her polity, but to the fact that these principles, especially that of liberty, were not fully carried out. Besides the mass of slaves that lay unregarded beneath the surface of all the states of heathen antiquity, the allies or subject states of Athens had no share in the liberties of the citizens, and it was the jealousy and irritation caused by this that led to the Peloponnesian war at first, and caused the final defeat of Athens in it. Had the liberty and fraternity that reigned within the city been extended to the allies and tributary states, so that they should all have been heartily united in one; the Athenian power would have been able to defy the assaults of the Peloponnesians, and to maintain its independence for ages. So far, its failure is due, not to a defect in the ideal, but to the incompleteness of its realization.

But though this may account for its external defeat, the internal decay of the Athenian constitution was undoubtedly due to the insufficiency of its fundamental ruling principles. If patriotism, and honour, and culture could be counted upon to be animating motives with all the citizens, Athens might have continued, even though deprived of its external empire, a free and well-governed city; but to a large and fatal extent patriotism was overborne by selfishness or faction; honour gave place to shameless impudence; and wisdom was overborne by artful flattery or sophistical declamation. The motives that were calculated to secure a free compliance with the laws of justice, sobriety, and prudence, proved quite inadequate; and liberty degenerated into licence and disorder, which in turn paved the way for oligarchy and tyranny.

Yet the Athenian polity, though it proved a failure, was surely much better than any government the world had then seen, better far than the cruel and crushing despotisms of the East, better in some respects than anything that had existed in Israel, either in the disorderly times of the judges, or in the semi-Oriental monarchy of David and Solomon; better in freedom, in culture, in humanity, than the oligarchy of Sparta. It aimed at least at government for the common good of all, and allowing the utmost possible liberty to all; and anticipated, though only in a transient way, the liberal constitutions of modern times.

The degeneracy and defeat of the liberal democracy of Athens exercised great influence on the philosophy of Socrates and Plato, who lived just at and after its fall. They perceived the need of some principle of order to correct the excesses and corruptions of unbridled liberty; and they looked in the direction of that rule of discipline that had given permanence to the Spartan government. But they did not attempt to reproduce the mere practical austere military training of Sparta, they sought for a training in the principles of philosophy; still it was in education that they looked for a principle that should be more powerful and permanent for the right guidance of a State, than those generous instincts had proved on which the Athenians had relied. A leading principle of Socrates' philosophy was, that all wickedness comes from ignorance, and that no man is willingly bad; if he could only be rightly instructed he would be in no danger of going wrong. For a perfect society, then, right education is the primary and all-sufficient requisite. This is the principle of Plato's ideal republic, it aims at training men by means of philosophy to their respective functions in the State; and is, as has been said, really a great university, since education is the main thing in it. The ideal is in one respect very different from that of the Athenian constitution. Instead of allowing, as that did, the freest scope to the individual, it would bring all into a certain uniform mould, which was deemed the best. Hence, like all systems that are mainly educational, it had a large admixture of the communistic element. Private interests are as much as possible discouraged, in order that the principles that are to rule the whole may have free scope; and in order to secure uniformity and harmony of action, goods and enjoyments must be, as far as may be, in common.

Plato's republic never was or could be realized; but it remains as a great and influential form of thought, the type of a conception that has been entertained by some in all ages, the notion that a perfect human society can be held together and guided by knowledge and education. Some of Plato's ideas have been reproduced in most of the ideal sketches of perfect States in later times; and some of these have even been attempted to be realized. Its principle still appears in the present day as the great rival of the principle of liberty and individuality that was adopted by ancient Athens.

Already Aristotle[1] pointed out the weak points in

[1] *Politica*, ii. c. 1, 2.

Plato's ideal republic, showing that it was impossible in practice, that it erred in carrying to an extreme the unity of the State, that it precluded the virtues of temperance and generosity, and that it proceeded from the idea that a State was to be made good by instruction alone, and not by character, and philosophy, and laws. This criticism shows an insight into the real state of the case, and has been confirmed by subsequent discussion and experience.[1]

These political efforts and speculations of the Greek states and philosophers may seem to have little or nothing to do with our theme; but they have at least this in common with the anticipations of the Hebrew prophets, that they contemplate, as the end to be aimed at, a social state, not merely the good of individuals, but the union of fellow-countrymen in a free, well-ordered, and stable society. The prophets of Israel looked for a reign of righteousness and peace, such as had never been fully established; the Greek sages desired a state in which the ideal of righteousness might be realized; and the history, both of Jews and Greeks alike, showed that the great problem to be solved in order to this is, to find some motive that shall be at once spontaneous and powerful enough to rule and guide men's conduct. The Hebrews passed from a state of anarchy, in which every man did that which was right in his own eyes, to a monarchical government, that united the nation under a king, but that very soon sowed seeds of discontent and fresh division; the Greeks either maintained a lasting order by a system of stern and austere discipline, or found freedom

[1] See Appendix, Note C.

and culture degenerate into licence and selfishness. Neither a divine law, nor a king ruling for God among the Jews, nor the strict discipline of Sparta, nor the liberal patriotism of Athens, could secure a perfect, or even a really permanent form of society. The need was felt; but how it was to be supplied did not appear. Plato's republic, even were it the best, could only be realized when either kings were philosophers or philosophers were kings; and the reign of God in Israel could only begin when Messiah should come.

Thus there were insuperable difficulties in realizing a right polity even within the narrow limits of the Hebrew and Greek nationalities: still greater then would be the obstacles in the way of a more comprehensive society embracing other nations and even all men, when that idea occurred to the mind. It was indeed involved, though only obscurely at first, both in Hebrew prophecy and in Greek philosophy; and it was perceived that the notion of a perfect State or kingdom of God would not be complete unless it was a universal State. Socrates is said to have called himself a citizen of the world,[1] and, according to Plato at least, laid down a principle of universal philanthropy.[2] Afterwards the Stoics had much to say of a universal society or community of men.[3] By the conquests of Alexander,

---

[1] Cicero, *Tusc.* v. 37. Zeller, however, thinks this story unworthy of credit. *Socrates and the Socratic Schools*, p. 136.

[2] *Crito*, 49 D. *Rep.* i. 335. Xenophon, indeed, puts the more limited and popular maxim in his mouth, so that it is doubtful whether the other is really Socrates' or only Plato's. See Zeller, *ib.* p. 139.

[3] They held, as stated by Schwegler, that "the separation of men into a variety of hostile States is a contradiction to the notion of the State; but the entire race ought to form a single community with the same principles and laws. Thus Stoicism originated the idea of cosmopolitanism" (*History of Philosophy*, p. 129).

Greek culture was brought into connection with the old Oriental world-empires; and this tended to enlarge the thoughts of men, and to bring together different nations. Alexander, the Hellenic sovereign of a non-Hellenic people, made it his aim, not only to conquer the world, but to spread the civilisation of Greece over the barbarian nations of the East. His policy was not to make Macedonians the ruling race over all the rest, but to treat all nations as equals, and mingle them with one another as much as possible. By the foundation of Alexandria and the maritime discoveries made in his distant expeditions, he did much to unite the nations by the bonds of commerce; and he also made the Greek language and culture a common possession of all his empire. But he established no constitution or organized government, he was not at all a legislator, he simply assumed the position of a Persian king, and governed all his subjects through satraps with a despotism that endeavoured to be equitable and wise. Hence, while his conquests did much to ameliorate the state of the world, and diffuse Greek civilisation and political ideas, he founded no empire, and immediately after his death his dominions were divided and contended for by his generals.

The Roman Empire was very different. It was the rule not of a man but of a people; a people which had been originally composed of different races of which at first one was dominant and had exclusive power, but which before it began its career of conquest had passed the crisis of transition to an obliteration of race distinctions. This principle, too, Rome continued to apply in its foreign victories. The conquered nations were after a time admitted to the privileges of Roman citizens; this was what secured the stability and constant progress of the Roman arms; and thus it came about, that what was imposed on the nations was not a Roman king or conqueror, nor the supremacy of a race or caste of Romans, but the authority of Roman law. Law was a subject studied by the Romans as by no nation before, as the rule of the rights and duties of citizens. Their fundamental idea of a republic was a consent and community of law,[1] and law was that to which they looked to secure the permanence of order and wellbeing in the community. The Roman law was influenced largely by the principles of the Stoic philosophy; to act according to nature, and to render to every man his due, being among its maxims. By establishing a system of jurisprudence based on such principles as these, the Romans did make an important and lasting contribution to the quest of the perfect society in which mankind has been always more or less consciously engaged. They laid down rules which have been very generally recognised in subsequent ages as the best fitted to secure the maintenance of righteousness and peace between man and man in civil society; and the philosophical basis on which they proceeded imparted to their work a cosmopolitan tendency, and made it a source of international as well as of civil law. Thus they gave a practical application to the doctrines of Greek philosophy, and showed in what way these might be applied to the manifold relations of actual life. Most of their work, too, was in the direction of that perfect social state which Christianity sets forth as

[1] Cicero, *de Rep.* i. 2. 25.

the kingdom or city of God, for in so far as the philosophical basis of the Roman law was true, it was at one with that of the Christian revelation.

But after all a code of law, even were it perfect, can but provide the machinery for a perfect government; in order to secure its actual exercise and enjoyment a motive force is needful; and the Roman law had no other force to maintain it but that of civil power. That power, too, long before the rights of citizenship had been extended to the provincials, had become first a military despotism veiled under republican forms, and then an undisguised absolutism of the Oriental type. Instead of the majesty of law, enforced by the officers of a sovereign and free state, there had come to be dominant simply the will of an unlimited monarch.

How crushing and humiliating that empire was to all that was noble, and enlightened, and free, we may learn from the pages of Tacitus or Juvenal. Not only was it oppressive to the provinces, which were plundered and desolated, so that the Jews on the one frontier and the Britons on the other were stung to fury and roused to mad efforts of revolt; but to the Romans themselves, the rule of a Nero and a Domitian seemed the lowest depth of slavery, when they had lost the very memory of former freedom. Better days might indeed come under a Trajan or an Antonine; but these were short and uncertain; the empire came to be in the gift of the Prætorian guards, and their favourite was made the deity practically worshipped by the civilised world. Was this what men's efforts at a perfect society had come to? Verily, no kingdom of God, but a kingdom of the worst and vilest passions of men, the kingdom of the beast, as John calls it in the Revelation. The benefits that the Roman law was destined to bestow on mankind as an auxiliary agency to the Christian kingdom of God were not realized then, and but for Christianity never would have been realized, since without Christianity the Roman Empire and law could not have survived the fall of the ancient world.[1]

Thus it should seem as if the attempts of mankind to establish a really good and lasting polity had been wasted in a sad and fruitless circle, returning to the point from which they started after having been driven by the failure of each successive plan to adopt another, which in turn broke down, and led them back on their wandering footsteps again. Neither family affections, nor loyalty to a divinely-endowed king, nor strict training in ancient and austere customs, nor free patriotism and sense of honour, nor philosophic education, nor reverence for law, had proved forces sufficiently strong to overcome those selfish passions of men, whether as rulers or subjects, that tend to the dissolution of civil society. Yet the path that mankind thus trod was not entirely a fruitless round. Every one of the forces called into play in the course of this long effort is good and useful in its place and degree; many of them have, either singly or in combination, preserved a tolerably good social order in single nations for considerable periods of time. Even in the ancient world they did not altogether fail in this; for many of its states did not fall from internal decay, and might have been lasting had they been safe from external attack. Where these principles absolutely broke down was in forming

[1] See Appendix, Note D.

any general society or friendly alliance among mankind. The nearest approach to anything of this sort was the mutual intercourse among the nations produced by the general diffusion of Greek culture and commerce in consequence of the conquests of Alexander. This did to a large extent give the civilised world a common language, common ideas, and common interests; but it did not produce universal peace or harmony. The ideas of despotism and forcibly constraining men to accept Greek manners and civilisation were still dominant; and the monarchs of the line of the Seleucidæ and Ptolemies were really but Oriental despots with a superficial tincture of Greek culture, but with nothing of the spirit of manly intelligent freedom that had marked the leaders of the Greeks in their best days, or even of the liberal and enlightened policy of Alexander himself.

So also, though the Roman conquests did do a certain amount of good to the nations, in uniting them by one system of law, as well as by language and culture, yet by the time the empire came to be consolidated into one, it had degenerated into a corrupt and oppressive despotism; and thus, notwithstanding the many and various attempts made in different parts of the world to establish a satisfactory political society, mankind had come back, after a fruitless circle of abortive schemes, to that despotism which was the earliest form of universal government attempted. Indeed the hopeful view of human history, according to which there is to be expected a gradual progress in an upward direction and an ultimate state of goodness and happiness, was entirely foreign to the ideas of the ancient world. Its philosophers and poets either regarded the course of mankind as a continual degeneracy from a golden age in the past, or as a vast cycle in which there was a continual return or reproduction of the same events and states of things. Cicero and others applied this theory to the succession of forms of government in different States; and philosophers such as Plato and the Stoics applied it more generally to all mundane things. So Virgil, even when giving loose rein to his fancy in the description of a golden age to come, and perhaps using Jewish materials, can only describe it as a return of the past, "*redeunt Saturnia regna*," and anticipates a reproduction of the former events, "*erunt etiam altera bella;*"[1] and so Celsus[2] derided the efforts and hopes of Christians for the improvement of the world on the ground that evil is inherent in matter, and all things must go round in a never varying cycle. The idea of the perfectibility of mankind, and of the gradual and steady improvement of the race in the course of time, which has been so largely used by those who reject Christianity, and which enables them to make light of the supernatural

[1] *Eclog.* iv. 6, 35. Bishop Horsley, in his *Dissertation on the Prophecies of the Messiah dispersed among the Heathen*, maintained that the anticipations of a golden age in Virgil's *Pollio* were derived from genuine Gentile Sibylline verses, which were mutilated and adulterated transcripts of ancient patriarchal prophecy. More recent writers on the subject, however, think that the resemblance between this poem of Virgil and the prophecies of the Old Testament must be explained by the assumption that some of the Jewish imitations of the heathen Sibylline oracles had found their way into the collection made at Rome to replace those lost in the time of Sylla. See Hengstenberg's *Christology of the Old Testament*, Appendix II. *Messianic Expectations among the Heathen;* Lücke, *Einleitung in die Offenbarung Johannis*, § 8; Friedlieb, *Oracula Sibyllina Einl.* § 17. The consideration of the contents of the extant Sibylline verses belongs therefore more properly to the next lecture, in connection with which they will be noticed.

[2] Origen, *c. Celsum*, iv. 65-68.

grounds of hope for the world that Christians cherish, was entirely strange to the pre-Christian ages;[1] and though it may be due in part to the progress of science, yet is much more to be ascribed to the promises and the truths of revelation. At least it may be said with truth that Christianity, and more particularly the Christian idea of the kingdom of God, furnishes the only solid ground for such hopes for mankind.[2] The idea of the ceaseless cycles of the world's history occurs also in Eccles. i. 9, 10, iii. 15, as part of Koheleth's complaint of the vanity of all things; but this clearly is not to be taken as the final and deliberate utterance of Israel's faith and hope.

How different from the heathen ideas was the view of the world's future that prevailed in Israel! There, a prospect of final blessedness was never absent from the minds of prophets and wise men, however dark and calamitous the present might be; and that prospect was not merely the return of something that had been in a golden age of the past, and that was to be brought round again in the circle of the suns, only to lead to the same consequences as before: what the Hebrew believer looked for was a new thing in the earth that would be a real, and satisfying, and everlasting good. In many of the pictures of this blessed time, it is not merely Israel, but all the nations that are to be thus blessed. There is hope for the world as well as for the chosen people of God. The hope for both alike, for the nation that God has taken into covenant with himself and for

[1] An exception to this statement may be found in the Zend religion, which in some respects was the least corrupted of the Gentile forms of faith.
[2] See on this subject Hare's *Guesses at Truth*, p. 313-339, ed. 1877.

all the nations of the earth that are to be blessed in it, rests ultimately on faith in the creative power and saving grace of God. This comes out in various places in the Old Testament, where God is praised as the Creator in immediate connection with his promises and the hopes of his people for the future. So we read in Amos, "Seek the LORD, and ye shall live . . . that maketh the seven stars and Orion, and turneth the shadow of death into the morning, and maketh the day dark with night: that calleth for the waters of the sea, and poureth them out upon the face of the earth; The LORD is his name: that causeth destruction to flash forth upon the strong, so that destruction shall come against the fortress" (vers. 6–9).[1] In a similar spirit Jeremiah says: "Thus saith the LORD, which giveth the sun for a light by day, and the ordinances of the moon and of the stars for light by night, which stirreth up the sea so that the waves thereof roar; the Lord of hosts is his name: If these ordinances depart from before me, saith the LORD, then the seed of Israel also shall cease from being a nation before me for ever" (xxxi. 35, 36). Again we read: "Thus saith God the LORD, he that created the heavens, and stretched them out; he that spread forth the earth, and that which cometh out of it; he that giveth breath unto the people upon it, and spirit to them that walk therein: I the LORD have called thee in righteousness, and will hold thine hand, and will keep thee, and give thee for a covenant of the people, for a light of the Gentiles;

---

[1] In quotations from the Old Testament, where it is necessary to depart from the Authorized Version, I adopt the renderings given by Cheyne and Driver in the *Variorum Teachers' Bible*, published by Eyre & Spottiswoode. 1880.

to open the blind eyes, to bring out the prisoners from the prison, and them that sit in darkness out of the prison house" (Isa. xlii. 5-7). So also in Ps. lxxiv., where the people call on God in distress, and appeal to his mighty works of old, the ultimate ground of their plea is creation (vers. 16, 18). It is also worthy of observation that the earliest express assertion in Israel of creation out of nothing occurs in the words of the mother of the seven sons who were tortured to death by Antiochus for their faithfulness to Judaism: "I beseech thee, my son, look upon the heaven and the earth and all that is therein, and consider that God made them of things that were not; and so was mankind made likewise. Fear not this tormentor, but being worthy of thy brethren, take thy death, that I may receive thee again in mercy with thy brethren" (2 Macc. vii. 28, 29). Reference is made to this story in Heb. xi. 35. Faith in their God as the Creator of the universe was a sufficient ground for the hope of Israel for themselves, for their nation, and ultimately for the world, such a hope as not even the most enlightened of the Gentiles had.

In modern times the discoveries of science in its investigation of the works of creation have tended to awaken in men's minds a similar hopeful spirit, so that the gradual and sure advance of mankind to perfection has been accepted almost as an axiom or self-evident truth by many who do not accept the religious basis on which it rested in Israel. But it may be doubted whether, apart from a belief in God as the Creator of the universe, and at the same time the God of grace and salvation, there is any solid foundation for such a hopeful view of the world's history. The rise and prevalence of pessimistic views in modern times serves to show this; and some of those who are most sanguine about the prospects of mankind, apart from revelation and Christianity, acknowledge frankly that there can be no certainty of this on a merely natural basis, and that possibly after all we may have to fall back into pessimism.[1]

The attempt at a perfect state in the heathen world failed, because it never could be a city or kingdom of God. Not that they lacked the idea of a divine Being, or failed to connect the laws by which they saw that states must be governed with such a Being. Nearly all the governments in the ancient world were regarded as in some way or other divine. Either the king was the vicegerent of the gods, or was himself worshipped as divine, or the laws were regarded as of divine origin and inviolable sacredness. Men in early ages did not doubt, and seldom perhaps failed to feel, that they were under law to a supernatural power. Whether the law was the ancient custom of a family or tribe, or the rules of a priestly caste, or the command of a powerful despot, or those dictates of nature and conscience that men heard in their own breasts, it was regarded with reverence as a law of deity. In this sense their governments were believed to be of God, and were doubtless really so as truly as that of Israel. For, as Paul says, there is no power but of God. But the fatal want in the heathen world was, that they did not know God. They identified the deities to whom they felt themselves under law with the powers of nature or the Providence

---

[1] See Appendix, Note E.

that guides human destinies; but when they attempted to see the deity who gave them laws in the course of nature, they fell into perplexity and darkness. Nature and history did not seem to follow the laws of justice; those who disregarded these laws often seemed to prosper, while those who sought to observe them suffered. If the powers of nature were worshipped as divine, many of these might be opposed to each other and to the laws of human society; or if the deity were a power above nature, it seemed a dark mysterious destiny. Evil came indeed upon sinners; but it seemed to come upon whole houses, generation after generation, involving the innocent with the guilty, and often falling with greatest weight on the purest and the best. Even if they believed that the laws which held together their states were divine, what assurance had they that the God from whom they came was really ruling in the world, and that it would be possible to establish and maintain a society in which they would be observed? They needed to know God, not merely as the giver of the moral law, but as making provision that it should be observed by men, and that they should attain their true happiness thereby; they needed to be assured of just what Paul proclaimed at Athens, that God has made of one every nation of men, . . . that they might seek him. If it be so that the God of righteousness, from whom the eternal laws come, is indeed ruling over all events, and arranging them all in order that men may seek him, then it is no vain hope that a city of God may be realized; and if he has so made all men of one blood, that city of God may be a universal and not a merely national one.

The idea of national deities watching over a city or race, and caring for their progress, was indeed familiar to the heathen world; and so also was that of a supreme power working for righteousness; but these were not conjoined; the local gods were mere nature-powers or deified heroes, and the supreme principle of righteousness was but a fate or destiny, indifferent about any particular men or states. There was no assurance that the tutelary god of any nation cared for its becoming a just and well-ordered state, or that the supreme power cared for any of the nations of men. As long as the two conceptions of deity could not be brought together, there could be no certain hope of a perfect human society; men could only raise altars to an unknown God. But let it be revealed that the God of righteousness is the Creator of all men, that he and no other watches over their life and habitations, and that he designs that they should seek and find him: then we may have a sure hope that human history is not to go on in a hopeless round of changes returning upon themselves, but that a perfect society may be realized in a kingdom of God which shall be the highest good of mankind.

Nay, we may see that there was some positive preparation even in the heathen world for such a kingdom. Not only was it made manifest that all human societies formed on a merely secular basis had in them elements of decay that led to their dissolution or fall; but some of the principles that must find place in any perfect commonwealth had been brought to light; and though only partially and ineffectually applied, had yet become the possession of mankind. Such was the Greek love of liberty, and conviction that in a true commonwealth men must not be slaves of a despot, but free citizens under equal laws: such was the teaching of Socrates and Plato, that righteousness is essential to the well-being of a State: such was the Stoic conception of a universal society. These were truths that were never entirely lost as ideas and things to be desired, however far they were from being realized in fact. Hence even when under the Roman Empire the world seemed to have returned to a despotism worse than that of Nimrod or Nebuchadnezzar, and the golden head of the image seemed to have given place to feet of iron and clay; still it was not entirely the same as then. There were more bitter cries of humiliation and misery, just because men had known better things; there was the longing for freedom, that could only be satisfied with the true freedom that the Son of God gives; there was the philosophy that told men to aim at likeness to God as far as possible, and would welcome the image of the invisible God; and there was the cosmopolitan spirit, that could understand a kingdom that was to embrace all nations. Such things the nations needed, and in so far as they were led in their struggles after a perfect commonwealth to feel their need, was not this the hand of God preparing for the establishment of that kingdom which cannot be moved?

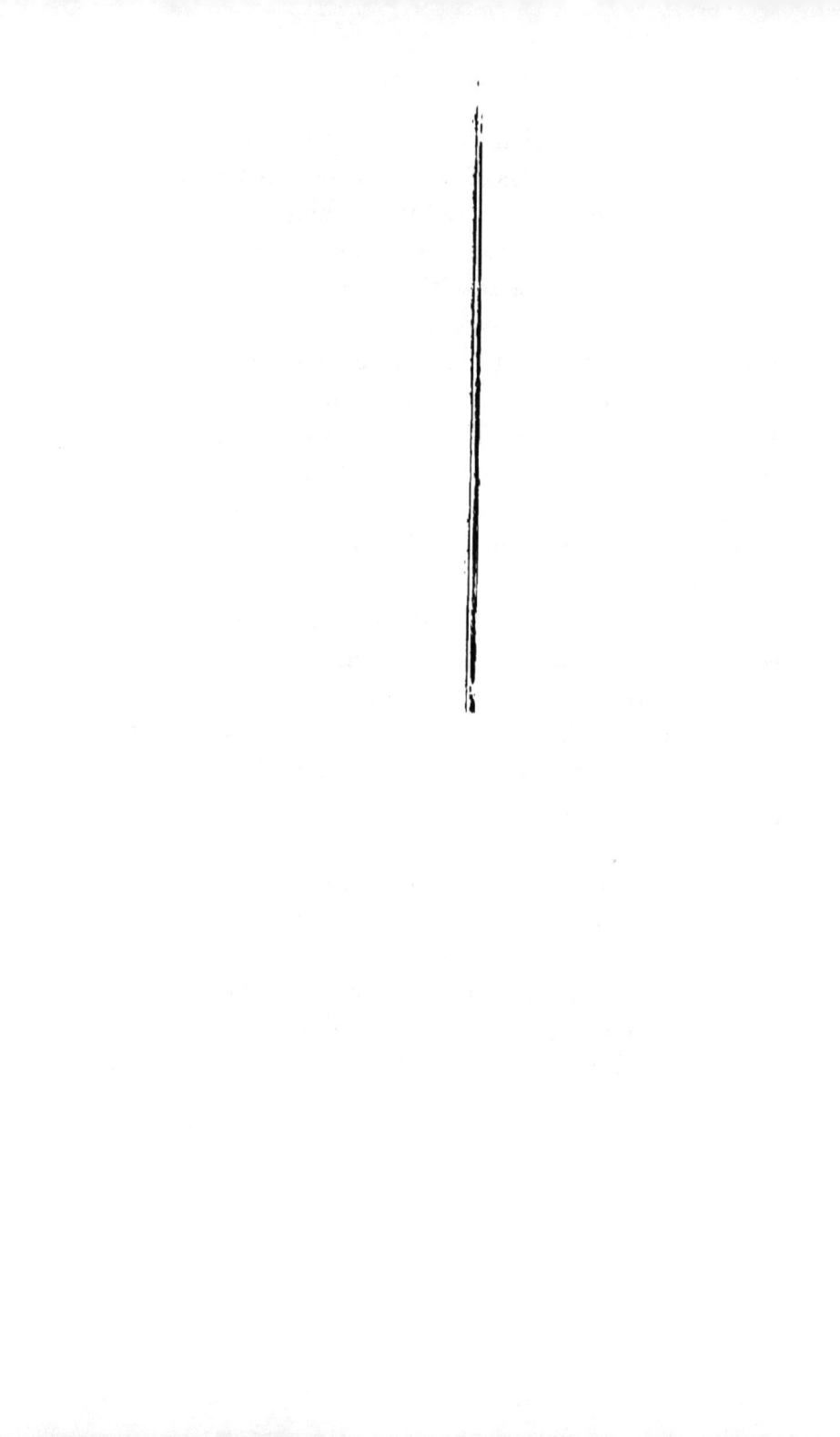

LECTURE II.

THE KINGDOM OF GOD IN THE OLD TESTAMENT.

Exodus xix. 3-6.—"And Moses went up unto God, and the Lord called unto him out of the mountain, saying, Thus shalt thou say to the house of Jacob, and tell the children of Israel. Ye have seen what I did unto the Egyptians, and how I bare you on eagles' wings, and brought you unto myself. Now therefore, if ye will obey my voice indeed, and keep my covenant, then ye shall be a peculiar treasure unto me above all people; for all the earth is mine. And ye shall be unto me a kingdom of priests, and an holy nation."

LECTURE II.

THE KINGDOM OF GOD IN THE OLD TESTAMENT.

THE natural foundation of the kingdom of God, or perfect society, is the divine institution of the family, as based upon the physical and moral nature of man. "The family," says Rothe, "is the primary institution of God for killing, or rather choking in germ, the natural self-seeking of the human individual; the further and only completely sufficient is the moral commonwealth as that of national humanity."[1] From the family, through the clan, sept, or tribe, have been formed the states of civilised men; from which should arise the brotherhood of the whole human race, which is the perfect moral society. Had the development and progress of mankind been normal, these successive stages might have been realized in a thoroughly satisfactory way; and states formed, securing to their members liberty, order, and peace, and drawing nations more and more together in mutual amity and good offices. But, as we have seen, the actual course of history has been very different. Nowhere have men found it possible, when left to themselves, to form really good and stable states, still less to construct a universal state, that should realize a brotherhood of

[1] *Theologische Ethik*, § 327, note.

mankind. Such a perfect moral society must be originated and erected by God, not only working in nature and providence, but revealing himself in grace.

God begins this work from the foundation. At the time when the families of mankind were forming themselves into peoples and empires, and wandering over the face of the earth in quest of habitations, God separated one family from the rest. The migration of Abraham and his household was in many respects, and to all outward appearance, just the same as the many similar movements of tribes or clans in that age; but it differed from them in this, that it was prompted, not merely by natural motives, but by a divine call and a divine promise. God made himself known to Abraham as gracious, showing a special favour for him, giving him special promises, and a special call. Abraham came to know God, not merely as a nature-power, but as a personal holy God, who was his shield and reward, and who trained him to avoid the sins of the people among whom he dwelt. From this God he received blessing in his own happiness and peace of mind in walking with him, and he had the promise that his seed should become a great nation and be a blessing to all the families of the earth. Through faith in these promises the family of Abraham was kept separate from the other tribes among which it dwelt, and grew into a people, which by its sojourn and oppression in Egypt was still preserved from being lost, and made ready for occupying a land of its own. The remembrance of the God of Abraham was revived by the mission of Moses and the wonderful events of the exodus; and so a people was formed with a faith in God's love to them, and promises of blessing to them, and through them to all mankind.

The name and the reality of the kingdom of God first appear in history after the exodus of Israel from Egypt, when the family of Jacob had grown into a people and gained independence by their deliverance from bondage. They recognised this as the work of their God, who thus showed himself to be greater than all the gods of Egypt, and faithful to his gracious covenant with their fathers; and now that they had become a free people, the title appropriate to their God in his relation to them was, not merely Lord, or Shepherd, as he had been called by the patriarchs, but King, as he is called in the song of Moses (Ex. xv. 18). But the formal beginning of the kingdom of God in Israel was made by the transactions at Sinai. In Ex. xix. 3-9 we read how God offered to become King of Israel, and how the people accepted the offer. It was made on the foundation of what he had done for them, smiting the Egyptians, and bearing them on eagles' wings to bring them to himself; it presupposed God's sovereign right of property over all the earth; but it proposed to bring Israel into a more special relation as his prized treasure, a kingdom of priests, and a holy nation. The meaning of this is, that Jehovah is Israel's King, and Israel is Jehovah's people; hence, as being in immediate relation to him, they are priests, *i.e.* servants of God, and they are holy, *i.e.* dedicated to him.[1] All the earth indeed is his; but the other nations have forsaken him and know him not; and as yet he has revealed himself in his grace only to

[1] See Appendix, Note F.

the seed of Abraham, and brought them near to himself. The establishment of God's covenant with Israel, which made them his kingdom, is ever represented as done in fulfilment of the promise to Abraham, that his seed should be a great nation and blessed of God. This implied two things, which Israel was very apt to forget; on the one hand, that this privilege was bestowed on them of God's free grace, and not on account of any merit by which they could claim it; and, on the other hand, that it was not given for their sake exclusively, but in order that through them all the families of the earth should be blessed, according to the promise made to Abraham. If the covenant had about it a character of exclusiveness, that was only temporary, for it was an integral part in a greater divine plan, which aimed ultimately at the whole world being included in the city which hath foundations, whose builder and maker is God.

By the solemn conclusion of the covenant at Sinai (Ex. xxiv.), Israel became the people of God, and he became their King. It is from this relation, for which Josephus (c. *Apion.* ii. 17) introduced the name *theocracy*, that the whole conception of the kingdom of God has arisen, and accordingly it is of great importance to understand rightly wherein the theocracy in Israel really consisted.

It did not consist simply in the nation having no human king; for though Gideon (Judg. viii. 22, 23) and Samuel (1 Sam. viii. 6, 7) regarded the proposal to appoint a king as inconsistent with Jehovah being their King; yet afterwards, when kingly government was established in Israel, it was not held that the theocracy had ceased. In psalms and prophetic books written long after the nation had become a monarchy, God is still spoken of as the King of Israel; and the Book of Deuteronomy, which emphasizes so strongly the theocratic idea, makes provision for a human kingship in Israel. The constitution was indeed modified when that was set up, and it may be called, as it is by Ewald, a *basileo-theocracy*, instead of a pure theocracy; but the kingdom of God, in the sense in which it was real and valuable in Israel, continued in spite of that change.

On the other hand, we cannot adopt the view that the kingship of God over Israel consisted in a special or miraculous administration of providence, according to which earthly prosperity came to the righteous, and adversity, suffering, and death to transgressors of the divine law. This was the theory of Warburton, on which he based his argument for the *Divine Legation of Moses*. He maintained that the Hebrew lawgiver was able to dispense with the sanctions of rewards and punishments in a future life, which all other legislators had deemed necessary for the stability of their governments, because there was in Israel a special providence of retribution in this life, which lasted till the fall of the Jewish nation; and that the complaints and questionings that we find in so many of the Old Testament books about the unequal distribution of earthly weal and woe, are due to the cessation of this special providence when the theocracy came to an end.[1]

---

[1] The same view was held by Dr. John Erskine (*Theological Dissertations: I. The Nature of the Sinai Covenant*); and it is still maintained by the Rev. Edward Garbett in his Boyle Lectures (*The Divine Plan of Revelation*, p. 350-354), mainly on the ground of the expression "he

But there is no sufficient evidence of such a special retributive providence having any existence; as the passages that seem to favour it may all be more naturally understood of those general principles of the divine government, in virtue of which, on the whole and in the truest sense, it is well with the righteous, and ill with the wicked, though the particulars of the earthly lot of each man do not always correspond to his character. There is no indication that individuals in Israel were under a more exact retributive providence than mankind in general; or that this was connected with their being the kingdom of God.

According to the Old Testament representations, the theocracy in Israel really consisted in this, that Israel was in covenant with God; they were his peculiar people, and he was their God and King. More particularly the privileges that they thus enjoy are indicated in Deut. iv. 7, 8, to be these, that they had God near to them, and had a righteous law given them by him. The same idea appears in Deut. xxxiii. 3, 4; Ps. cxlvii. 19, 20, cxlviii. 14. This certainly implied a providential government exercised over the people, such as is signalized in the Book of Judges, where it is specially brought out, that God chastised Israel for their unfaithfulness to him by giving them up to their enemies, and again had mercy on them, when they were humbled and penitent. This is what is brought out in Amos iii. 1-8, when the prophet protests against the idea that God's relation to

shall be cut off from his people," used as the sanction of many laws, which he understands of a judgment to be executed by God himself on secret sins. But the phrase seems simply to mean separation from the people of Jehovah, which would imply the loss of all blessing and salvation; and is too narrow a foundation for a theory which assumes a continual miracle.

Israel was a merely natural one, such that he must be on their side no matter how they acted. It is a moral relation, requiring agreement, and implying chastisement for iniquity. It also appears from that passage, that it was through prophets that God's dealings in this way were explained: the people were to look for guidance, not to diviners or such as practised magic arts, but to those men whom God should raise up from among them to declare his will as taught them by God. The promise of a prophet in Deut. xviii. is closely connected with the prohibition of imitating the heathen divinations. It was by these that men sought some supernatural guidance for their life and conduct, and such guidance is indeed needful; but God promises to give it to his people through men from among themselves, speaking plainly and intelligibly as they have been taught of God.[1]

What distinguished Israel from other nations was, not the idea that their God was their King and they his people, for that was common to almost all ancient nations; not the fact that the power of their leaders and kings was limited by the authority of laws reverenced as of divine authority, for that also was usual in early societies; but the fact, that in Israel these laws did come in a special sense from God, and were interpreted and developed by men who were in spiritual communication with God. We say the laws of Israel came in a special sense from God; and the proof and test of that is their pure and healthy morality. Whatever was

---

[1] Cf. Num. xxiii. 23: "Surely there is no enchantment in Jacob, neither is there any divination in Israel: at the (due) time shall it be told unto Jacob and unto Israel what God worketh."

good and true in the laws of any nation must be regarded as in a sense from God; and when the heathen reverenced such laws as divine, and did by nature the things of the law, they were obeying God as their King, by whatever name they called him. But in none of the heathen peoples was the traditional code which was reverenced as the law of the deity morally pure: along with some sound elements, they all contained much that was perverted and wrong; and so the peoples that followed them were not really under divine law in a great part of their conduct, but very much the reverse. In Israel, however, the law was really the result of a divine communication, and though in some respects its morality was not the very highest, yet it was not in any way positively impure or perverted, and was the best possible then, suited for their stage of moral development, and fitted to lead them on to higher things. The proof that this is so, that Israel was under a specially revealed divine law, and so was really a theocracy, while other nations only fancied themselves to be such, is to be found in the lasting and salutary effect which their law had on the moral character of the people.

But the reign of God over Israel implied, not only that the law had been originally in a special sense given by God, but also that he raised up from time to time prophets to develope its meaning and guide the people in their course. Prophecy served to keep up a living connection between Jehovah the King and Israel as his people. Such a connection was supposed to be effected in other nations by magical arts, auguries, divinations, and the like. These all wrought, or were believed to work, through the lower faculties of man's nature and the world of sense: for as heathenism was essentially nature-worship, so heathen divination consisted in men bringing themselves into some communication, real or fancied, with the powers of nature, in dreams, or madness, or ecstatic trance. In Israel the messengers of the Divine King to his people were men whose higher nature was enlightened, who had communion with God in clear intelligence and sound mind, and whose words appealed, not to the superstition and credulity of the people, but to their consciences and hearts.[1]

Thus Israel was truly in fellowship with the one living and true God, having a law which really came from him and expressed his character and will, and enjoying the guidance of men who were really in communication with him, and were sent to them from time to time. But still the mass of the people were not directly taught of God themselves, but only instructed and guided by those who were. This appears from the course of the history of Israel. In the earliest periods of that history, even after the people as a whole had been taken into covenant with Jehovah, there was little or no national unity among them. During their migration to Canaan they were kept together by the pressure of common dangers without, and the powerful personal influence of Moses and Joshua as their leaders. But when they settled here and there in Canaan, each tribe and family in its own allotted portion, they were divided by separate interests, and each cared only for itself, and was often at feud with its neighbours. There was no central government, and very little patriotism or public

[1] See Appendix, Note G.

feeling among them. They were in danger of losing their distinct existence entirely, and being merged in the tribes among whom they dwelt. From this peril it was their faith in Jehovah as their God that saved them. The Judges were men raised up in times of oppression, rallying the tribes in the name of Jehovah to battle against their enemies; and it was only through them that Israel obtained any measure of freedom and peace. Their final safety was not achieved till the general religious revival under Samuel, which brought the mass of the people to a more living faith in Jehovah, and so knit them more together as a nation than they had ever been before. Now perhaps Samuel hoped the reign of God was to be established in Israel. Jehovah would be acknowledged and followed, not only as their leader in war against their enemies and oppressors, but as their King, ruling them in righteousness and peace. But the nation was not ripe for that. They thought it necessary to preserve national unity and good order in the same way as all other nations had endeavoured to do so, by putting themselves under the government of one man as king. They had not yet enough of faith in God and loyalty to him as their unseen King, to make it sure that when he raised up for them a deliverer and leader the people as a whole would obey and follow him: it would still too probably be as before with Gideon or Barak, that his own tribe or clan would follow him, but others would be indifferent or jealous. Had they such faith and public spirit as to discern and follow the men whom God would raise up as their leaders from time to time, marked out by nothing but fitness and signs of God being with them, Israel might have been really a nation governed directly by God as its King. But they were not able to rise to such an ideal; and their safety and order had to be secured by the appointment of a king, who would command the allegiance of all the tribes in virtue of his official position and the visible symbols of authority with which he would be invested. The demand for a king was thus a sign of the failure of Israel to rise to the position of a kingdom of priests, having Jehovah alone as its King, and being directly governed by him. But it cannot exactly be called a declension.[1] It was simply, as the narrative indicates (1 Sam. viii. 8), the continuance of the same spiritual incapacity that they had shown all along. The mass of the people had failed at first to recognise their heaven-sent deliverers, or to be obedient to them when their personal interests were affected; and it was just the same danger of failure that made them seek a king. They were now conscious of their weakness; and though the kingly government came short of the ideal, it was a real and great blessing to Israel. The reigns of Saul and David freed them from the attacks and domination of the Philistines, and welded the tribes into one nation. Nor did it make them less the people of Jehovah than before. The king was chosen by the Lord, and endowed with special kingly gifts of his Spirit; he was the Lord's anointed, and ruled in his name.

That in the hands of David at least the kingly government was exercised in this spirit, as under the authority of Jehovah recognised as a holy and righteous God, and as carrying out his will in the enforcement

---

[1] So Riehm represents it. *Messianic Prophecy*, p. 61.

of a law of righteousness among the people, seems evident from the Psalms, especially those that may with reasonable probability be ascribed to David. In Ps. xviii., which is generally admitted to be his, there is a warm expression of devotion to Jehovah, followed by a vivid and sublime description of his interposition to deliver the psalmist and raise him to be king. In a way that was to him as wonderful a theophany as that on Sinai of old, Jehovah has delivered him from the floods of ungodly men (or "torrents of wickedness," ver. 4), and has raised him to rule his people, and to be head of the heathen (vers. 42–47). And God has done this, not merely in special favour for his servant, but in righteousness, because of his obedience, his innocence, his uprightness. Jehovah is most distinctly recognised as having a moral character, purity, righteousness, mercy (vers. 20–26). These expressions in this psalm, which have caused perplexity to many evangelical expositors, because of their seeming tone of self-righteousness, are really most valuable, as showing David's view of the character of God, and the nature of the rule he was to exercise for him. He does not exclude his grace; on the contrary, that is implied throughout; but in those days, when heathen kings and nations appealed to the favour of national deities, apart from any moral considerations at all, it was more important to show that the God of Israel was essentially righteous, and saved and exalted a righteous king to enforce righteousness on his people. Even more striking are the last words of David, recorded in 2 Sam. xxiii. 1–7, where in beautiful poetic language is described the blessing of one ruling over men, just, and ruling in the fear of God; and the prospect of this is declared to be the object of David's chief desire and hope, founded on the sure covenant God had made with him. The king seems pervaded with the consciousness that his government had not brought to the people all the blessedness that should flow from this ideal, but yet he has the full confidence that it shall one day be realized, and that in the monarchy of his house. Very similar in tone and spirit is the 72nd Psalm, though that is a prayer for the king, not by him. It presents the picture of what a king of Israel should be, ruling for God, administering justice and judgment, protecting the poor and oppressed, and so proving a blessing to the people. The 101st Psalm is also the language of a king, either David himself, or one of his successors, expressing the two ideas that are the fundamental principles of the monarchy in Israel, that the king owes his elevation to God, and rules in his name, so as to establish righteousness in the nation. He sings of mercy and judgment, not merely as shown by God to him, but as the peculiarly kingly virtues in which he desires to be God-like. The same thing appears in Ps. xlv., to whatever king it may have been originally addressed: "Thou lovest righteousness and hatest iniquity, therefore God thy God hath anointed thee."[1]

David was the king of Israel who most nearly realized the theocratic ideal of a king ruling in the name of Jehovah, and securing the observance of his righteous law among the people. He was called to the kingship by the voice of God through Samuel; but he took no step himself to gain the throne; what he did was

[1] See Appendix, Note H.

simply to use faithfully and courageously his powers in the cause of God and of Israel, with a childlike faith in God's help. He goes to meet Goliath in the strength of faith; he does all the work assigned him by Saul diligently and wisely; he is forced into exile, but raises no rebellion, and spares the king's life when in his power, and waits patiently, following the guidance of Providence, till he is called to be king, first by the tribe of Judah and then by all Israel. When on the throne he recognises that he has been raised to it by God, and that it is for his people Israel's sake (2 Sam. v. 12). His first care, after defeating the Philistines, and securing the external peace of the land, was to provide in his own capital a national sanctuary for the ark of the Lord's covenant, and so to make the unity of the people religious as well as political. He was for the most part in thorough sympathy with the prophets Nathan and Gad, and had himself the prophetic spirit; yet even in his hands the royalty began to show some of the evils of an Oriental despotism. David apparently thought it necessary, in order to keep up the state and dignity of a king, to take many wives and concubines; and this not only proved the occasion of the worst blot on his character, but introduced the system of court intrigues and palace conspiracies that makes the most important pieces of public policy depend on the most unworthy persons. When the king had to be influenced by such devices as that of Joab and the widow of Tekoah, we cannot doubt that there must have been ground for the complaints of lack of justice which Absalom used to steal the hearts of the people from David. Also the numbering of the people must have been intended to lead to a consolidation of the nation's power, such as would have made it a military monarchy like the great empires of the East. Solomon began his reign with anxious care for the administration of justice, and by the building of the temple completed David's plan for the religious unity of the nation. He also by his alliances and commercial undertakings drew an influx of foreign commodities into the land, and brought Israel into relations with other and distant nations. But the tendency to keep up a splendid court and large seraglio that had begun in his father's reign increased, with all its attendant evils, and the intercourse with foreigners brought in foreign customs and foreign religious rites. Thus this peaceful and brilliant reign was not an unmixed blessing; and it left the people at its close oppressed with taxation and pervaded with secret discontent.

The Old Testament theocracy had reached its highest point; it could not retain permanently its power, and speedily began to degenerate. Though it sought the security of civil order and peace in the fear of Jehovah as the righteous God of Israel which animated the best kings, the mass of the people was still far from such a moral and spiritual conception of Jehovah, and it was only by the authority of the king that they were made more obedient to the law than formerly. The theocracy worked on them by means of external force, by the commands of civil law enforced by pains and penalties; and what is brought about merely by such means never can be permanent. Force always, sooner or later, awakens a reaction, by which what has been gained is either overthrown or made the subject of conflict between opposing powers. More particularly a separate nation, having the law of God as its civil constitution, and tolerating no violation of it, could not continue to exist among the nations unless it had power enough to resist or conquer them all. Israel did, under David, through the strength that union and moral discipline gave, conquer the tribes immediately surrounding it, and made them tributaries. But when it came into contact with the more powerful nations of Tyre, Syria, and Egypt, it must either enter into alliances on equal terms with them, and in that case, if there was to be any intercourse at all, their idolatrous religions must be tolerated in Israel, as was done under Solomon and under the house of Omri in the northern kingdom; or else Israel must stand aloof from alliance and commerce with all other nations, in order to keep pure its monotheistic and moral religion; and in that case it ran the risk of provoking enmity and hostility, and in the end being crushed by more powerful neighbours.

This at least was the actual issue of the history. Whether or not it may have been possible, had Israel consistently maintained from the first the position of isolation marked out for the nation by its religion and law, to have remained independent, a monotheistic people of pure morals, among nations following a licentious nature-worship; the fact is that they compromised themselves deeply with these other nations and their religion, so that when they attempted to go back to a severer policy, as they did under the influence of Elijah and Elisha, it was too late to arrest the operation of those causes that were disintegrating and destroying the nation. It proved impossible to restore the old state of things; and in consequence of their internal divisions and corruption, first the northern kingdom and then the southern fell before the advancing power of the empires of the East, and the people were carried captive out of their land. Thus it might seem as if the whole of what had been done by the deliverance of Israel from Egypt was undone. Israel was again merely a tribe of captives, and the theocracy, that had been established at the exodus, seemed to have come to an end, and vanished, leaving no trace behind.

But it was not so. The kingdom of God in Israel, though it had not proved, and could not prove permanent, had yet important and imperishable effects on the character of the people, and formed a necessary preparation and a sure foundation for something higher. It produced in Israel a moral sense, such as we do not find in other nations. Among the heathen, religion had no connection with morality; the favour of the gods was propitiated by ritual observances, often of a licentious or cruel nature, and there was no deep sense of the obligation of moral right and the evil of wrong. The wrath of heaven might be provoked by the neglect of some ceremony or offering as easily as by a moral offence, and required to be appeased, not by repentance and confession, but merely by some arbitrary and external sacrifice. Hence we do not find in heathen literature any controlling sense of the authority of conscience and the moral law, or any deep conviction of sin. How different in this respect is the Hebrew literature! We find in it that religion is ever connected with morality. In the Psalms, for example, we meet with such expressions of the authority and

E

excellence of God's law, and such acknowledgments and confessions of sin, as show that the people by whom such hymns were composed and used, whatever may have been their moral defects and faults, had yet a deeper sense of right and wrong, of the obligations of moral duty, and of the evil of sin, than any other ancient nation. The same thing appears to a certain extent in the historical books. The way in which the sin of David with Bathsheba, and that of Ahab in regard to Naboth, are treated in the narratives, testifies to the existence of a strong moral sense in the people.

The law, given and received as the will of God, the King of Israel, did produce a knowledge of sin, a sense of obligation to the great moral duties, and a feeling of guilt and ill-desert when these were neglected or transgressed. Thus, though the theocracy did not secure the actual observance of the divine law, or the permanent continuance of a nation ruled by it, it did establish the conviction that the moral law ought to rule, and train up a people impressed with the idea that that law is the will of their God and King, to which they are bound to be obedient.

But there was in Israel, not only a strong sense of the obligation of moral duty as the law of Jehovah, but also a belief and hope that the fulfilment of that law would be realized in the future. The Hebrew religion was distinguished, not only as one of morality, but as one of hope; and this was founded on the belief of the grace of Jehovah to them and their fathers. This comes out especially in the prophets. They not merely rebuked the sins of the time, and denounced the judgments that would come on these, but they called the people to repentance, and gave promises and predictions of the future obedience and prosperity of Israel. Even in the worst times and amid the most awful denunciations of judgment, there is ever a background of hope in their pictures; and blessing is almost always their last word. These hopes for the future only became more prominent as it became increasingly evident that the theocracy of the time then present was unable to secure its end, and was doomed to extinction.

In the earliest prophecies of Israel's restoration, those given in the times of division and war between the two kingdoms, it is simply a return of the reign of David that is promised, when the people have been sifted by judgment. The happy time contemplated is one when a king shall reign over Israel in the manner and spirit of David, and shall be crowned with blessing and success as David was. Amos and Micah seem to contemplate nothing more than this, a people reformed and reunited by a new David, protected by divine power, and dwelling securely in the midst of the nations, drawing them all to Jehovah. The deliverance from the Assyrians is portrayed as a repetition of the deliverance from the Philistines under David, and a restoration of the reign of David in its better aspects, in which it appeared idealized in the popular memory. In this prophetic picture there was a great truth; for the spirit in which David wrought the deliverance of Israel in his day is that in which all true deliverance must be wrought; and that deliverance was a type of the highest and most perfect of all. But a literal reproduction of the past there could not be: if the work of David was to be really done over again, something more must be done also; for the very evils of the time, which make Amos and Micah long for a new Davidic kingdom, were a proof that the Davidic kingdom had not been perfect. Hence the people must not be allowed to forget that the Davidic kingdom itself came far short of the ideal of the kingdom of priests, of whom Jehovah himself and he alone was king; and so in the prophecy of Hosea we find it pointed out, not merely that the rule of the kingdom is to become once more like that of David (iii. 5), but that the people are to return to Jehovah, and enter anew into covenant with him (ii. 15-20, xiv.). The ideal is now pitched higher up: it is not merely a restoration of the kingdom of David, but of the covenant of Sinai. The same thing is presented in Isaiah's prophecies from a somewhat different point of view. In his picture of the future blessedness of Israel, one great element is a king and princes ruling wisely and justly, every one of whom shall be as a hiding-place from the wind and a covert from the tempest (xxxii. 1, 2). But over and above this just and beneficial civil government he places the promise that the Lord himself shall reign over his people (xxiv. 25, xxxiii. 22), and the earth shall be full of the knowledge of the Lord (xi. 9), and he recognises that this can only be when the Spirit of the Lord is given not to the king only, but to all the people (xxviii. 6, xxix. 24, xxx. 21, xxxii. 15-17). What he looks forward to is still in substance the restoration of the government and prosperity of Israel as it had been before; but it is its restoration in a more perfect and durable form ; and he gives at least hints that it is to be more perfect and durable, because Israel as a whole shall have learned to know, and trust, and obey Jehovah as their true King.

But the ideal of prophecy must be carried higher up still. The kingdom of God cannot be the restoration of the covenant, unless it is a better covenant than that of Sinai. The renewal of the covenant with Jehovah by the godly and reforming kings Hezekiah and Josiah might seem to many to be a fulfilment of Isaiah's prophecies of the king who was to reign in righteousness and peace, and through whom Jehovah was to rule Israel. But the issue proved that it was not so. The improvement effected by these reformations was but partial and transient ; and hardly had the personal influence of these godly kings been removed, when the old moral and social evils showed themselves in as great force as ever. Thus it became clear to Jeremiah, that for a true kingdom of God there must be a new covenant, with better promises than the former, in which God would write his law on the people's hearts, and be merciful to them and forgive their sins (Jer. xxxi. 31–34). In the same strain Ezekiel and Joel predict the pouring out of the Spirit of God on all the people, and the giving of a new heart, that they may love and serve the Lord continually (Ezek. xxxvi. 25-28 ; Joel ii. 28–32). Thus then, after the fall of the state of Judah, the kingdom of God appears, not merely as the restoration and perfection of David's government, nor even as the realization of the theocracy of the Sinaitic covenant, but as something higher and quite distinct. Then, too, it would begin to be seen why the founder and king of this kingdom of God must be so great as the prophets represented him. To restore the rule of David, a mere man, Hezekiah or Josiah, might suffice; to restore even the Sinaitic theocracy, a second Moses might be found in an inspired prophet like Isaiah; but to be the mediator of a new covenant, to dispense blessings greater than it gave, needed one whose name should be called Wonderful, Counsellor, the Mighty God, the Everlasting Father, the Prince of Peace.

Yet even in the highest views of the kingdom of God it is not severed from the nation of Israel. It is in his people Israel that God is to reign, and through them he is to bless all nations. The promises of the new covenant are connected with the house of David (Isa. lv. 3; Jer. xxiii. 5–8), and in a series of prophecies of this period the promised deliverer and king seems to be viewed as the representative of the people and called by their name.

In the views of the future of Israel given by the prophets there are two different lines that seem to be at variance with each other. On the one hand, we find the representation, that Israel is to be sifted by judgment, the sinners among the people destroyed, and a remnant who remain faithful saved. This is the issue contemplated by Amos, Micah, Habakkuk, and Zephaniah. On the other hand, however, there is the view, that Israel is to be converted, humbled, and brought to repentance by God's chastisements, and renewed by his Spirit. This prospect is presented more or less fully by Hosea, Jeremiah, Ezekiel, Joel, and Zechariah. The key to the reconciliation of these apparently conflicting views may be found in Isaiah, by whom they are both given, especially chap. vi. 13.[1] The vision in that chapter is to be regarded as the final sentence of the Divine King of Israel on the theocracy. It occurred in the year that king Uzziah died, *i.e.* at the end of the last reign under which the people enjoyed anything like independence and prosperity, and after which their career was one of inevitable declension towards final subjugation. The prophet sees the true King of Israel, who dwells in the temple, and hears the proclamation of his holiness, and of his glory filling all the earth. He is pierced with a sense of his uncleanness and that of his people, but his lips are touched with a live coal from the altar, *i.e.* with sacrificial fire, and he is cleansed. Then he hears the King inquiring for a messenger, and he offers himself and is accepted. The effect of his message is described as that of hardening, but the contents of it are not mentioned; it must, however, consist in an announcement of what he had seen, that the King of Israel is the Holy One, and that the whole earth is full of his glory. The issue of the rejection of this message by Israel is to be the entire desolation of the land, and the removal of the people far away; and the vision closes with these words: "And if there should yet be a tenth in it, this shall again be consumed: yet as the terebinth and the oak though cut down have their stock remaining, even so a sacred seed shall be the stock thereof" (Isa. vi. 13). Here it is not said merely,

---

[1] The meaning and importance of this passage are beautifully brought out by Maurice, *Prophets and Kings of the Old Testament*, p. 224-229.

that a remnant of Israel shall be saved from the impending judgment, and that that remnant shall be the better part of the people and the stock of a new Israel. On the contrary, the judgment is described as universal. All the outward community of Israel is to be carried away; it is compared to a tree entirely stript of leaves, and cut down to a bare stump; but yet in that stump there is a germ of life, a seed of holiness. That seed of holiness is not merely a section of the people, who have kept themselves from the prevailing sins, but what lies beneath that, and is far more precious, the presence of the Holy One as the true King in Israel. He had purged Isaiah's lips; and he was ever there to purge the lips of all who sought him like Isaiah; and even though the judgment should leave no remnant at all, though the tenth part that escaped should again be consumed, yet there was hope that the bare stock would again revive. Thus, though, as Isaiah elsewhere describes it, the judgment was to be indeed a sifting one, showing the vanity of all worldly confidence, and leaving no help, except for those who would trust in the Lord, and who should be but a remnant of the people; yet they were to be saved, not because they were better than others in their own character, but because God brought them to himself by means of judgment and grace: and those who were thus converted and saved in virtue of the holy seed in the midst of Israel would be not a mere fragment of the people, but the people itself, restored to new life. Thus the two apparently opposite representations are but two different aspects of that new kingdom of God that gradually dawned on the eyes of the prophets of Israel.

In the following prophecies of Isaiah, given in the reign of Ahaz, we find the actual historical realization of what the Lord had said of the holy seed being the stock of Israel. The assault upon Judah by Syria and Israel combined, under Pekah and Rezin, was one of the signs and beginnings of the downfall of the nation; and when king Ahaz, instead of trusting in Jehovah, sought help by calling in as an ally Tiglath-pileser, king of Assyria, the doom of his kingdom was sealed. Once drawn into the vortex of Eastern politics, and brought within the range of Assyria's ambitious plans, there was no hope of such a small and poor kingdom retaining its independence. Jehovah would bring upon Judah, as an overflowing flood, that very empire of Assyria from which they now sought help (Isa. vii. 17, viii. 10). Seeing the king and people bent on this infatuated course, Isaiah is instructed by God to hold aloof from their confederacies and fears, and to wait on the Lord, even when he was hiding his face from the house of Israel. He and his children and disciples form a little band, fearing and trusting Jehovah, and among them the testimony and instruction, that God has given, but the nation has rejected, is to be bound up and sealed, *i.e.* kept safely and handed down to the time when it would be received by the people (viii. 11-20).

This event marks a turning-point in the history of Israel. A society or church is formed within the nation, having faith in God for its uniting principle, and treasuring his word as its guide; and the existence of this prophetic party, nourishing its faith on God's revelation, is what made it possible, that the religion of

Jehovah should survive the utter destruction of the nation. This was actually in history the stock of Israel, formed by the holy seed, *i.e.* the presence and recognition of the Holy One, in the midst of it, which made it possible that a new and better kingdom of God should spring up after the earthly one fell.

The hopes based upon this ground speedily extended beyond the people of Israel, and became universal in their scope. It is true, indeed, that the most immediate subject of Messianic prophecy is the restoration of Israel as the people of Jehovah, and of Jehovah's reign over them, which is described in various ways. But this is sure to the prophet's mind, only in so far as he recognises Jehovah as the only living and true God, the God of all the earth; and therefore the prospect of the re-establishment of his kingdom in Israel carried with it that of a universal dominion over all nations. Such a dominion was indeed looked for even before the fall of the monarchy of David's house. The 2nd Psalm, whatever its exact date or original occasion, must have been composed while the kingdom was still standing, and it predicts a universal sway for the King of Israel, who is the Lord's anointed and his Son. In Psalm lxxxix., similar promises are looked back to from a time of humiliation and overthrow, as having been given before. Of this kind are Amos ix. 11, 12, and Micah iv. 11, v. 15. In these places what is foretold is simply a dominion of Israel and her theocratic king over the heathen nations that had been rebellious or hostile. The king is to crush his enemies in battle, and to establish an empire that shall include them all. But along with these there are also prophecies that indicate that the Gentile nations are to be joined to the people of Jehovah in worship, and allegiance to the king who is to save Israel. Such are Micah iv. 1, 2, where a direct reign of God is spoken of, and the union of the nations under him is a religious one; Ps. lxxii., where the king is described as feared and obeyed by all nations because of the gentleness and benignity of his sway. But above all, the catholicity of the predicted reign of God is seen in Ps. lxxxvii., and in the oracle in Isa. xix. 23–25, on which that psalm seems to be based. In these places it is distinctly declared that Egypt and Babylon are to be included in the city or kingdom of God, and that not merely as conquered and tributary subjects, but as citizens, with a right equal to that of birth, and privileges equal to those of Israel. These are the most distinct references to a universal kingdom of God, in the Christian sense, that are to be found in the Old Testament. Other psalms, that invite all nations to praise and worship Jehovah, and declare that they all see, or shall see, his glory, may have been simply expressions of the monotheistic faith, that found such striking manifestation in Israel after the exile. Because Jehovah is the only living and true God, he is to be recognised by all mankind; and his judgments on Babylon make him to be thus recognised; but it does not obviously follow, that other nations were to be admitted to the privileges of Israel, or that the special blessings of the kingdom of God were not exclusively to belong to the chosen nation. Yet, even if the utterances of such psalms as the 96th, 98th, 100th, do not directly teach the admission of all nations into the covenant people of Jehovah, they at least imply that the worship of Jehovah is to be universal. That seemed to be made possible by the signal interposition of God for the deliverance of his people by the world-famous event of the fall of the Babylonian Empire with all its idols. This is the view given, in the second part of the Book of Isaiah, of the conquests of Cyrus. He is Jehovah's servant, his shepherd, his anointed, whom he has girded, and to whom he has given victory over the nations, "that they may know, from the rising of the sun, and from the west, that there is none beside me. I am Jehovah, and there is none else" (Isa. xlv. 6). The confusion of all the heathen gods and their worshippers will lead all the ends of the earth to look to Jehovah and be saved; and he has sworn that all shall do homage to him, and so enjoy blessing from him (Isa. xlv. 22–25).

But the conversion of the nations to the true God is not described in this prophecy as due merely to the wonderful manifestation of his power and glory in the triumph of Cyrus over Babylon, but to the ministry of the servant of Jehovah, spoken of in that series of oracles. The servant of Jehovah is called Israel (xli. 8, xliv. 1, 21, xlix. 3), yet in some places he seems to be clearly distinguished from the mass of the people (xlix. 5, liii. 8). Indeed, the whole passage, lii. 13–liii. 12, can only be understood as speaking of some one distinct from the people. The person thus spoken of must have some intimate relation to Israel as a nation, since he bears the name of Israel: and it would seem as if he were introduced as its representative, after the literal Israel had failed in the work to which it was called by God. That failure is described in chap. xlviii., which closes with a bitter lamentation of God over Israel's disobedience (vers. 18, 19), and then a new series of oracles begins with the announcement of one who bears the name of Israel, and is to accomplish perfectly the work of bringing the salvation of God to the Gentiles, even to the ends of the earth. Now the prophecies of a personal Deliverer and King of Israel had been given before, Isa. xi. 1–9, Micah v. 2-5, and also in Jer. xxiii. 5, xxx. 9, Ezek. xxxiv. 23, 24, xxxvii. 24, 25, which, on the supposition of the later date of the second part of Isaiah, were also earlier. Since the Jews were undoubtedly led by their prophecies to expect a personal Messiah, as they did in the time of Jesus, there seems no reason to doubt that such a passage as Isa. xlix. would naturally be understood of that great Deliverer, whom the people had been taught to expect, and through whom Jehovah was to establish his kingdom over Israel and all nations.

In this prophecy, too, we find the picture of a Saviour and King who is to accomplish his work and attain his kingdom, only through deep humiliation and severe suffering. This is nowhere so fully depicted in the Old Testament as here; yet the idea is one which is quite in harmony with the suggestions and analogies of other places. The servants of God had often to endure hardships, opposition, and affliction in their life of faith in him, before they were raised to positions in which they were means of blessing to others. So it was with Abraham, Jacob, Joseph, Moses, David. There were always ungodly men and hostile nations, whose enmity caused such sufferings to the servants of God. That the great and final Deliverer, of whom these were types, should have to encounter similar opposition, and suffer in the conflict, could not be thought strange or impossible.[1]

In several of the psalms the establishment of the kingdom of God over all the nations is connected with the suffering of one or more of his people, and his deliverance of them from that suffering (Ps. xxii., xl., lxix.). In each of these the psalmist speaks as a servant of God, trusting in him, and suffering, on account of his faith in Jehovah, from the persecution of enemies. He pleads with the Lord for deliverance, and confidently hopes that it will come, and that he shall have cause to praise God for his salvation. It is also anticipated in these psalms, that the deliverance wrought by God for his afflicted and persecuted servants will be the means of making his name known far and wide, and leading all the ends of the earth to turn to him. Thus we find here the idea of the reign of God being brought in through the suffering of his servants and his deliverance of them; but in Isa. liii. we have the additional ideas, that the suffering of the servant of Jehovah is to be even unto death, and that he, sinless himself, bears their sins as a sacrificial victim, and makes intercession for them. The only approach to this in the Old Testament is the prayer of Moses to be blotted out of God's book for the sake of Israel after their sin in the worship of the golden calf. What he had offered, but could not be permitted to do, the servant of Jehovah, of whom the prophet speaks, is really to do, and so save his people from their sins.

But while these anticipations of a universal kingdom

[1] See Appendix, Note I.

of God appeared in the prophets, and the events of the exile showed that the religion of Jehovah, as the one living and true God, could be kept alive in Israel, even when their independent nationality was destroyed; the time had not yet come for the true religion to be set loose from its connection with a nation. The seed of Abraham was beginning to be a blessing to the nations, by diffusing among them the knowledge of the true God and of his promised salvation; it began to be possible and not uncommon for proselytes to join themselves to Israel; but the nations of the world were as yet too isolated and mutually hostile for the formation of a catholic Church as a purely religious community: the society of the true religion must still for a time be a political or national one; and therefore Israel's first task, when delivered by Cyrus, must be to return to their land, and re-establish their national and religious institutions. These formed a centre for the whole people so far as they retained any national identity, not only for those who actually returned to Judea, but also for the greater number who remained in exile. In their relation to these Israelites of the dispersion, we may see the importance of the stand which those who returned took against the offer of the Samaritans to work along with them. That is apt to look like a narrow-hearted action, putting away from them an opportunity of gaining over a Gentile nation to the service of Jehovah along with them. But, apart from the danger of corruption from their half-heathen religion, the Jews could not have fraternized with the Samaritans without cutting themselves off from their brethren of the dispersion, and it was of more service, even for the ultimate conversion of the Gentiles, that the Jews scattered everywhere among them should be kept in connection with the historical centre of their religion and its hopes, than that one nation, who sought to join them from interested and worldly motives, should be admitted at that time to their fellowship. We need not therefore doubt, that the policy of Zerubbabel and his associates was a wise and right one. The Samaritans at first knew Jehovah only as " the God of the land," and desired to be associated with the Jews only because they dwelt in the land, not because they desired to know what Jehovah was to Israel, or to share in the spiritual hopes that the better part of the Jews had. If they had come in the spirit in which the heathen are described as coming, impressed with a sense of the greatness of Israel's God above all idols (Isa. xlv. 14), it would have been a different matter; but they showed nothing of that spirit, and to have accepted their offered help would have been to become lost among them, and to forfeit the position of the people of God. For the same reason it was necessary to exercise severity, as Ezra did, against those of the Israelites who had married heathen wives, and to preserve the purity of their race. There was the more need of such rigid separation from other peoples, because the restored Jewish colony had no separate political existence. It was, along with the neighbouring tribes, merely a part of the Persian Empire; and though it was allowed to regulate its own internal affairs, yet it could only maintain its distinctness by so ordering these, as to keep up and enforce its peculiar position as the people of Jehovah.

Accordingly the people under Ezra and Nehemiah entered into a solemn covenant to observe the law of Jehovah, as they had never done before (Neh. viii.–x.). They still regarded themselves as the people of God, and recount, as the ground of their faith, all that God had done for their fathers from the call of Abraham onwards (Neh. ix. 7–31). But they acknowledge that they have lost the kingdom that God gave them (vers. 22, 24, 25), and are now servants to the kings whom God has set over them, *i.e.* the Persian monarchs (vers. 26, 27). But as that subjection consisted mainly in the payment of tribute, and in a general control by which the king might prevent any movement that was displeasing to him, it allowed them in many respects to carry out the provisions of the law of Jehovah as their true and heavenly king. The aim of the most patriotic and religious among them now was to make that law an actual power, ruling them as much as possible.

After the final establishment and acceptance of the law as the constitution of the people, the voice of prophecy in Israel ceases. There appear no more of those messengers from God, who by their utterance of words from him maintained the present connection of Israel with Jehovah as a living God. It would seem as if they were now left merely to the rule of the letter, the book of the law, interpreted by the priests and the scribes, who now begin to appear and to play an important part in the history of Israel. So among the things which the Jews say were wanting in the second temple, were the Urim and Thummim, and the spirit of prophecy; yet it is remarkable that the prophets of the restoration speak of the continuance of the Spirit of God with his people, as guaranteed by his covenant, and as the basis of their encouragement and hope of success. Jehovah says by Haggai (ii. 5): "The word which I covenanted with you when ye came out of Egypt, and my Spirit remaineth among you: fear ye not;" and Zechariah has the vision of the candlestick ever supplied with oil, explained by the words: "Not by might, nor by power, but by my Spirit, saith the LORD" (Zech. iv. 6). We cannot but connect these sayings with the references in Neh. ix. 20–30, and Isa. lxiii. 10, 11, to the Spirit of God as given to Israel in the wilderness. Yet we cannot interpret these sayings, either as promising a continuance of prophecy, or as pointing directly to the New Covenant, promised by Jeremiah and Ezekiel. They seem rather to refer to a work of the Spirit even then, not on prophets or specially commissioned men, in the way of supernatural inspiration, but on ordinary Israelites in the way of gracious enlightenment and influence, though that was not as yet to be so general as after the Messiah came. For we cannot suppose that Paul's distinction between the Old Covenant, as that of the letter, or law, and the New, as that of the Spirit (2 Cor. iii. 6–18), is an absolute one; or that such a statement as John vii. 29 is to be literally understood. The Holy Spirit was given in Old Testament times, not only to prophets and kings, but to many simple and unknown souls; and when the prophetic revelation was no longer given, because it had done its work, there was still a channel of direct communication with God for humble and believing souls. The Spirit of God made his word, as far as then revealed in the law and the prophets, a sufficient means of keeping up a personal communion with him, and we can see this in the expressions of faith and devotion in the psalms and other religious literature of the Jews. But before the full revelation of God in his incarnate Son, the full power of the Spirit could not be put forth, and comparatively few would be taught by him; while the mass of Israel could only be governed by an external code of law. It was the error of the scribes, that they did not look for the teaching of the Spirit, and enforced the law in a merely external and literal way.

The position of Israel as a nation under the Old Testament theocracy may be regarded as analogous to that of an individual man under the law or covenant of works. Conscience is, as Thomas Goodwin[1] strikingly says, the faculty through which God exercises his moral government over men: it is as it were a castle or fortress in the soul, that is ever open to communications from God, and that never can be overthrown or taken by the power of evil. This gives the knowledge of good and evil, issues commands in the name of God, and condemns, yea executes sentence in the feelings of remorse for wrong-doing. Yet it cannot secure the obedience of the will or the love of the heart to what is right; and in the covenant of works the law is only written on the conscience, not on the heart, as God promises to do by his Spirit in the New Covenant. So in the corporate body of Israel, the prophets were, as Delitzsch well says, the conscience of the state.[2] They had direct communi-

---

[1] *Works*, vol. vi. *The Work of the Holy Ghost in our Salvation*, Bk. vi., especially p. 259, 260.
[2] *Messianic Prophecies*, § 9.

cation with God, and were taught by him, and spoke his word to the people with a power that could not be silenced; they were as a defenced city and a brazen wall. But they could not always influence the people to obey the will of God, which they proclaimed; often they were disregarded and opposed by the party in power in the state. From this came the many judgments and calamities which the nation incurred in consequence of their unfaithfulness to their God and violation of the principles of their religion. The last of these, the Babylonian captivity, had, along with the words of the prophets, the effect of weaning them from idolatry and the idolatrous worship of Jehovah, and establishing the law of the Pentateuch as the supreme and authoritative code. The people now solemnly bound themselves to the service of Jehovah at the one sanctuary according to the Levitical ordinances, and to observe the moral and social precepts of the law. The last of the prophets enforces this as the great duty of Israel, and promises God's blessing to them in connection with this (Mal. iv. 2-4); and from thenceforth the greater part of the people were earnestly and resolutely set on carrying out the provisions of the law. They became the people of the Book; the law as read in the synagogues Sabbath by Sabbath took the place of the messages of the prophets, and was to them the voice of God. But still the gift of the Spirit was not bestowed on all the people, and the voice of God in the law was to the nation as a whole but as the voice of conscience in a natural man, commanding with divine right, but not securing obedience with divine grace and power. As the law had to be interpreted and enforced by priests and scribes, the theocracy assumed the form of a hierarchy; and as those who were the organs of the government were not necessarily or always spiritual men, their interpretations and regulations were often wrong and misleading, and a false view of the law was brought in.

Under the teaching of the scribes the Jews gradually lost sight of those prophecies that spoke of a new covenant, the peculiar blessing of which would be the gift of the Spirit of God to all his people, to write God's law in their hearts, and give them all a direct knowledge of him and access to him (Jer. xxxi. 31-34; Ezek. xxxvi. 26, 27; Joel ii. 28, 29). Failing to understand these promises, the utmost that they sought was the outward observance of the law, and so much freedom from foreign domination as would enable them to carry that out; and the prophecies of a happy and universal reign of God they interpreted as meaning a restoration of the glories of David and Solomon, and a subjugation of all nations under their king. This notion of an earthly kingdom is found in connection with different views of the way of its establishment in different sections of the people. The Sadducees, or party of the priestly aristocracy, looked for it in the reign of the Asmonean princes and high priests that had been established by the Maccabees, but was threatened and finally overthrown by Herod and the Romans: the Nationalist party of the Zealots sought it also by human means, only not by wise policy, but by a popular enthusiastic rising and war of liberation: the Pharisees thought the great requisite was to secure the perfect fulfilment of the law, and then God would miraculously deliver his people and set up his reign: while the Essenes gave themselves to the study of apocalyptic prophecies, to determine the successive kingdoms that were to precede that of the Messiah, and the signs of its coming.

From an examination of the nature and history of the theocracy in Israel, it appears that it really was simply the special moral and religious training of that people by God, its speciality consisting in this, that it was a training not merely by nature, in which God is hidden, but by revelation, in which his grace and mercy is unveiled. God is training all nations, did they but know it: he has determined "the seasons and the bounds of their habitation; that they should seek God, if haply they might feel after him, and find him" (Acts xvii. 26, 27). He says to Cyrus, "I have called thee by name: I have surnamed thee, though thou hast not known me" (Isa. xlv. 4). But Israel knew God: he was not merely guided in darkness and unconsciousness, but called to the knowledge of God and of his work and way. This essential privilege, to know the living God and to be known of him, is what is described, from different points of view, by the terms covenant, theocracy, revelation, education. Each of these names describes a different side or aspect of the thing; but the thing itself that is denoted by them is one and the same; and accordingly we find expressions corresponding to them all in Scripture. The one great word the Law (Torah), so dear to the true Israelite, implies them all. The Law is God's revelation of himself; for it is equivalent to the Word of the Lord, "The commandment is a lamp; and the law is light; and reproofs of instruction are the way of life" (Prov. vi. 23). This also shows that the idea of education or training is contained in it, as is expressed in such a passage as Deut. viii. 10 as well. Then, further, the Law was the covenant between God and Israel; the tables of the Law are also called the tables of the covenant; and the Law is also the heart and soul of the theocracy, since it is by the Law that God rules over Israel. Only if we give the Law this central position, we must understand it in its true sense as God's instruction to his people, and as including all his words and revelations of himself; and not like the Jewish Rabbis, limit it to the mere written record of the Pentateuch, or even of the Bible as a whole. This had the effect of shrivelling up their notion of God, and making them incapable of seeing the perfect reign of God when it came; and it will have a similar effect on us. If we take the wider view, we can see both the reality of the preparatory kingdom of God in Israel, and its fitness to lead on to the true, and universal, and everlasting reign.

Israel seemed indeed to have failed in its striving after a national society just as much as the other peoples who had been working at the same problem in so many different ways; and in a sense it did fail, in so far as it did not completely solve it. But it contributed elements that formed the basis for its real solution, and made that possible. This people acquired a sense of the obligation and sacredness of morality, and a hope of the realization of a perfect moral society, such as were not to be found among the heathen. There are noble moral sentiments in the ancient heathen writers, and some great philosophical principles of ethics have been discussed and established by these sages; but their practical moral code lacked authority; and even in their most enlightened and pure-hearted writings we do not meet any of those expressions of a conscience feeling the guilt of sin that are so frequent and so touching in the Hebrew psalms and other Scriptures. The deep spiritual sense of the evil of sin was indeed obscured and perverted by the teaching of the scribes; but it was not entirely obliterated, and even under that superficial and literal teaching the moral state of Israel was less degraded than that of the heathen.

Israel also had a hope of better things, to which the Gentile world was strange. Even in the darkest times there is no tone of despair in the Jewish literature. The Book of Ecclesiastes is the only one in which anything like it can be perceived; even here it is corrected and renounced at the close; and elsewhere the expression of hope and confident expectation of ultimate deliverance and blessing appears amid the most terrible denunciations of judgment. The issue was indeed often conceived by the common mind in false and unworthy ways, and sought by wrong and bad means; but still the hope was there; and those who were guided by the genuine teaching of the Law and the prophets might learn to look in the right direction, however obscurely they might see. The history of this nation under the influence of their law and prophets gave them these two things, a moral sense and sensitiveness to sin, and a hope for the future, that the heathen world had not. In this we have the historical proof that they were under the special teaching of a holy and gracious God, and that his law was to them, and to the world, a schoolmaster to lead to Christ, the shadow of good things to come, though not the very image of the things.

SUPPLEMENT TO LECTURE II.

THE KINGDOM OF GOD IN POST-CANONICAL JEWISH LITERATURE.

IN order to understand the various views of the kingdom of God that prevailed among the Jews when Jesus appeared, and to estimate the relation of his teaching both to them and to the prophetic teaching, we must take notice of the period that intervened between the last of the Old Testament prophets and the appearance of John the Baptist, and see what information we can gather from the history and literature of that period as to the hopes and expectations of the Jews on this subject.

The expectations of a time of deliverance and blessedness under the reign of Jehovah that were awakened in Israel by the teaching of the prophets continued to be cherished by the godly; and after the voice of prophecy had ceased, were moulded into various forms in the post-canonical literature by the reflection or imagination of writers, taking hold now of one and again of another side of the prophetic teaching. In the various productions of this literature we may trace the incipient divergence of the great parties of the Pharisees and Sadducees. But little is to be gathered from what is probably the earliest of these, the Wisdom of Ben Sirach. It professes to unfold the instruction contained in the Scriptures, and does so in the form of practical precepts of religion and morals, with exhortations to trust in God's providence watching over the pious.

Wisdom is described, as in the Book of Proverbs, as dwelling with God in the beginning and coming from him; and this divine wisdom is identified with the law given to Israel (chap. xxiv.). There appears in the book no very keen sense of oppression; and the longing for deliverance finds decided expression only once, in a prayer (chap. xxxvi. 1–17, E. V., xxxiii. 1–11, xxxvi. 16–22, Gr.) that God would have mercy on his people, and remember his covenant, smite in sunder the heads of the rulers of the heathen, gather all the tribes of Jacob together, and inherit them as from the beginning, fill Zion with his oracles, and his people with his glory, raise up prophecies in his name, and hear the prayer of his servants, "according to the blessing of Aaron over the people, that all they which dwell upon the earth may know that thou art the Lord, the eternal God." These hopes are connected with the blessing of Aaron, and the writer seems to attach special importance to the priesthood. In chap. vii. 29, 31, reverence for the priest and giving him his dues is joined with the fear of the Lord as a condition of the blessing for individuals; and in chap. xlv. 24–26 the covenant of the priesthood to Aaron and Phinehas is closely associated with that of the kingdom to David, and it is added, "God give you wisdom in your heart to judge his people in righteousness, that their good things be not abolished, and that their glory may endure for ever." Then the book closes with an enthusiastic description of the high priest Simon, son of Onias, in the glory of his sacerdotal functions. It would seem, therefore, that Ben Sirach looked for a time of blessedness, in which the priesthood and kingship should both exist in Israel, and be together the means of its wellbeing and happiness. These ideas are most closely connected with the prophecy of Zechariah, and there is also taken from Malachi the expectation of the coming of Elijah to turn the heart of the fathers to the children. In the special prominence given to the priesthood in this book, we may see a beginning of that line of thought afterwards followed by the Asmonean princes and the Sadducees, looking for the kingdom of God, in Israel being an independent nation, in which the priests should have authority beside the princes, or, as it came to pass, have secular authority in their own hands.

The Book of Baruch is probably of nearly the same date, and is one of the earliest in which the literary artifice is used of putting imaginary discourses in the mouths of ancient worthies, as in this case of Baruch, the companion of Jeremiah. It too contains hopes for the restoration of Israel, founded on the old prophecies; but the only thing that is emphasized as the necessary condition or means to that, is the faithful observance of the law. That is described more fully than by Ben Sirach as the eternal wisdom, which was with God, and which he has given to Jacob his servant (chap. iii. 9, iv. 2). Israel has been afflicted and oppressed because they did not keep the law; but they are called to repent and obey it anew, and assured that, if they do so, God will have mercy on them and restore them (chap. ii. 29-35, iii. 7, iv. 1, 2). The views and hopes of the kingdom of God in this book are chiefly founded on Deuteronomy and Jeremiah; and they have a leaning towards the Pharisaic rather than the Sadducean ideal, though the divergence at this point would hardly be noticeable were it not for the light that subsequent history throws upon it. The course of that history turns largely upon the ideas held as to the kingdom of God in Israel, and serves in turn to illustrate these.

The First Book of Maccabees describes the conflict of the Jews with the Syrians under Antiochus Epiphanes, and the subsequent struggles and political movements that led to the establishment of the independence of Judea; and the writer seems to sympathize with the aims and policy of the Asmonean princes, whose history he records. The movement at first set on foot by Mattathias was a purely religious one, roused by the attempt of Antiochus to force Greek customs and religion on the Jews. Mattathias was moved by zeal for the law (1 Macc. ii. 19-26); and he and his followers were strict in observing its precepts. They would not at first even defend themselves on the Sabbath (chap. ii. 34-38), and they followed the law as exactly as possible (chap. iii. 46-56). Those who joined them were a company of Assideans[1] (*Hasidim,* pious), those who were voluntarily devoted to the law (chap. ii. 42). What they desired was not political independence, but freedom to observe the law. This no doubt implied the possession of the temple of Jerusalem, and also power to carry out the sentence of death against Jews guilty of idolatry; but it was not inconsistent with their being subjects as before to the civil government of the Syrian

---

[1] This reading seems well supported, and is given in Fritzsche's text.

kings. But practically, in the circumstances, the religious liberty that they desired could best be secured by gaining political independence as well; and this was the more felt, because, though they had gained their first successes by the heroism of a devoted people taking advantage of the natural strength of their mountainous country, they had latterly owed their safety to the skill of Jonathan the wary, taking advantage of the feuds and civil wars of the rival claimants of the throne of Syria, and being careful to be on the side favoured by the Romans. The issue was, that Jonathan, and after him his brother Simon, not only succeeded to the high priesthood, but were invested by the Syrian kings with the authority of princes of Judea. On the final establishment of Simon in this dignity, the writer of First Maccabees says: "Thus the yoke of the heathen was taken away from Israel in the hundred and seventeenth year" (*i.e.* of the Seleucid era = 143 B.C., 1 Macc. xiii. 41). Two years later a great assembly at Jerusalem resolved that Simon should be their governor and high priest for ever, until there should arise a faithful prophet, *i.e.* Messiah (1 Macc. xiv. 41). Evidently the tendency of the historian was to regard this as a restoration of the kingdom of Israel, and to make little or no account of the hopes connected with the Messiah, whom he only speaks of as a prophet. The main object of the priestly party certainly was, to maintain their ascendency and independence of foreign powers. But a government that owed its origin to a wise policy in relation to foreign and heathen powers, could not be very strict in carrying out the requirements of the law, and so, though it never went back into anything like the Hellenizing ways of the party originally opposed to the Hasidim, yet the more earnest maintainers of the law became gradually disaffected to the Asmonean government. The Pharisees, or separatists, as they began to be called, did not share the political aims of the priests; they did not care much for civil independence; they desired to have the law fully and perfectly observed, and in order to attain this, the scribes had begun to make a hedge round the law, and enlarge it by traditions which must be observed with equal care. The first indication of an open breach between the two parties occurs towards the end of the reign of John Hyrcanus, the son and successor of Simon. According to Josephus, he had been attached to the Pharisees, and endeavoured to please them; and when he had reigned twenty-eight years, he assembled them at a feast, and after protesting his desire in all his government to act according to the law, he invited them to point out anything in which he had failed to do so. They all bore witness to his faithfulness; but one, Eleazar, said, that if he desired to obey the law, he should lay down the high-priesthood, because his mother had been a captive among the Gentiles. The rest repelled this charge, which Josephus says was false; but as they did not pronounce so severe a sentence on Eleazar as Hyrcanus thought necessary, he suspected them all of secretly sympathizing with the charge, and thereupon went over to the party of the Sadducees (*Ant.* xiii. 10).

Josephus' representations are somewhat distorted by his mistaken idea of the Pharisees and Sadducees of that time being theological sects; and it would perhaps be more correct to say, that the Pharisees, *i.e.* the party of the scribes, left Hyrcanus, than that he left them. The Sadducees were simply the party of the priestly aristocracy, and were not distinguished at first by those negative theological opinions that were their chief characteristic in New Testament times. They differed indeed from the scribes, in seeking the deliverance of the people by political means, instead of expecting that a perfect obedience to the law would be rewarded by a supernatural interposition of God to give them the Messianic kingdom. They did not need to lay much stress on the resurrection of the dead, which formed a prominent and essential element in the Pharisees' ideas of the future ; and as their opposition to the Pharisees grew more decided, they might be led to reject this doctrine entirely. How the idea of a present external theocracy tends towards the omission of the doctrine of a future life, appears in Warburton's once famous but now exploded theory of the Jewish theocracy, in which an essential position was, that the Mosaic revelation contained no teaching about a state after death, because it was sanctioned and supported by a special providential government in the present. The connection of ideas may have been similar in the system of the Sadducees. The political character of the Sadducees appears even after the fall of the independent Asmonean princes. In the days of Jesus, while the scribes and Pharisees were offended at his transgressing the traditions of the elders (Matt. xv. 1), and being in their view not careful enough about the Sabbath law, the chief priests, who were Sadducees, were concerned lest, in consequence of the movement raised by Jesus, the Romans would come and take away their place and nation (John xi. 48), and afterwards lest the apostles' preaching Jesus as the Messiah should bring his blood on them (Acts v. 28).

Alexander Jannæus, the second son of Hyrcanus, who succeeded his elder brother Aristobulus as high priest and king of the Jews in 105 B.C., was strongly opposed to the Pharisees, and engaged in violent contentions and civil wars with them. They still maintained the objection to the legitimacy of his priesthood from the alleged servile birth of his father. But when he died in 79 B.C., he advised his wife Alexandra to endeavour to gain over the Pharisees by giving them the direction of affairs. This was accordingly done. Her elder son, Hyrcanus, a man of peaceful and unambitious character, was made high priest, and the party of the scribes held sway in the state, re-establishing the observance of the traditional law. After the death of Alexandra (69 B.C.) came the civil war between her sons Hyrcanus and Aristobulus, the former being supported by the scribes and Pharisees, the latter by the priests and Sadducees (Josephus, *Ant.* xiv. 2). When Pompey appeared as arbiter between the rival claimants and parties at Damascus in 63 B.C., the body of the people, who were animated by the Pharisaic principles, desired that the kingly power should be abolished, and complained of both the brothers as attempting to bring them into servitude. They would acknowledge Hyrcanus as high priest, but neither him nor his brother as prince; and they would have the civil power in the hands of the Sanhedrin (Joseph. *Ant.* xiv. 3. 2). When Aristobulus afterwards took up arms against the Romans to restore the old Maccabean independence, Hyrcanus and the Pharisaic party admitted Pompey's army into Jerusalem; and while the priests defended themselves in the temple until it was taken by the Roman general, were willing to submit to the political sovereignty of Rome, though they were offended at the desecration of the holy place (Joseph. *Ant.* xiv. 4).

The views and aspirations of the Pharisees about this time are expressed in the remarkable collection of poems called the Psalms of Solomon.[1] These psalms must have been written after the death of Pompey, as they refer to his capture and profanation of the temple, which is regarded as a judgment on the wickedness of Israel, but for which the haughty Roman is to be himself punished. This is expressed thus in the second of these psalms:—

1 When the wicked man was exalted, he cast down with the ram strong walls,
   And thou didst not hinder.
2 Strange nations have gone up on thy altar:
   They have trampled with their shoes in pride;
3 Because the sons of Jerusalem polluted the holy things of the Lord,
   Profaned the gifts of God by lawlessness.
4 Because of these he said: Cast them far from me,
   I have no pleasure in them.
5 The beauty of their glory was set at nought;
   Before God it was dishonoured for ever.
6 Our sons and our daughters are in an evil bondage,
   Their neck under a seal, a sign among the Gentiles.
7 According to their deeds he hath done to them,
   For he hath left them to the hands of the mighty;
8 For he hath turned his face from mercy on them,
   Their young men, and their old men, and their children together;
9 For they did evil together, not to hear.
10 And the heaven was indignant,
    And the earth abhorred them;
11 For no man did upon it what they did.

---

[1] Ψαλμοὶ Σαλομῶντος. *Libri Apocryphi V. T. græce*, ed. O. F. Fritzsche. Appendix.

12 And the earth shall know all thy judgments that are righteous.

 . . . .

16 I will justify thee, O God, in uprightness of heart;
 For in thy judgments is thy righteousness, O God!
17 For thou didst render to the sinners according to their deeds,
 According to their sins that are exceeding wicked.
18 Thou didst discover their sins, that thy judgment might appear.
19 Thou didst blot out their memory from the earth.
 God is a righteous judge, and will not regard persons.
20 He tore down her beauty from the throne of glory,
 For the Gentiles put Jerusalem to shame in trampling her down.
21 She girded herself with sackcloth instead of goodly raiment,
 A rope round her head instead of a crown.
22 She took off the glorious mitre which God put upon her.
23 Her beauty is cast away to the earth in dishonour.
24 And I saw, and besought the face of the Lord, and said,
 Let there be enough, Lord, of thy hand being heavy on Jerusalem in bringing up the Gentiles;
25 For they mocked and spared not in anger and fury with animosity;
26 And we shall be consumed, unless thou, Lord, rebuke them in thine anger;
27 For they did it not in zeal, but in the desire of their soul
28 To pour out their own anger on us in rapine.
 Delay not, O God, to recompense upon their heads,
29 That the pride of the dragon may yield in disgrace.
30 And God delayed not, till he showed me
 His insolence pierced upon the mountains of Egypt,
 Set at nought by the least upon land and sea,
31 His body rotting upon the waves with great insults,
 And there was none to bury.
32 For he set him at nought in disgrace.
 He considered not that he is a man;
 And he regarded not the latter end.
33 He said, I shall be lord of land and sea:
 And he knew not that God is great,
 Strong in his great might.

The reference to Pompey is unmistakable, and the poem shows the view that the writer took of the reason of the calamities of his people. It is a view very similar to that of many of the prophets, and doubtless derived from them. The Gentile invasions are judgments on Israel for their sins; but, on the other hand, God's mercy continues over his people, and the selfish ambition of the heathen brings down in turn judgments on them.

What were the particular sins for which he regarded the afflictions of the time as a judgment, appears in some measure from other passages of these psalms. The fourth is directed against those who live in hypocrisy among the saints, the men-pleasers, who are described as sitting in the Sanhedrin, though their heart has departed far from the Lord, abundant in words of fair profession, hard in judgment against sinners, but secretly practising licentiousness and fraud. The character of severity in judgment is one that is ascribed to the Sadducees in contrast with the Pharisees, one of whose maxims was to lean ever to the most favourable side;[1] and the other features would naturally be those of a wealthy and politic aristocracy. A similar description is given in Psal. viii. 7-14; and thereafter it is said that on this account God brought against Jerusalem from the end of the earth him that strikes mightily (*i.e.* Pompey), and poured on them a spirit of error, so that they opened the gates to him, and received him in peace, whereupon he shed much blood and carried many away captive. In point of fact it was the Pharisees who opened the gates to Pompey, while the Sadducees resisted him in the temple; so that this representation does not seem to be quite accurate. But it is not perhaps necessary to identify the "rulers of the land" (Psal. viii. 18) with the sinners before described, and after all that which caused the calamity was, not the admission of Pompey by the Pharisees, but the resistance of the Sadducees. The writer of these psalms seems to have been led by his patriotic feelings of indignation at Pompey to a somewhat

---

[1] Weber, *System der altsynagogalen palæstinischen Theologie*, p. 11.

rhetorical rather than strictly accurate representation of the events. In another passage he expresses the objection that was taken by the Pharisees to the rule of the Asmonean family as not of the line of David (Psal. xvii. 5) :—

> 5 Thou, Lord, didst choose David to be king over Israel,
> And thou didst swear to him concerning his seed for ever,
> That his kingdom should not fail before thee.
> 6 And in our sins there have risen upon us sinful men ;
> They set upon us and thrust us out ;
> They to whom thou didst not promise robbed with force,
> 7 And they did not honour thy glorious name ;
> They set a palace in glory for their loftiness ;
> 8 They desolated the throne of David in the haughtiness of their boasting ;
> But thou, Lord, shalt cast them down,
> And shalt take away their seed from the earth ;
> 9 When there rises upon them a man foreign to our race ;
> 10 According to their sins thou shalt render to them, O God.
> Let it be found to them according to their deeds.

Then follows another description of the foreign invader, who desolates the land and sends its children captives to the west; and then again there is a reference to the sins of the princes, judges, and people, that deserved such judgments. After this comes the principal Messianic passage in this work, showing the writer's view of the kingdom of God in the future :—

> 23 Behold, Lord, and raise up to them their king,
> The son of David, for the time which thou knowest, O God,
> To reign over Israel thy servant :
> 24 And gird him with strength to crush unrighteous rulers.
> 25 From Gentiles treading it down in destruction cleanse Jerusalem
> In wisdom, in righteousness :
> 26 To thrust out sinners from the inheritance,
> To root out the haughtiness of sinners,
> As potters' vessels with an iron rod to crush all their substance,
> 27 To destroy lawless nations by the word of his mouth,
> That nations may flee from his face at his threat,
> And that he may rebuke sinners in the word of their heart.
> 28 And he shall gather a holy people, which he shall lead in righteousness ;
> And he shall judge the tribes of a people sanctified by the Lord his God ;

29 And he shall not suffer unrighteousness to harbour in the midst of them.
  And there shall not dwell with them any man that knoweth vice;
30 For he shall know them that all are sons of their God;
  And he shall divide them in their tribes upon the earth;
31 And a sojourner and a stranger shall no more dwell with them.
  He shall judge peoples and nations in the wisdom of his righteousness:
32 And he shall have the peoples of the Gentiles to serve him under his yoke;
  And he shall glorify the Lord with an ensign for all the earth;
33 And he shall cleanse Jerusalem in sanctification as at the beginning,
34 That nations may come from the ends of the earth to see his glory,
  Bringing as gifts her sons that are weakened,
35 And to see the glory of the Lord with which God hath glorified her.
  And himself shall be a righteous king taught by God over them,
36 And there is no unrighteousness in his days among them;
  For all are holy, and their king is the Lord's anointed.[1]
37 For he shall not trust on horse, or horseman, or bow;
  Nor shall he multiply to himself gold and silver for war,
  Nor shall he gather hopes with arms for the day of battle.
38 The Lord himself is his king; the hope of the mighty is by hope in God.
  And he shall raise up all the nations before him in fear;
39 For he shall smite the earth with the word of his mouth for ever.
40 He shall bless the people of the Lord in wisdom with joy;
41 And he is himself pure from sin to rule the great people,
  To rebuke rulers, and to remove sinners by strength of word.
42 And he shall not be weak in his God all his days;
  Because God made him powerful in holy spirit,
  And wise in counsel of understanding, in strength and righteousness.
43 And the blessing of the Lord shall be on him in strength,
  And his hope shall not be weak on the Lord.
44 And who can resist him,
  Strong in his works and mighty in the fear of God,
45 Shepherding the flock of the Lord in faithfulness and righteousness?
  And he shall not suffer any in them to be weak in their pasture.
46 In piety he shall lead them all;
  And there shall not be in them haughtiness to be overpowered in them.
47 This is the comeliness of the king of Israel, which God decreed,
  To raise him over the house of Israel to chasten it.
48 His words are tried in the fire above the most precious gold;
  In assemblies he shall discriminate the people, the tribes of the sanctified.
49 His words are as words of holy ones among sanctified peoples.
50 Blessed are they that live in those days,

---

[1] The Greek is Χριστὸς κύριος; but this is in all probability a mistranslation of יהוה משיח, as in the LXX. of Lam. iv. 20.

> To see in the assembly of the tribes the good things of Israel, which God shall bring to pass.
> 51 May God hasten his mercy upon Israel,
> Deliver us from the uncleanness of profane enemies!
> The Lord himself is our king for ever and ever.

Here we have obviously an echo of some of the prophetic descriptions of the Messianic times, and a reproduction of some of the leading ideas of the Old Testament. That Israel is the people of God, that their prosperity depends on their faithfulness to him and to his law, that he chastens them for their sins by means of the heathen nations, but will ultimately judge these nations and sift his people, separating the hypocrites from those who truly trust in him, that God is to raise up a son of David to reign over Israel in righteousness and peace, and to have dominion over all nations, and that this kingdom of God is to be established, not by worldly might or policy, but by a divine power, which is to be rested on by faith: these ideas expressed in these psalms are genuine utterances of a heart that has taken in a large portion of the prophetic oracles, especially those of Amos, Micah, Habakkuk, Zephaniah, and parts of Isaiah, which speak of Israel being sifted and purified by judgment, the sinners being destroyed, and the believing remnant saved. But there is no echo in these poems of that other line of prophetic teaching that is given especially by Hosea, Joel, Jeremiah, Ezekiel, and Zechariah, and foretells the conversion of Israel by God's gracious chastisement, and the pouring out of his Spirit. In the picture of the Messianic kingdom given in these psalms, there is no word of the new covenant, or of God's gift of the new heart, as necessary in order to real obedience to the law, or of the writing the law in the heart. So far from this, the writer looks for deliverance by a judgment that shall destroy the sinners and save the righteous. Even these, indeed, are not perfect or free from sin, they are chastened, and that is a blessing to them. But it is by their own will that they turn from sin, and by their repentance and confession to God they obtain his mercy. This appears in Psal. ix.:—

7 O God, our works are in the choice and power of our soul,
  To do righteousness or unrighteousness in the works of our hands.
8 And in thy righteousness thou visitest the sons of men.
9 He that doeth righteousness treasureth life to himself with the Lord;
  And he that doeth unrighteous things is himself the author of his soul's destruction.
10 For the judgments of the Lord are in righteousness on each man and house.
11 To whom shalt thou be good, O God, but to those who call on the Lord?
12 He shall cleanse his soul from sins, in confession, in praise.
13 For to us and our faces is shame for all things.
14 But to whom shall he forgive sins, but to those who have sinned?
15 Thou shalt bless the righteous, and not exact for the sins they have done,
  And thy goodness is to sinners in repentance.

The mercy of God is indeed spoken of, but it is to the righteous as forgiving their shortcomings and sins, but there is no word of salvation and grace for those who have more grievously sinned. All that is looked for is a coming of the Messiah to judgment, to destroy the wicked and to establish his kingdom with the righteous. So, also, the attitude of the author towards the Gentiles is an exclusive one. Messiah's reign is indeed to be universal, but only in the way of subduing all nations and crushing all who oppose him, not by extending to them the blessings of the kingdom. Those prophecies that describe the kingdom of the Son of

David in the language of war and conquest are re-echoed and apparently understood in a literal sense; but there is no trace of the influence of those that speak of outside nations as incorporated among the people of God, and sharing their privileges as equals and brethren. It is just what might be expected from the other features of these psalms, that there does not at all appear in them that idea of a suffering Messiah, which, in the later Book of Isaiah, Zechariah, and some of the Psalms, is closely connected with the representation of the deep moral renewal of the hearts of the people needed for their regeneration.

In short, we find here self-portrayed the Pharisaic spirit, both in its strength and in its defects. There is a real zeal for God, a genuine enthusiasm in the utterance of his praises, and in the confidence expressed in him. But there is a spirit of legalism about the piety thus expressed; and the blessedness of the future is looked for as something entirely apart from the present, that is to come by an abrupt, supernatural, and, as it were, magical interposition of God.

Another apocryphal writing, probably somewhat earlier than the Psalms of Solomon, may be referred to here, as indicating the transition towards the Alexandrian form of Judaism, afterwards more fully developed by Philo. The Wisdom of Solomon speaks of the righteous as sons of God (ii. 13, 18, v. 5), and declares that they shall reign with him (iii. 8); and in one remarkable passage (v. 15-23) it describes how God shall establish his kingdom. In language closely resembling Isa. lix. 16 – 18, he is represented as arming himself with a panoply of zeal, a breastplate of righteousness, a helmet of judgment, a shield of holiness, and a sword of wrath. But then, instead of the declaration of the moral work of God's word and Spirit that follows on this in the evangelical prophet (Isa. lix. 19-21), the Alexandrian author of this book merely portrays physical convulsions, in which the world fights along with God against his enemies. The righteous raised from the dead are to take part with God in judging their enemies and reigning over the world; but there is a curious mixture of Platonic and Jewish notions, which makes it impossible to gather from this book any distinct idea of what the author conceived the kingdom of God to be. We see here the historical notion of the kingdom of God fading away into an abstract idea, which is all that we find in the writings of Philo corresponding to it.

In the course of the conflict between Hyrcanus, whom the Pharisees supported, and Aristobulus, with whom were the Sadducees, the former party proved successful, chiefly through the energy and policy of Antipater the Idumean, and father of Herod the Great, who, availing himself of the necessities of the contending factions in the Roman state, and taking the side of the most powerful, succeeded in bringing to an end the Asmonean line of priest-kings in Israel, and the domination of the Sadducean priestly aristocracy. But Antipater and his sons, especially Herod, were far from being animated by the Pharisaic principles, and it soon became plain that their ambition aimed simply at establishing a rule of their own. They paid no regard to the law, for which the Pharisees were so zealous; they defied the authority of the Sanhedrin; and they adopted and introduced among the people foreign and heathen customs. Thus they established a dynasty that was as much opposed to the Pharisees' ideas as that of the Asmoneans had been, and that was besides of foreign origin, and reigned in entire subjection to Roman power. Hence the party of the Herodians in the time of Christ seems to have been distinct alike from the Pharisees and the Sadducees, though it had some points of affinity to both.

Along with those great ecclesiastical parties, there are also to be considered the ideas about the expected reign of God held by those who were rather visionary dreamers, without any definite practical scheme to propose or carry out. Their expectations are to be found in the apocryphal apocalyptic literature of the Jews in the times before Christ.

In the later times of Old Testament history, the utterances of prophecy assume in some cases what has been called the apocalyptic form. By that is meant the mode or garb in which the future of the Messianic kingdom is represented in the Book of Daniel, and parts of Ezekiel and Zechariah, in the Apocalypse of John, and such apocryphal writings as the Book of Enoch, Sibylline oracles, the Testaments of the twelve patriarchs, the Fourth Book of Ezra, and the Ascension of Isaiah. What all these have in common is the allegorical style of representing historical events by fanciful symbols, artfully woven into imaginary narratives. Such a use of symbols must have formed part of the art of interpreting dreams, so common in all ages; for the lawless fancies of the sleeping brain could only be made to correspond to any real events by being treated as symbols. The same thing must have been done in all other kinds of divination. Then the converse process of representing actual events by symbols became a literary fashion, of which instances may be found in most languages, and which came into use especially when artificial kinds of composition were admired rather than the more simple. Such a period seems to have come in Hebrew literature about the time of the captivity, and it was therefore natural that prophecy should adopt it.

It was also suitable to the circumstances of the times that the essential hope of the ultimate establishment of a world-wide kingdom of God should now be presented in such a form. Israel was then under the dominion of the Babylonian Empire, and the triumph of the kingdom of God, of which Israel had the promise, must imply the fall of that empire. Any prophecy of the kingdom, therefore, which should be suited to the times, must include the future of the Babylonian Empire as well. The history of the people of God, from this time on, was interwoven with the general history of the world, in a way in which it had not been before; and the symbolical mode of representation was not only suited to the taste of the time, but the best adapted for giving a view of the general outline and leading principles of the future, without furnishing a detailed history beforehand. The symbols were used partly to describe events of the past or relations of the present, and by these their meaning was made intelligible; and then the representation was projected into the future, and the eye of the seer looked onwards to the final consummation of all things, or at least to the triumph of the good cause. So we may observe in the parable of the two eagles and the vine in Ezek. xvii., representing Israel between the empires of Egypt and Babylon, part of it refers to past events, and part points forward to the future. In general, such apocalyptic visions are clear and precise only in reference to the past and the present of the writer; and in reference to the future give nothing more than general outlines. This is true, not only of the apocryphal compositions of this kind, but also of many of the biblical ones, such as that parable of Ezekiel, and the visions of Zechariah (i.-vi.). If the Book of Daniel in its present form was written between the reigns of Nebuchadnezzar and Cyrus, it would afford an exception to this, for chaps. viii. and xi. undoubtedly describe with much precision of detail the events of the time of Antiochus Epiphanes. It is possible that this was so, and reasons have been suggested why there should have been this exception to the general rule; but it is difficult to avoid the suspicion that these chapters were composed in the Maccabean time.

The idea that a kingdom of God was to succeed the last of the world-kingdoms, and that this last world-kingdom was to be the most wicked and ungodly of all, was taken into the popular mind of Israel from the visions of Dan. ii. and vii., and made the basis of further imaginative development in apocalyptic literature, such as the Sibylline oracles, the Book of Enoch, and the like. But these popular anticipations overlooked one feature in the visions of Daniel, the remarkable distinction indicated between the kingdom of God and the world-kingdoms. In chap. ii. they are parts of an image, *i.e.* a work of man, degenerating in excellence from gold to iron and clay; it is a stone cut out without hands, *i.e.* a work of God. In chap. vii. they are wild beasts rising out of the sea, each more fierce and cruel than the last; it is a son of man, coming in the clouds of heaven. This contrast might have taught men that the kingdom of God was to be different in its nature and in the way of its establishment from the empires of this world; and had the visions of Daniel been taken in connection with the plainer utterances of other prophets, it might have been seen that God's kingdom was to be set up by spiritual means, and not by mere power. But the expectation of many was that a divine judgment should destroy the last of the world-empires, and that the king of the new theocracy should literally come in the clouds of heaven, raise the godly dead from their graves, and reign with them on the earth in peace and plenty, with abundance of all earthly delights.

This is the view generally presented in the apocryphal apocalyptic books, and it was doubtless widely current. Any great outburst of wickedness, oppression, or persecution, on the part of heathen rulers, awakened in enthusiastic minds the thought, this must be the worst and last outbreak of evil, it will soon end, and then will come the Messiah and the kingdom of God. This idea found literary expression in imaginary prophecies by some ancient seer or patriarch, leading up to the times of the writer, and describing the future as he expected it.

This view of the kingdom of God, which is generally known as the chiliastic or millennial, would seem to have arisen from a onesided and superficial study of the book of Daniel; onesided, because it looked at it apart from the utterances of the earlier prophets; and superficial, because it overlooked the indications in these visions themselves, that the kingdom of God was to be essentially different from the earthly kingdoms. That the book of Daniel does not really teach such a view of the kingdom of God, appears from the fact, that Jesus, whose teaching was most decidedly opposed to such chiliastic ideas, referred with special frequency to that book, and borrowed some of his favourite expressions from it. He may have done so indeed, just because the book of Daniel had been made the basis of such earthly ideas of the Messianic kingdom, and in order to vindicate its true meaning; but anyhow, the teaching of the book was in his eyes very different from those wild enthusiastic anticipations, and we can easily see a vast difference between its brief and comparatively simple pictures and their extravagant fancies.

The Sibylline oracles are one of the most curious and interesting relics of antiquity, and have had a very remarkable history. Ancient legends give different accounts of the number and country of those women believed by the heathen to have been prophetesses, and called Sibyls or revealers of the will of the gods. There were from an ancient time verses current under this name in different countries; and at Rome there was a collection, believed, according to the well-known legend, to have been bought by Tarquinius Priscus, preserved under the care of special priests, and consulted on emergencies. These books seem to have contained, not predictions of future events, but directions for appeasing the deities in times of public distress; and were probably consulted by drawing out a leaf at random. They were destroyed in the burning of the Capitol in 82 B.C.; and thereafter envoys were sent to collect from various cities in Italy and Asia Minor such Sibylline oracles as could be found, to replace them. Many seem to have been found, and others were brought forward from time to time; several of the Roman emperors gave orders for examining those that were current, destroying the spurious, and keeping under the control of the priests those deemed genuine. What was the character of the new collection at Rome is not easy to say. Cicero seems to admit that they contained predictions of a great and universal king, and that they were not favourable to the Roman religion (*De Divinatum*, ii. 54); and Virgil professes to derive from the Sibylline oracles the picture of a golden age about to begin, which he draws in his fourth eclogue, and which has such a remarkable resemblance to some of the Old Testament prophecies.

Many of the Christian fathers regarded the Sibyls as true prophets of the Gentiles, and quoted from poems extant under their name; others thought that there had been a Hebrew Sibyl, who had given true oracles, though the others were deceivers. In modern times there have been recovered twelve books and some fragments of Sibylline oracles. This collection is very varied in character and date. Some parts are obviously forgeries by Christians, generally of a Judaizing tendency; others are the work of Jews, and these again are of widely different ages. There seem also to be intermixed or interwoven with the mass some ancient heathen oracles; and the whole is thrown together without any order or arrangement. The greater part of the third book, which is the oldest portion, is a Jewish composition, not later than the time of the Maccabees; and it is quite possible that this, or something like this, may have found its way into the collection made and preserved at Rome. But its chief interest lies in the insight it gives into the Messianic views of a portion of the Jews at that time.

The writer was a Jew in Egypt, whence most of such literary productions seem to have proceeded, and either for the purpose of deceit, or merely as a rhetorical exercise, composed a poem in the style and verse of current heathen Sibylline oracles, as an imaginary prophecy by one of these legendary seers. It contains descriptions of successive kingdoms that are to reign in the world. The Macedonian Empire is expressly and distinctly spoken of, and the Roman power more vaguely hinted at, described as still republican; then it is said, the people of the great God shall again be strong and be guides of life to all men (*Sib.* iii. 194, 195). This is considered by critics to refer to the establishment of Jewish independence in the time of the Maccabees. Then there is an outline of the history of Israel from the exodus to the seventy years' exile; and the restoration by Cyrus and rebuilding of the temple are described. Then comes a series of denunciations of calamity against various cities and countries for idolatry and immorality, and the Greeks especially are exhorted to repent and worship the true God, bringing sacrifices to his temple. There shall be terrible wars and battles, in which the ungodly nations shall be destroyed. Then God shall send a king from the east, who shall put an end to war and enrich the people of God with all wealth and glory. But the kings of the earth shall again invade the holy land; and when they approach the sacred city, God shall scatter them with his voice, and overwhelm them with fire and hail from heaven. Thereafter comes the kingdom of eternal peace and happiness, when all men shall serve and worship God, and all creatures shall be at peace (vers. 702–94).

A piece of much later date, though placed earlier in the collection, predicts that a holy prince shall come, who shall wield the sceptres of the whole earth; that then an adversary, called Beliar, shall come showing false miracles; but that God shall destroy him and all who follow him; and by tremendous cosmical changes shall melt down all the elements, and bring out of them a new and pure world (vers. 46-96). This portion bears evidence of having been written about the time of the second Roman triumvirate.

In these curious poems we see the popular form of the Messianic expectations of the time. Many parts of them are copied very closely from some of the prophecies, especially of Isaiah; but they have imitated chiefly the more external features of his description of the future kingdom of God. It is conceived simply as a worldly dominion, in which peace and plenty, wealth and prosperity, abound; and it is to be ushered in by terrible judgments against the heathen enemies of God's people, and terrible convulsions of nature. No spiritual promises are given, and there is no indication of a change of the law and ordinances of Israel. Sacrifices are still to be offered, and a temple still kept up as the place of worship. The personal Messiah, too, is of very little importance. He is indeed mentioned, but no special work is assigned for him to do; the conflict with the evil power is described as merely physical; and the final result is expected to be attained simply by mighty supernatural works of divine judgment. Naturally therefore we find no trace of a suffering and atoning Messiah. It is a onesided reflection of the prophetic teaching, in which what is outward, striking, and attractive to the eye of sense is made exclusively prominent; and while we must recognise in the writers of these poems moral and religious earnestness and strong hope, such as distinguish them from heathen poets, we see also a want of spirituality that would make them most unsafe and misleading guides to those who might form their thoughts of the promised kingdom of God on them.

The book of Enoch, though similar in its general form, is in some respects very different in its contents from the Sibylline oracles. In it the person of the Messiah, instead of being thrown into the background, is remarkably prominent: he is called the Elect One, the Son of man, and in one place the Son of God: he is described as pre-existent, and is associated with God in a way that closely approaches the Christian doctrine of the Trinity. The symbolical representation of the history of Israel seems to extend down to the time of Herod, or even to that of the Jewish war; and there are some passages in which it is very difficult to avoid seeing the hand of a Christian, while other portions would seem to be the work of a Jew, who had gained some knowledge of Christian phrases and ideas, and been partly influenced by them. It seems impossible to appeal with any confidence to this extraordinary production for the opinions of the Jews before the time of our Lord. In its general features, indeed, it is thoroughly Judaic, and may be regarded as a specimen of that class of Messianic anticipations that looked for a sudden supernatural catastrophe, and a divine judgment that should overthrow the wicked and establish a kingdom of God. But where so much is fanciful and extravagant, and there is so strong suspicion of interpolation, it is hardly possible to form any distinct idea of what sort of a kingdom the writer expected.

At the time when the Baptist appeared, there was a general expectation of the coming of the reign of God; but very different ideas of the way in which it was to come. At the head of the nation was the priestly aristocracy, which had indeed lost much of its power since the rise of the Herodian family, and the subjection of Judea to the direct government of Rome, but was still a strong and wealthy body, with the greatest influence in the Sanhedrin. Their aim was to maintain as carefully as possible what remains of independence Israel still had. Their Sadducean views left them no faith in any supernatural divine interposition or miraculous appearance of a kingdom of God; that must be looked for, they thought, through ordinary political means; and as political wisdom gave no encouragement to a popular uprising, they were shut up to a cautious temporizing policy, and deprecated any violent excitement. Then there were the scribes, who aimed at the rigid observance of the letter of the law, with the traditions that they had raised up as a fence round it, and who looked for a sudden miraculous interposition of God for Israel, if only it would perfectly keep the law. This party had the favour and support of the great body of the people. Some, however, were not satisfied with waiting in peace and inaction for a miraculous deliverance; but, zealous for the law, and provoked to action by public violations and insults offered to it, took up arms, and attempted to imitate the deeds of Mattathias and his sons, who had delivered Israel from the yoke of Antiochus Epiphanes.

John's proclamation did not agree with the programmes of any of these parties. It was too open and bold an announcement of the kingdom of God to please those who thought that the hope of Israel lay in wise and cautious policy, and in avoiding anything that might provoke the suspicion or jealousy of the Roman Empire. A popular preaching of the reign of God at hand would create disturbance; and once the unstable equilibrium of the national existence were disturbed, no man could tell what might be the issue. To provoke a conflict with Rome would be to lose the last poor remains of independence, and that in their view was the only hope of the promised kingdom of God. To the Pharisees, the movement might not be so immediately obnoxious. As they looked for a supernatural deliverance, a prophet like Elijah might be its herald; nor was a call to amendment of life in their view an unsuitable mode of preparation, if only it had been a call to strict observance of the law, oral as well as written. Had John given himself out as a literally supernatural being, Elijah, or one of the prophets actually risen from the dead, they might have more readily acknowledged him (see John i.

19-25). But he made no such claim; and it was not legal observances, but moral goodness, that he insisted on; and so the Pharisees soon found that his movement was utterly opposed to their ideas. Still less could the Zealots sympathize with one who did not enjoin publicans and soldiers to leave the service of the heathen, but only to be honest and contented.

But while differing from all these ideas and plans of the time, the Baptist's teaching was just in the line of the old prophets. They, too, had precisely the same tendencies to contend against. The politicians of Israel and Judah, who sought the safety and establishment of the kingdom from alliances with Egypt and combinations of neighbouring states against Assyria, were the forerunners of the Sadducees of that day; those who thought that by many sacrifices, fasts, and ritual observances they would win the favour of Jehovah, were of the same principles and spirit as the scribes and Pharisees of John's day; while the Zealots were animated by the temper of their last kings, who rushed fanatically into a mad and fatal rebellion against the Chaldean Empire. In the face of all these, the prophets had urged the duty of true humiliation before God for moral evils, repentance and reformation of these, and trust in God; and it was precisely these things that John inculcated.[1]

[1] See Appendix, Note J.

LECTURE III.

THE KINGDOM OF GOD IN THE TEACHING OF CHRIST.

MARK i. 14, 15.—"Now after that John was delivered up, Jesus came into Galilee, preaching the gospel of God, and saying, The time is fulfilled, and the kingdom of God is at hand : repent ye, and believe the gospel."

LECTURE III.

THE KINGDOM OF GOD IN THE TEACHING OF CHRIST.

WE have to proceed now to the central and most important part of our subject, the kingdom of God as proclaimed and established by Jesus. The phrase *kingdom or reign of God, or of heaven,* was often on his lips; and he spoke of it as a thing that had been indeed promised and expected, but was now to be made a reality by him and his work. The object of our inquiry must be, not to ascertain all that he taught about the kingdom of God, for that would imply an exposition of his whole theology, but to learn what was the actual thing that he brought into existence, and called by that name; and more particularly, whether it was indeed that kingdom, or blessed society of men, for which Gentile nations had been craving, and Israel had been taught to hope. Did he use the name merely by way of adaptation to the ideas of his countrymen, while his work would be more truly described as teaching a new religion, founding a church, or giving spiritual life and salvation to individual souls? In that case, the name would be a mere form of representation, and the study of it would only illustrate our Lord's mode of teaching. Or is it the most proper and literal designation of what Jesus actually brought in, giving a more adequate view of its nature than any of these other descriptions, true and important as they are? Then in studying it we are actually studying, not merely how Jesus sometimes described his work, but that work itself as a great reality; and as the Old Testament theocracy was, as we have seen, a real and active training of his people by God, so the Christian kingdom of God is the higher and more universal training for which that was designed to prepare.

We must pursue this inquiry by considering the substantial meaning of the sayings of Jesus, especially of his main and central ones, in which he gave, not mere incidental statements, but announcements of his great and chief work, and by observing whether, when we apprehend these as realities in the most direct way, the idea of a kingdom or reign of God falls off as inadequate and confusing, or whether it shows itself to be still appropriate, and, indeed, comes into view where we would not expect it, and proves to be the very thing that gives reality and consistency to varying figures and descriptions. If we find the latter alternative to be the fact, we cannot hesitate to conclude that the kingdom of God is not a mere figure of speech, but the direct designation of a great reality.

According to Matthew (iv. 17) and Mark (i. 14, 15), Jesus began his public work by repeating the same proclamation that had been made by John the Baptist, "Repent, for the reign of heaven[1] (or of God) is at hand." The only difference, if any, in the initial announcement would seem to be, that in Jesus' mouth it is more distinctly described as glad tidings. This is suitable to the circumstance, that while John declared

[1] See Appendix, Note K.

himself to be merely the herald of the approaching reign of God, Jesus appeared as invested with authority and power actually to establish it. John did not aim at forming a new community; his aim was to prepare the people as a whole for the reign of God, which he who came after him should set up. He baptized those who confessed their sins and professed repentance, but he did not form them into a distinct body.[1]

But Jesus from the beginning of his ministry attached disciples to himself, and these not only as the pupils of a Rabbi, but as the members of the kingdom of God which he proclaimed. His disciples were not only the few who followed him personally and received his instruction from day to day, but a much larger number, from whom he chose the twelve (Luke vi. 13), and who were found in Judea and Samaria (John iv. 1, 41) as well as in Galilee. The Sermon on the Mount is addressed to his disciples in the larger sense, and it addresses them as members of the kingdom of heaven. It seems clear that Jesus represents the reign of God either as already present or at least as so near at hand that men could truly enjoy its blessings and come under its power. His call to the people was to believe the glad tidings about the reign of God, and to yield themselves to it. In order to understand our Lord's teaching about the kingdom of God, we may consider—

I. The nature of the kingdom.
II. Its righteousness or fundamental constitution.
III. Its king.

I. When Jesus began his public work with the pro-

---

[1] See Weiss, *Leben Jesu*, i. 302, 303.

clamation, the reign of God is at hand, he was not introducing a new idea, but announcing the advent of what had long been expected and longed for, the blessed time foretold by the prophets when God would manifest himself as the deliverer of his people, and reign over them in righteousness and peace, defending them by his power, and giving them perfect and everlasting happiness. But there was no outward token of the sort of deliverance that they expected, no appearance of the downfall or removal of the Roman supremacy, no signs from heaven indicating supernatural judgments impending, like the plagues of Egypt, on the heathen power. At first those who looked for such things might be content to wait in the hope that by and by they would appear. The miracles of Jesus might even seem to them precursors of the more glorious things they looked for, though they were not themselves the signs from heaven that were to be seen when Messiah should come. But soon it became apparent that Jesus did not contemplate at all such an earthly deliverance as they expected; and that while he was declaring the prophecies of the reign of God to be fulfilled, it was in a very different way from what they looked for.

The chief points on which our Lord's teaching about the kingdom of God contradicted that current in his day were these :—

1. He represented its blessings as not external but spiritual.

2. He declared the way of entering it to be, not by works of the law, but by faith in himself as revealing God's grace.

3. He described the power that rules in it as being not force but life.

In all these points his teaching was in the line of the Old Testament prophets, and carried out their spirit; but in them all he went beyond what had been distinctly revealed or understood in the former dispensation.

1. We have very little information as to how Jesus explained the kingdom of God to those whom he addressed for the first time on the subject, since in most of his discourses some knowledge of it is presupposed; but what throws most light on his way of introducing men to it, is the account of his discourse in the synagogue at Nazareth (Luke iv. 17–30). Though he had before this been preaching and doing miracles in other places, and the evangelist may not have put it in its chronological connection, yet it was evidently his first address to that audience. He read part of Isa. lxi. and declared that prophecy to be then fulfilled. Now that passage is one of those that describe the glory and blessedness of the restored people of Israel under a new reign of God.[1] That expression does not indeed occur in the place read by Jesus, but it is found in Isa. lii. 7, where the whole announcement of the coming deliverance is summed up in one sentence.

What Jesus declared to the Nazarene congregation to be fulfilled before them was, not merely the proclamation of the blessings described in the passage that he read, but the actual bestowal of them, or at least such a pro-

---

[1] It is pointed out by Dr. Edersheim (*Life and Times of Jesus*, i. 454) that Isa. lxi. 1, 2 was regarded by the Rabbis as one of the three passages where the Holy Spirit is connected with the promised redemption, the others being Isa. xxxiii. 14, 15, and Lam. iii. 50.

clamation as is also a bestowal. When, too, he says afterwards, "Ye will surely say unto me this proverb, Physician, heal thyself," he assumes that he presented himself to them as a physician, *i.e.* one who brought a remedy for the evils under which they suffered, and that they were unwilling to accept him as such, because he did not seem to have delivered himself from these evils. For they thought only or mainly of the outward evils that they suffered, since the independence of their nation was gone, their religious feelings wounded by heathen customs, and themselves impoverished by the extortion of Roman tax-gatherers, and liable to have their blood mingled with their sacrifices by Roman soldiers. This preacher of the reign of God was as poor as they, he was making no attempt to shake off the hated yoke; the only thing about him that could incline them to regard him as a deliverer was that they had heard of mighty works done by him elsewhere; but these he was not doing among them; and yet he was asking them to believe, that they might have even now the blessings described by Isaiah. Jesus answers these thoughts of theirs by pointing out, from instances in Old Testament history, that divine works of outward blessing were done, not for Israelites as such, but for the widow of Zarephath, who trusted Elijah as a prophet when he was a poor and houseless wanderer, and for the Syrian Naaman, when he brought himself to take Elisha at his word.

All this shows that what Jesus proclaimed was a reign of God whose blessings were spiritual, and could be enjoyed at once. This attracted to him those who really cared and longed for spiritual blessings; while it repelled those who only cared for earthly things. He proclaimed that the reign of God was come, not because God was delivering his people from the heathen yoke by a new David or a new Moses, but because he had sent him to dispense to them spiritual blessings, forgiveness, rest, joy, freedom, righteousness. When men give themselves to Jesus for these blessings, God reigns over them and in them, and theirs is the kingdom of heaven.[1] It was not enough that people should come to him for earthly blessings, such as healing of sickness in themselves or their families; he would have them feel their need of blessings for their souls, and look to him for these. He did indeed do many cures for those who did not become his disciples, since whenever he found the sick trusting in his power to heal, he seems to have healed them; but in such cases he generally forbade them to make it known (Matt. viii. 4, ix. 30, xii. 16); for he did not want to become famous as a mere physical benefactor or wonder-worker. Where there was more than mere trust in his power of healing the body, he gave no such injunction, as in the cases of the centurion and the paralytic; and after curing the Gadarene demoniac, which was a distinctly spiritual deliverance, he bade him tell it to his kinsmen and neighbours.

Jesus' teaching in regard to the blessings of the kingdom he proclaimed is most fully and emphatically expressed in the beatitudes with which he opened his Sermon on the Mount (Matt. v. 3-10; Luke vi. 20-26).

The blessing on the poor in spirit is just an expression of the principle repeatedly declared by Jesus, in full accordance with the Old Testament, " He that humbleth

[1] See Appendix, Note L.

himself shall be exalted," most strikingly illustrated in the parable of the publican, whose humiliation expressed itself in the prayer, "God be merciful to me a sinner" (Luke xviii. 13). The poor, the humble, the afflicted, are often in the Old Testament designations of the people of God as a whole in times of oppression and trouble; and such a time it surely was then. None who had any genuine interest in the cause of God or the people of God could be really happy in such a state of things, when Israel was in subjection to the Gentiles, and there was so little real fear of God or appearance of his blessing. The priests and rulers indeed were wealthy and luxurious, clothed in purple and fine linen, and faring sumptuously every day. The Pharisees were satisfied with their own legal righteousness, and thought that if they only maintained that, the kingdom of the Messiah would speedily come, and they at least would enjoy its blessings. Such were like those described by the prophet Amos (chap. vi. 3–6), enjoying themselves, and satisfied with themselves; "but they were not grieved for the affliction of Joseph." Such as really waited for the consolation of Israel would not generally be found among the rich, at least they would not be those that trusted in riches; they would be really poor in all that enriches the spirit, whatever their outward lot might be.

The following beatitudes describe them as reduced still lower, mourning, *i.e.* feeling their poverty, meek, *i.e.* weaned from all haughtiness of heart, even absolutely hungering and thirsting for righteousness. This is surely that conversion and becoming as a little child that Jesus elsewhere speaks of, that change of mind for which both John the Baptist and he called. Does it not just describe what had been promised by the prophets of old, that God would take away the hard and stony heart from Israel, and give them a heart of flesh? The beatitudes really announce the fulfilment of those promises, which were connected with the New Covenant and kingdom of God, but were precisely those aspects of it that the Jewish scribes had overlooked and neglected. If there is a hungering and thirsting after righteousness, is not the law written in the heart, as God had promised to do; and does not this exactly correspond with what Jesus said to Nicodemus about the new birth? Yes! when such a state of heart is produced; God has really given new life to dead souls, and the graces mentioned in the following beatitudes, mercy, purity, peace-making, are the fruits and proofs of that.

Then, when Jesus goes on to say, that those who are thus described are the salt of the earth and the light of the world, does he not show how by means of this new birth of souls they become the nucleus of a community, and the means of extending the blessings they enjoy far and wide? The beatitudes speak of states and experiences that are individual, and from them alone we could not see how a kingdom is to be set up; but taken in connection with what follows, they present to our view a clear picture of a community of renewed souls, checking corruption, and diffusing light among those around them, and thus forming a people or kingdom of God in the world, a stone cut out without hands, that is to become a great mountain and fill all the earth.

The announcement that the kingdom of God is to be established by men being brought into such a state of spiritual poverty as is described in our Lord's beatitudes, is in perfect accordance with the sayings of the prophets. By Hosea the Lord says of Israel, "I will allure her, and bring her into the wilderness, and speak to her heart, and give her the valley of trouble for a door of hope" (Hos. ii. 14, 15; cf. iii. 4, 5, v. 14, 15, xiv. 1–3). Isaiah says, "The lofty looks of man shall be humbled, and the haughtiness of men shall be bowed down; and the Lord alone shall be exalted on that day" (Isa. ii. 11, cf. 17; also, v. 15–17). The blessing is to come "when the Lord shall have washed away the filth of the daughters of Zion, and shall have purged the blood of Jerusalem from the midst thereof, by the spirit of judgment, and by the spirit of burning" (Isa. iv. 4). Promises are continually given to the poor and needy as distinct from the proud and self-reliant; and God's dealings alike in his judgment and in his grace are designed to produce such a poverty of spirit. So by Zephaniah he describes the final salvation thus: "Thou shalt no more be haughty because of my holy mountain. I will also leave in the midst of thee an afflicted and poor people, and they shall trust in the name of the Lord. The remnant of Israel shall not do iniquity, nor speak lies," etc. (Zeph. iii. 11–13). In a similar way the process of humiliation and repentance is described by Jeremiah (chap. xxxi.) as the preparation for the New Covenant. Of the same kind are the representations of Ezekiel (xvi. 52–64, xx. 23–44).

Thus the conception of the kingdom of God implied in the opening of the Sermon on the Mount, however different it might be from the ideas of it then current among the Jews, was in full accordance with Old Testament prophecy; and if Jesus' words seemed strange to his hearers, it was only as those of Amos, Isaiah, and Jeremiah seemed strange and seditious to those who in their days placed all their hopes on earthly policy, or thought that God must save them because they were in covenant with him.

Yet there was in Jesus' teaching something more. The idea of the blessings of the kingdom of God being really enjoyed in the midst of outward poverty and affliction was one never fully apprehended before. Prosperity was the blessing of the Old Testament; and in the earliest times that was the only token of God's favour that men could appreciate. As the divine grace and faithfulness came to be more and more known, there was a gradual rise to more spiritual views. Men were taught that they might often have to wait long for the blessing that God would surely bestow on them. So they lived in hope, still regarding prosperity as the only thing that could give them complete blessedness, but resting meanwhile on the expectation that it would be theirs in due time. Such is the spirit of Ps. xxxvii. The Book of Job marks, and perhaps indeed effected, the transition to a higher view. Not only will God deliver his people out of all their afflictions, but he will be with them and bless them even in their afflictions, so as to make them really happier than the most successful wicked men. This idea and experience is expressed in Ps. iv. 6-8, lxxiii. 23-28, and also, though more from the moral point of view, in Prov. xv. 16, xvi. 8. Yet even at its highest point of spirituality Old Testament piety never rose so high as to see that the enjoyment of God's blessing and the light of his countenance is the all-sufficient blessing of his kingdom. For the people of God was still a nation; and even when the full enjoyment of God's salvation was dissociated from earthly prosperity in the individual, it could not be conceived separate from the prosperity of the nation. The Israelite must seek the peace of Jerusalem, and put that above his chief joy; and as long as his Jerusalem was an earthly city and nationality, he could not conceive of perfect blessedness apart from outward prosperity, if not to himself at least to the nation. When Jesus proclaimed the fulfilment of the Messianic promises apart from a restoration of the kingdom to Israel, and announced the blessings of the kingdom as belonging even now to the poor, the mourning, the oppressed; he took a step beyond any advance that had been made before, though it was directly in the line in which the earlier revelation had been leading godly men onwards. Now that which enabled him to do so was the conception of the kingdom of God as spiritual.

For the Christian doctrine of the blessedness of the believer even in suffering is essentially distinct from what might seem a kindred doctrine of the Stoics, the happiness of the wise man in whatever state he may be outwardly. The Stoic ideal is gained by denying any real goodness in outward things, and holding happiness to consist only in what is within the power of the soul itself; the wise man despises alike pleasure and pain, and finds his only good in reason and virtue, his happiness is from within himself; he is self-sufficient, and therefore proud and arrogant; while, on the other hand, his morality is of an ascetic, unreal character. He seeks to triumph over the evils of the world around him by denying them to be really evils at all, and finding the only true good within himself. Besides the fatal objection that this theory does violence to facts and outrages nature, it tends to deaden sympathy, since he who trains himself to despise pain will be so much the less able to feel for it in others. How possible it was for Jews in times of adversity to adopt such ideas, appears from their occurrence in some of the apocryphal books, more especially 4 Maccabees, where a philosophical argument for the supremacy of reason over the passions, conducted on Stoical principles, is illustrated by a rhetorical account of the martyrdom of Eleazar, and the mother and her seven sons under Antiochus Epiphanes. At the same time the divergence of this philosophy from the genuine spirit of the Old Testament may be seen by comparing this with the simpler and earlier narrative of the same events in 2 Maccabees. In the older record, the endurance of the martyrs is made to rest on faith in the creative power of God; in the later, it is grounded upon philosophical principles, and used to illustrate the power of reason to subdue and overcome the strongest passions and feelings of human nature.

Now when Jesus announced the blessings of the kingdom of God as present even in adversity and affliction, he did so not at all in the Stoical spirit. He did not teach men to seek their happiness only within themselves and in what is in their own power, to become independent and self-sufficient, despising pain and sorrow as no evils. No! he represented the blessedness of the poor, the mourning, the destitute, as consisting in this, that theirs is the kingdom of God; they can look to God as caring for them, and if they see God, and are the children of God, they have all sufficiency, not in themselves, as the Stoics would say, but in God. This comes out in that section of the Sermon on the Mount (Matt. vi. 19-34) which speaks of the relation of the children of the kingdom of God to the things of the world, which Keim thinks was originally a separate discourse delivered probably earlier than the other parts. The treasure we are to seek is not, as the Stoic would say, virtue in our own minds, but it is in heaven; and it is really the blessing of fellowship with and enjoyment of God as our Father. This secures and involves perfect blessedness, whatever be our lot in this world, not because earthly things are indifferent to a wise man, but because they are all in the hands of God who is our Father.

The blessings belonging to the kingdom of God, which make it worthy of being sought as the chief good, are described by Jesus very fully both in figures and in direct language. It is compared to a treasure for which a man would joyfully part with all he has, a pearl of great price, a great feast, a marriage entertainment. It is described as giving forgiveness of sins (Matt. ix. 2, 6, xviii. 23, 27, xxvi. 28), for when forgiveness is emphatically said to be given by the Son of man, and his blood said to be that of the covenant shed for the remission of sins, that blessing is certainly connected with the kingdom. Peace and rest to the weary and burdened soul is closely connected with this as its fruit. See Matt. xi. 28-30. Life, eternal life, is also identified with the kingdom, or used as a parallel and synonymous expression (Matt. vii. 14, 21, xix. 16, 23, 24, xxv. 34, 46). The same parallelism is found in the Gospel of John (iii. 3, 5, 15, 16), and this is one of the points of contact between the synoptic Gospels and that of John. The former represent Jesus as speaking most commonly of the kingdom of God, but in several places show that the same thing may be denoted by the phrase eternal life. John reports discourses of Jesus in which this latter phrase habitually occurs, but in one place shows that it was also called by him the kingdom of God. Sonship to God is another blessing made very prominent by Jesus among the good things of the kingdom he proclaimed (Matt. v. 9, vi. 4, 8, 9, etc.); and with this is connected freedom from anxiety about earthly things (Matt. vi. 25-33).

These blessings are all inward and spiritual; and Jesus' teaching includes no chiliastic views of earthly enjoyments in the kingdom of God, but rather implicitly excludes them. Heaven and earth are to pass away, while the children of the kingdom inherit eternal life; their life cannot therefore be in this world, nor can their enjoyment consist of earthly blessings. Jesus asserts indeed the resurrection of the dead; but he clearly explains that it is not to an earthly life, but to one like that of the angels.

2. In regard also to the way of entering the kingdom of God, Jesus' conception was utterly opposed to the views that prevailed among the Jews of his time; and from the beginning of his career he set his teaching in opposition to that of the Scribes and Pharisees. To them the law as an external code of duty had become everything: God's reign was the reign of the law; and

when all its precepts were perfectly fulfilled, then deliverance and happiness would come to Israel. Jesus said that that observance of the outward letter of the law, on which they laid all stress, was nothing, for God looks to the heart; and he also said, that the blessings of the kingdom come now to all who repent and turn to God, and are not to be purchased by obedience to the law. Thus, on the one hand, he set up a higher standard of duty than that of the Pharisees; but on the other hand, he brought a more gracious message of mercy to the sinful and lost than they could.

It was this last-mentioned point of contrast that came out most prominently in the work of Jesus, as is seen in the fault found by the Pharisees with him and his disciples for eating with publicans and sinners, and in the way in which Jesus vindicated his conduct in so doing, on the ground that he came as the physician of souls, not for the whole, but for the sick, not for the righteous, but for sinners.

Yet, with all its contrariety to the received teaching of the time, Jesus' proclamation of the kingdom of God was founded on the Old Testament, and was the genuine outcome of it. He did not introduce foreign ideas, but founded his teaching on the law and the prophets, and made continual appeal to them. At the same time he appeared not merely as an interpreter of the law, he was taken notice of from the beginning as speaking with authority, and not as the scribes. He called men to follow him, and, if need be, forsake all things in order to do so. The following or coming after him did not always imply a literal going along with him in his journeys about the country. It meant that in the case of the twelve, who are sometimes called especially his disciples; and they actually left their worldly occupations, and lived with their Master on charity. But as he had many disciples in a wider sense who did not thus follow him, he seems often to have used the expression, "forsake all," in a less literal sense, to denote a severance of heart and affection from all outward things. It is parallel to hating one's father and mother, and one's own life also (Luke xiv. 25, 33), not loving father or mother more than him (Matt. x. 37), denying oneself. This again corresponds with the warning in the Sermon on the Mount against laying up treasure on earth. The requirement of an actual abandonment of all might be used as a test, as in the case of the rich young man; but it does not appear that it was actually required in every case, and the essence of the condition was a heart detached from the world, and ready willingly to give up all for Jesus, and to suffer anything, even to the death of the cross, for his sake. This giving up all for him is elsewhere described as taking on his yoke; but it is coming to him as sent by God, and so is also spoken of as doing the will of his Father in heaven. This brings men into fellowship with him as brethren, and makes them partakers of true and lasting blessedness. If they have to give up all that they have, they shall have treasure in heaven; if they lose their life for his sake, they shall find it.

Such seem to be the fundamental elements of Jesus' teaching, and if we put them together we may see how they make up the notion of the kingdom of God. When men became his disciples, they entered on a state of things in which God indeed was their King; they gave their hearts to him through Jesus his Son, and they did so because they had also, through Jesus, the present enjoyment of forgiveness and rest to their souls, and the assurance of all they needed to have from God's fatherly love. This was in fact the realization of the Old Testament idea of the kingdom of God, so far as it could be realized by individual men. It was not as yet the full realization of it, for that implies a society whose members are all divinely ruled and blessed; indeed, ultimately it implies that this society shall be coextensive with the world. But every one who believed in Jesus and accepted him as Lord and Master, did really enjoy the blessedness of being guided and defended by God as his King and Lord, which was the special blessing of the theocracy.[1]

3. A further difference from the current idea, and a very essential element in Christ's idea of the kingdom of God, is indicated by his comparing it, or the word of it, or the members of it, to seed, in the parables recorded in Matt. xiii., Luke viii., Mark iv. At a certain stage of his teaching, Jesus seems to have begun the use of this form of instruction; and he told his disciples that the reason why he did so was the dulness of comprehension in his hearers (Matt. xiii. 11-13). Though they heard his teaching, they did not understand it, and they were not influenced by his exhortations. They thought only of an earthly kingdom of God, and looked for Jesus to raise a war of independence against the Roman power, and claim the throne of Israel. The more he spoke in plain language of the kingdom of God, the more would they think of this, and misunderstand all that he said.

[1] See Appendix, Note M.

The only way in which he could safely go on with his teaching about it was by clothing what he had to say in figures, the meaning of which would be dark to those who had such earthly ideas, but which would be more intelligible to those who were willing to learn that what he promised were spiritual blessings. At least those who really desired to learn of him would be led to inquire the meaning of his parables; and he was ever ready to explain them to those who were in earnest to know the truth.

Now, in at least four of these parables, he employs the image of seed. In that of the sower, the word of God, of the kingdom, is compared to seed. It is the word of God, as coming from him,—the word of the kingdom, as proclaiming it; and it is sown by being proclaimed to men. What the fruit of this seed is to be is not said in this parable, but there can be no doubt, from our Lord's use of the same image elsewhere, that it consists of works pleasing to God, righteousness and goodness. The parable teaches that the word of the kingdom has a living power in it, when received into the heart, to develop and work itself out in a holy life, adorning a bare and barren soul with a crop of virtues and good works. In the parable of the seed growing secretly, preserved only by Mark (iv. 26–29), it is the kingdom itself that is compared to seed, and its gradual and imperceptible growth is brought out; and the comparison is the same in that of the mustard seed, which makes prominent especially its great progress from a small beginning. In the wheat and the tares, the good seed represents the children of the kingdom, sown by the Son of man.

But these different representations are not hard to combine. The kingdom of God comes to men by being proclaimed in the word; when they believe and obey that proclamation, they receive the kingdom itself, and become its members or children. If it were merely an outward power by which this kingdom rules, then these things might be distinct, the rule itself, the proclamation of it, and the subjects of it. But since the power of the kingdom is a vital one, a power of life; those who receive it, and bow to its proclamation, receive it not only as a power over them, but as a power in them, which as a power of life is inseparable from their own life.

This general principle has several important applications in Jesus' teaching. It appears in his repeated declarations, that any real moral improvement in man must be from within outward, and not from the outside inward. So he says in the Sermon on the Mount, that good fruit must come from a good tree (Matt. vii. 27, 28), and this was one of the main points of his controversy with the Pharisees, that while they laid stress on outward purifications and acts of righteousness, they thought little or nothing of the state of the heart (Matt. xv. 1–20, xxiii. 25, 26; Luke xi. 39–42). They thought to secure the righteousness of the people by a strict observance of the outward precepts of the law: he taught that there was no true righteousness that did not begin in the heart and proceed from it.

With this is also connected another contrast between Jesus' teaching and the Pharisees'. They taught that the law must be perfectly observed by them and all the people, and then the reign of God would come; God would in a miraculous way deliver Israel from subjection to the heathen, and give them independence under his own reign. Jesus taught that the reign of God is not the reward of perfect obedience, but the means of securing that, that it is established in each heart that is willing to yield to him, and will bring them more and more under its influence. Hence his teaching was good news to the guilty and sinful, the publicans and harlots, for whom the Pharisees had no message of glad tidings, and whom they could only exclude from the kingdom they looked for.

With this is connected further his sayings about the need of being converted and becoming as little children. If the heart is to receive the seed of God's reign, it must be an honest and good heart, not like the trodden wayside, that will not even attend seriously to the word; nor like the stony ground, that admits only a superficial impression; nor like the thorny ground, preoccupied with the love of the world. From the heart of man proceed all evil thoughts and deeds (Matt. xv. 19, 20), and in order that it may become a source of good, there must be a poverty of spirit, mourning for sin, meekness, hungering and thirsting for righteousness; in a word, a new life in the soul, springing from heartfelt dissatisfaction and abhorrence of the old life. When the revelation of God's grace that Jesus brings is received in faith, and awakens love, filling the heart, then there is a new life, in such as Zacchæus the publican and the harlot in Simon's house.

These various sayings of Jesus, and the incidents recorded in the synoptic Gospels, fully bear out and illustrate his teaching about the new birth or regeneration, in John iii. 3-15. To be begotten again, or from above, is to have a new principle of life imparted to the soul, a principle that is secret and mysterious in its own nature and working, but manifest in its effects, as it makes one a member of the kingdom of God, *i.e.* a willing and loyal subject of God as his King. This life comes from the Spirit of God, and implies a cleansing of the whole man as by water. It is received by us when we believe the love of God to the world, as revealed in Christ's life and death, and trust in him for our salvation. Such, in brief, is the teaching of Jesus to Nicodemus, and it just sums up, in a striking form, what is implied in various sayings and doings scattered through the other Gospels.

Another feature, still more obviously implied in the representation of the kingdom as seed, is that it has stages of growth and development. This admits of its being spoken of in different aspects, as both present and future at the same time. Some of our Lord's sayings clearly imply that the reign of God which he announced was already, in the experience of his disciples, a present reality (Matt. xi. 12, xii. 28); at other times again he speaks of it as coming in the future (Matt. vi. 10; Mark ix. 1). It is not necessary to suppose that the kingdom is used for two different things in these various statements, nor to explain away the natural force of either set. For if the kingdom of God is a vital principle, it must necessarily have its growth and its various stages. The time of our Lord's personal ministry was especially the seed-time of the kingdom; but God's reign was to come, both in the world and in the hearts of his people, by a growth of the vital inward principle of the new life implanted by Christ; and it was to have its harvest-time when it should come to maturity and full manifestation.

II. We have next to consider the righteousness of the kingdom of God that Jesus proclaimed. For the idea of a kingdom requires for its completion not only a supreme authority exercising itself over the subjects, but also certain relations of these among themselves, fixed by the law of the realm, and making them one organized whole. So, when God set up his kingdom in Israel of old, immediately after the covenant by which he made them his people, he gave them a body of laws regulating their mutual relations and rights, in virtue of which they became, not a mere host under a supreme leader, but a body politic. In like manner Jesus, setting up the kingdom of God in the New Covenant, laid down, especially in the Sermon on the Mount, the laws, or in Old Testament phrase, the righteousness of the kingdom. In doing so, he solemnly disowned any intention to subvert the law or the prophets, *i.e.* the fundamental constitution of the old theocracy; and declared that the object of his coming was in general not to destroy, but to fulfil, or to ratify in its full extent and intended meaning. He does indeed go on to give precepts that go deeper and reach further than what is expressed in the Old Testament; but in no case do these overturn the old law, but conserve its principle, and secure its observance. He is, however, directly opposed to the current interpretation of the law.

The points in which the righteousness of the kingdom is to exceed that of the scribes and Pharisees are mainly two, its inwardness and its universality.

The former appears in that not only murder, but anger is forbidden; not only adultery, but unlawful desire. This was the best and truest way of securing the observance of the law. The Pharisees tried to do this by making a hedge round the law, as they phrased it, *i.e.* adding a number of outward positive precepts, that might keep men from coming near the act of transgression; but Jesus does it by enforcing the application of the law to the first beginning of evil in the heart.

But what he thus enforces is the Old Testament law of love, as comprised by him in the golden rule (Matt. vii. 12), which is expressly given as the sum of the law and the prophets. Only he extends the application of that principle beyond that generally given to it by the Pharisees, and distinctly makes it include all men, strangers as well as fellow-countrymen, enemies as well as friends (Matt. v. 38-43; Luke x. 25-37). This is the second point of difference between the righteousness Christ inculcated and that of the Pharisees.

Now the laws of a state determine the rights of its subjects and their mutual relations. In Israel each Israelite owed certain duties to others, and could claim certain rights from them. Within this law he might stand in various relations to his fellow-citizens, as ruler or subject, master or servant, creditor or debtor, but in each he had certain rights as an Israelite, which other Israelites were bound to respect. Others outside the nation did not share these rights; the resident strangers had certain partial rights, and other foreigners none at all. In these the nationality consisted, and from the nature of them it derived its specific form. Now the law that Jesus laid down for his kingdom very much simplified the relations of its citizens. Each owed to each to abstain from even a desire or emotion tending to injure them, and positively to do for them what he would have them do to him. That is, as he put it on another occasion, they are to be all brethren (Matt. xxiii. 8). This excludes all distinctions, as of masters and servants, in the kingdom, and gives equal rights to all. It does not, indeed, abolish all distinctions. Jesus very expressly took up into his kingdom the natural and domestic relations, vindicating the sanctity of marriage and parental authority against the teaching of the Pharisees, which infringed on it (Matt. v. 31, 32, xv. 3-6). He also speaks of differences in the kingdom, some in it being great and others less or the least. But he says, he is great who most perfectly fulfils the law of the kingdom (Matt. v. 19), who humbles himself as a little child (Matt. xviii. 4), who is willing and able to do most service to his brethren (Matt. xx. 26-28). Thus, in respect of rights and privileges, there are no distinctions at all; there are no castes, ranks, or orders, in this band of brothers.

Now, how was it possible to make such a kingdom a reality, and not a mere ideal of what ought to be? Only by making men really brothers, revealing God to them as the Father, and bringing into their hearts the assurance of his forgiving love, so implanting in them the germ of a new life. Thus the constitution of the kingdom is determined by the nature of the power that originated and upholds it, as in general the fundamental laws of any state are to be explained by its origin. So the various orders of the people of Rome, and their mutual legal relations in the commonwealth, are understood by the circumstances from which they originated. So, too, the constitutional laws of the people of Israel may be seen to depend on the creation of the nation by God's deliverance of them from Egypt, and giving them possession of Canaan. Because they are redeemed from bondage by God, all Israelites are his servants, and are not to be slaves of men; because their land is God's gift to them, it is not to be sold for ever, and so on. But that outward redemption could found only outward rights; the inward deliverance from sin, and bestowal of a new life, by which the Christian kingdom of God is founded, lays a basis for those spiritual heart-searching laws that Christ gives, and provides a motive and a power by which they can be fulfilled.

This law of the kingdom may indeed be transgressed, as long as the new life has not reached its full maturity and perfection; and some provision must be made for that. The provision that Christ has made is the law of forgiveness (Matt. xviii. 15-35), flowing from the forgiveness that all the members of the kingdom have received. If any one of them has been wronged by another, he is to forgive him as a brother, however often the wrong may be repeated. Not that he is to be indifferent to the wrong as an act of sin on the part of his brother: he is to seek to lead him to repentance by faithful brotherly remonstrance and expostulation, first speaking to him personally and alone; then, if that fail, taking one or two others as witnesses, that he may see that it is not merely one individual who has been grieved and offended by his conduct; and finally bringing the matter before the congregation or assembly of the kingdom as a whole. It is not necessary to inquire here more particularly how this is to be done; we are only concerned at present with the general precept here given. It is the only thing in our Lord's teaching at all resembling the setting up of a system of jurisprudence for his kingdom, providing for the way in which offences are to be dealt with. They are to be, if possible, removed by the faithful efforts of Christian love, seeking to bring the sinning brother to repentance; but the possibility is admitted that these may fail, and what is to be done in the last resort is, that the impenitent offender, who will not give heed to the voice of the Church, is to be no longer treated as a Christian brother, but as a heathen man or a publican, *i.e.* one outside the kingdom of God. In giving these directions, Jesus assumes that a brother has really been guilty of sin, and on that assumption he encourages his disciples to the performance of the necessary acts of discipline, by assuring them that, when they are thus putting away an impenitent sinner from among them, their action will be ratified in heaven. He is not here contemplating a case in which, by mistake or ill-will, they might condemn an innocent brother; but the proper effect of what he said would be not only to strengthen them for the faithful exercise of discipline when sin was clearly proved, but also to solemnize them and guard them against a rash exercise of it, by the assurance that their Master would be with them in all their meetings. We must remember also what he taught on other occasions about the judgment that is to be when his kingdom has reached its maturity, and he comes to sit on the throne of his glory. Then he will right all wrongs that may have been done in his name, and gather out of his kingdom all that offend and such as do iniquity, while he gathers his own from the ends of the earth. Meanwhile his people are to deal one with another's sins in the spirit of brotherly love, and in the last resort, if sinners are still impenitent, simply to treat them as no longer brethren.

But another peculiarity of the constitution of the kingdom here comes into view. It prescribes the same love and kindness to those outside as to those within it (Matt. v. 43-48). Jesus speaks indeed of an impenitent brother being to us as a heathen man, and that implies that we make a certain difference; but the difference is not to lie in our love or willingness to do him good, but only in what we think and say of him. We dare not call a man a brother or a child of God, if his conduct makes it clear to us that he is not so; that would be to call darkness light, and evil good. But we are not to love him less on that account, or be less ready to pray for him and to do him good. Thus the law of the kingdom not only gives all its citizens equal duties to each other, but extends that even to those who are not its citizens at all. It is thus a universal society in a very peculiar sense; for it not only offers but actually gives equal rights and privileges to all men, to strangers and enemies, as well as to its own members; it lays its citizens under the same obligations to those outside as to one another. The kingdom of God is therefore a universal society in a very high and emphatic sense. It makes its members not only brethren among themselves, but brethren to all men, even to those who will not be brethren to them. It claims all men as its citizens; but inasmuch as the power by which its rule is established and enforced is that of love, it carries out that claim by seeking, not to subdue all men by force, but to win them by love. The duties and obligations of the citizens of God's kingdom are just those that would be theirs if it really embraced all men. The blessings of the kingdom are not only offered to all men, but in so far as these consist in the love of the citizens, they are really extended to all, whether they become members of it or not.

But if, as we saw before, the brotherly love required in the kingdom of heaven is only made possible by the fact, that through the new birth in Christ all Christians are really brothers; how, it may be asked, can the same brotherly love be extended to those outside, unless it be assumed that they also are really brothers in Christ? The answer is, that the possibility of brotherly love depends not upon him whom we love being born of God, but upon our being so ourselves. We can love one another as brethren, in the spirit required by Christ, not because our brethren are born of God, but because we are. The fact of a man being outside the kingdom, and an enemy to it and its citizens, prevents him from loving them, but does not prevent them loving him. He is a stranger and an enemy by his own fault and will, not by the will of God. The King would have him to be a citizen; he calls, invites, and entreats him to come in, and he is ready to give him all the blessings of citizenship; and as one of the same nature as themselves, and for whom their King and Father has such good will, the citizens of the kingdom are called to extend their love and interest to every brother man. The believer is indeed a child of God, in a sense in which the unbeliever is not, but he is a child of that Father who makes his sun to rise on the evil and the good, and sends rain on the just and the unjust; he enjoys a love of God to which others are strangers, but that is the love of God to the world, to man as such, not to Jews, or to Christians, or to good men, or to believers, but to man. Unbelievers do not enjoy that love, not because it is not theirs, but because they forsake their own mercy. The love of the brethren is theirs, the love of God seeks them; and would they but accept it, they need no other right to the highest blessings of the kingdom, than just this, that they are men.

The universality of the kingdom of God proclaimed by Jesus appears also from all those sayings of his, which declare it to be an inward, vital, spiritual power, not coming with observation, but working like leaven hid in the mass of meal, or seed hid in the earth, and also from the fact that he gave no instructions about any outward organization for the society that he founded, but laid exclusive stress on those great moral principles and precepts that have regard to the state of the heart. These things plainly implied that the kingdom which was so described could not be limited to Israel, or conditioned by the acceptance of Israel's external law and ritual. But Jesus did not himself explicitly draw those conclusions, as it was not his part to exhibit the systematic and logical connections of divine truth, but to proclaim and accomplish the great work of redemption. He even asserted the inviolability and perpetual obligation in his kingdom of the law (Matt. v. 17-20; Luke xvi. 17). From these sayings, strictly pressed, we might deduce the position held by the Pharisees who believed, that all Christians must be circumcised and keep the law of Moses (Acts xv. 1, 5); and this would imply that the national theocracy of Israel was still to be maintained, as seems to be assumed in a saying recorded in different connections by two evangelists (Matt. xix. 18; Luke xxii. 29, 30). These sayings, along with our Lord's express limitation of his own and his disciples' ministry to the house of Israel (Matt. x. 5, xv. 24), have led some to hold that Jesus had really no idea of a universal kingdom, but was merely a Jew, with all the narrow and exclusive notions of his race. This view, however, cannot be maintained without disregarding sayings to an opposite effect, that are as well attested as these (*e.g.* Matt. viii. 11, xxi. 43, xxii. 9, 10), and also doing violence to those ideas, which, as we have seen, are not merely expressed in single statements, but form the most central and characteristic elements of Jesus' teaching. It is to be observed also, that when our Lord asserts the perpetuity of the law, he conjoins it closely with the prophets, and proceeds to interpret it in such a way as to show that he regards not the letter but the spirit of it. In what way he meant it to be maintained in his kingdom, is illustrated by his mode of dealing with the Sabbath law, in defence of which he appealed to God's saying by the prophet: "I will have mercy, and not sacrifice," putting the moral above the ceremonial part of the law. That Jesus extended his gifts of healing on certain occasions to Samaritans and Gentiles who sought them, is attested by all the records of his life, though, on the other hand, his limitation of his own proper work and that of his disciples to the house of Israel, is confirmed by the subsequent conduct of the apostles and Church of Jerusalem. He found the Jewish nation the field plainly marked out to him by Providence, as that in which he should carry on his work and found his kingdom. In it were those previous convictions and hopes that formed the basis of his teaching, and should have prepared a soil for its reception, the belief of one only living and holy God, and of his moral government of the world, the sense of the evil of sin, and the hope of redemption from it through God's mercy. His glad tidings of the kingdom of God were really in harmony with the spirit of the religion of Israel, as shown in the law and the prophets, although opposed to the Pharisaic interpretation of the law. The people of Israel, as the nation to whom God had given this revelation of himself, ought to have been the first to receive such a message, and by their receiving it, it might have gone forth with the utmost purity and power to other nations. But there are clear indications that Jesus did contemplate the ultimate extension of the gospel to all mankind. Especially in the later period of his ministry, when it became apparent that Israel as a whole was to reject him, he indicated in various parables that the kingdom which they rejected would be given to the Gentiles (Matt. xxi. 41-43, xxii. 9, 10, xxiv. 14, with the parallels in Luke). It is possible, indeed, that our Lord's last commission to his disciples, to go into all the world and preach the gospel to every creature (Mark xvi. 15), to make disciples of all nations (Matt.

xxviii. 19), was not given in such plain and unmistakeable terms as these. It was certainly not so understood by the early Church at Jerusalem (Acts x. 45, xi. 2, 3, 18, 19, 22), when they had so much doubt and scruple as to the preaching of Christ to the Gentiles. Neither in Paul's argument with the Galatians, nor in the recorded discussion of the apostles and elders at Jerusalem (Acts xv.), is appeal made to any saying of Jesus, but only to the general spirit of revelation, and the manifest teaching of God in the conversion of Gentiles. It may therefore be the case, that the actual sayings of Jesus were more obscure and less fitted to decide the question than they seem to be, as given in the Gospels, and that the evangelists, writing after the freedom and universality of the gospel had been fully established, gave to our Lord's words a form more distinctly expressing the meaning they were then seen to have. But if so, then we can hardly doubt that the form into which they cast them is substantially true, and faithful to their real meaning and intention. For the whole spirit and tendency of Jesus' teaching about the kingdom of God as a spiritual society, having as its law love to strangers and enemies, pointed to a religion not limited to one nation, or bound by ritual observances, but open and free to all mankind. If he could not openly proclaim this at once, because of the necessity of building his teaching on the ground prepared for it in Israel, this reserve was only for a season, and it was a true development of his principles, by which his disciples were led to throw down the barriers of Jewish ordinances, and invite all men to the full privileges of Christian fellowship. The universalism of Paul was but the full logical following out and justification of the principles that underlay the teaching and work of Jesus, though by many believers in him they were not perceived or recognised.

III. It remains that we consider what light is thrown on the Christian kingdom of God by our Lord's teaching about himself as its king. While the great subject of Jesus' teaching was the kingdom or reign of God, there can be no doubt that he also spoke of himself as king of Israel. He thus seems to have conceived the kingdom of God, at least in its initial and growing stage, not as a pure theocracy, in which God should rule directly, but as one in which God should rule through him as his representative. In that view he speaks of himself as in a special sense Son of God, and of God as his proper Father ($\pi\alpha\tau\acute{\epsilon}\rho\alpha$ $\acute{\iota}\delta\iota o\nu$, John v. 17, 18); he declares that all things have been given to him by the Father, and that none knows the Son but the Father, and none knows the Father but the Son (Matt. xi. 27; Luke x. 22). The sonship which he claims is not a mere title belonging to him as king; it indicates that perfect oneness of mind and heart with God that makes his reign the reign of God. The claims that Jesus made in this connection were on several occasions (Mark ii. 7; John v. 18, viii. 51, x. 31, 33, 39) regarded as implying divine honour, and therefore, if not true, as blasphemous; and this was the ground on which he was formally condemned by the Sanhedrin at last (Matt. xxvi. 63-66). These facts form the basis of the evidence for the deity of Christ as believed by the Christian Church. But Jesus' main object was, not to teach a theological doctrine about his person, but to show his moral oneness with God. He speaks of himself as the representative and embodiment, as it were, of righteousness, which is the character of God and aim of his kingdom. To be persecuted for righteousness' sake is the same thing as to be persecuted for his sake (Matt. v. 10, 11; Luke vi. 22); he places his own saying on a parallel with that of God in the law (Matt. v. 21, 22,[1] 27, 28, 33, 34, 38, 39, 43, 44), and thus he was recognised as teaching with authority, and not as the scribes. Still it is his Father's will that is to be done in the kingdom (Matt. vi. 10, vii. 21, xxvi. 39, 42); and when he sits on the throne of his glory, it is his Father's blessing that he pronounces on his true disciples (Matt. xxv. 34). He speaks of himself also as the bridegroom whose presence is necessary and all-sufficient for the joy of his people (Matt. ix. 15); he claims supreme affection (Matt. x. 37; Luke xiv. 26, 27); and he offers peace and rest to all (Matt. xi. 28–30).

We may thus gather from our Lord's teaching that his position in the kingdom of God is a necessary and fundamental one. He is not merely a teacher who has revealed it, and who may then pass away, or one who has by a great act founded it, and then left it to stand by itself. He is not merely like Moses, who received the laws of the Old Testament theocracy from God, and gave them to Israel. Jesus is the king of the new

[1] I accept the rendering of the Revised Version, "to them of old time," as grammatically preferable to the old translation. But it is to be observed that Jesus does not say that the sayings which he quotes and supersedes with his own were really what God had said to the fathers, but what his hearers had heard, *i.e.* from the scribes, that God had said. Still he does not merely correct their version of an old law, but gives a more explicit law by his own authority.

theocracy, in and through whom God reigns. This would seem to be indicated, really though not obtrusively, in the name by which he habitually designated himself, the Son of man.

The phrase Son of man (בֶּן אָדָם, בֶּן אֱנוֹשׁ, בַּר אֱנָשׁ, υἱὸς ἀνθρώπου) is frequently used in the Old Testament as a synonym for man, and in contrast to בֶּן אִישׁ (Ps. xlix. 3) it denotes man as frail, weak, mortal, *homo* as distinguished from *vir*. So it is used in Ps. viii. 4, cxliv. 3, for man in contrast to God, where, however, the honour and dignity bestowed on mortal man by God are described. The phrase in the vocative בֶּן אָדָם is habitually used as the address of God to the prophet Ezekiel in his book, and as that book begins with a full description of a most glorious appearance of God to the prophet, and the address " Son of man " occurs first in the midst of that vision (Ezek. ii. 1, 6, 8, iii. 1, etc.), its use may very naturally be explained as being for the purpose of making it plain that one so highly favoured with visions and revelations of God was still a man. Anyhow, there as in the Psalms, it means simply man, mortal, as distinct from God. In Dan. vii. 13 it occurs in a different contrast. After the vision of four beasts, there appears in Daniel's dream " one like a son of man " (כְּבַר אֱנָשׁ), *i.e.* a human figure, for that is all that is directly meant by the phrase. But here the contrast is not with God, but with the lower animals. The four beasts symbolize (ver. 17) four kings or empires, and the bestial form of the symbol indicates that they are empires of brute force and wild rapine. The human figure represents the kingdom that shall succeed them, which is that of the saints of the Most High (ver. 18), the kingdom of God (see Dan. ii. 44, and particularly vii. 27). It is symbolized by a human figure, to show that it is to be of a nobler and more humane nature than the kingdoms of the world, a kingdom imbued with reason and humanity, in which the rights of man are respected, and " a man is more precious than gold, even the golden wedge of Ophir." Thus " son of man " is here expressive, not of lowliness and weakness, but of excellence and dignity, but it still has its proper and original meaning as a synonym for man; and in this, as in all the places where it occurs in the Old Testament, it is indefinite or generic merely, not the name of a particular person or office. It may be that the figure described in Dan. vii. 13 is meant for an individual person, the same who is afterwards called Messiah (ix. 25); but this is not certain; and in any case, the name " Son of man" does not by itself mean more than simply man.

The peculiarity of our Lord's use of the title is, that in his mouth it is uniformly definite, both nouns having the article, ὁ υἱὸς τοῦ ἀνθρώπου, the Son of man. As we know that Jesus regarded Dan. vii. 13 as about to be fulfilled in his establishment of the kingdom of God, there is a probability that the definite phrase referred to it. "The Son of man" would thus be equivalent to "that human figure seen in vision by Daniel, the representative of the kingdom of God," and so would denote the Messiah, though it was not one of the usual titles by which he was known. Such a reference as this seems to be necessarily implied in those sayings of Jesus in which the title is used in connection with claims and privileges as their ground, as, for instance, when he says, " The Son of man hath power on earth to forgive sins" (Matt. ix. 6; Mark ii. 10; Luke v. 24). The forgiveness of sins is one of the blessings of the new covenant (Jer. xxxi. 34), by which the kingdom of God is founded, and therefore is properly dispensed by him who proclaims and founds that kingdom. On the other hand, however, there are sayings of Jesus which show that while he had regard to the passage in Daniel, he understood also the meaning of the appearance of a son of man there. It denoted that the kingdom of God was to be, not one of brute force, but of a truly human character. The representative of such a kingdom must also be the representative of humanity, a true and genuine man, ruling his fellows by reason and moral power, not domineering over them by force. This is, in a sense, a humble view of the kingdom, and so the title Son of man, while it is used by Jesus as a Messianic name, is one that brings out the lowliness of his mission. That it is a title peculiarly adapted to the humiliation of Christ, is proved by the fact that after being so constantly employed by Jesus himself, it was entirely disused by his disciples, the single exception of its use by Stephen (Acts vii. 56) being fully accounted for by his design of calling attention to Jesus' own saying before the very court that was judging him.[1]

Regarding it as a title of humiliation, we can understand both why it was so frequently used by Jesus of himself, and why his disciples nevertheless avoided using it of him. It has, in fact, two sides, denoting on the one hand the Messiah as the founder and representative of God's kingdom, and, on the other, the true and

---

[1] The phrase in Rev. i. 13 is not Jesus' self-designation, "the Son of man," but simply the indefinite, "one like a son of man," *i.e.* a man.

perfect man, the representative of humanity. This latter idea is implied in such a saying as Mark ii. 27, 28, and is more distinctly expressed by Paul when he calls Jesus "the last Adam," "the second man" (1 Cor. xv. 45, 47), "the man Christ Jesus" (1 Tim. ii. 5). Both ideas are combined by the consideration that the kingdom of God is a universal one, embracing mankind as such, and giving all equal rights. Jesus is the true sovereign of God's kingdom, just because he is the head and representative of that humanity that is its realm. Hence even to himself as king he applies the principle of unselfish love that is the fundamental law of the kingdom. He that is great in the kingdom is he who does the law of love, he that is the servant of his brethren. So he, "the Son of man, came not to be ministered unto, but to minister, and to give his life a ransom for many." He is king because he has made the greatest sacrifice, and done the greatest service for the kingdom; indeed, by that service he has founded the kingdom. His blood is that of the new covenant, and in Scripture the covenant and the kingdom are correlative terms. The old theocracy began with the covenant of Sinai, and if Jesus by his voluntary laying down his life establishes a new covenant, by that very act he erects a new kingdom of God.

Another form in which he represents his work in founding the kingdom, is as a conquest of Satan. Jesus speaks of Satan having a kingdom (Matt. xii. 26), and compares him to a strong man armed keeping his house (Luke xi. 21), who must first be stripped of his arms, and bound, by a stronger (Luke xi. 22; Mark iii. 27), before his possessions can be rescued from his power. Thus

Jesus appeals to the fact of his casting out devils by the Spirit of God, as a proof that the kingdom of God is come. It is to be observed that the force of our Lord's argument is derived from the moral character of his work, as opposed to Satan. It was conceivable enough that Satan might enable a man to cast out some demons, in order thereby to deceive men; but one who not only systematically cast out demons, but carried on a successful warfare against the moral influence of the evil one, could not possibly be in league with him. It is the same argument by which Origen meets Celsus, ascribing the miracles of Christ to magic. "There would indeed be a resemblance between them, if Jesus, like the dealers in magical arts, had performed his works only for show; but now there is not a single juggler who, by means of his proceedings, invites his spectators to reform their manners, or trains those to the fear of God who are amazed at what they see, nor who tries to persuade them so to live as men who are to be justified by God."[1] The victory over Satan, to which Jesus alludes as enabling him to deliver those who were his captives, seems most probably to refer to his resistance to the temptation at the beginning of his public work. Thereby he maintained his invulnerability to all his attacks; the prince of this world came, and had nothing in him (John xiv. 31); and his refusal of all the offers and seductions of Satan virtually determined the whole course of his life and work. He chose, in spite of all temptation, a course that implied his gaining his kingdom by no compromise with Satan or the world, but by triumphing over them in the endurance of the cross.

[1] *Against Celsus*, I. c. 68.

The motive power by which Jesus would draw men to himself was the revelation of the grace of God to sinners. He carefully avoided the use of any political hopes or ideas of a Messianic kingdom; he discouraged those who were attracted merely by his miracles, or by external benefits received from him; but he freely admitted to fellowship with himself, and treated as his friends those who felt their need of forgiveness as sinners, and were willing to trust to him for it. Jesus is thus the king of God's kingdom, because he is the perfect representative of God, both in that forgiving grace by which he draws men to himself to be subjects of the kingdom, and in that perfect righteousness by which he rules and directs them in it. In both he is also one with men as their head and representative, because the Spirit of God, which was given to him and dwelt in him as Messiah, is also given to them to animate them with new life as members of his mystical body, and to enable them to live as he lived, serving and glorifying God as he did. This notion of the vital and spiritual union between Christ and his disciples is indeed fully brought out in our Lord's teaching only in the discourses of the fourth Gospel, especially those in chs. vi. and xiv.-xvii., where it is illustrated by the figures of the bread of life and the true vine. But there are in the synoptic Gospels some indications that point towards it, as when Jesus speaks of what is done to his disciples as done to him (Matt. x. 40, xxv. 40–45), and of being with them always (Matt. xviii. 20, xxviii. 20). In view of this, and also of the fact that the mystical union is not a peculiarly Joannine idea, but one found as prominently in the writings of Paul, there seems good ground to believe that it was originally derived from the teaching of our Lord himself.

Thus the representation that Jesus gives of himself, as the king who is at once the Son of God, and therefore the perfect representative of his Father in his forgiving grace and absolute righteousness, and the Son of man, and therefore one with mankind, and able to make all who believe on him sharers in his Spirit, harmonizes perfectly with his teaching about the kingdom of God, as being in its nature a spiritual dominion over the hearts of men, and in its character a fulfilment of that righteousness which consists in supreme love to God as our Father, and equal love to men as our brethren.

Jesus was to enter on his glory as Messiah through his sufferings and death, and important light is thrown on the nature of his kingship by what passed at his two trials, before the Sanhedrin and before Pilate. By the Sanhedrin he was condemned on the ground of his own statement (Matt. xxvi. 64; Mark xiv. 62; Luke xxii. 69, 70), in which he confessed himself to be the Messiah, and applied to himself the prophecy in Dan. vii. 13, 14. The figure of the Son of man in that vision seems to be explained in vers. 22 and 27, as representing simply the saints of the Most High who are to possess the kingdom; but apparently it had come to be understood as pointing to the person of the Messiah as their King and Head. Jesus spoke of the fulfilment of that prophecy as about to take place soon, and within the observation of his hearers ($\dot{a}\pi$' $\ddot{a}\rho\tau\iota$ $\ddot{o}\psi\epsilon\sigma\theta\epsilon$). This seems to require us to understand his words as pointing to a spiritual event in the immediate future. He was to be raised by God to supreme power, and they were to perceive it. Do we not find in the 2nd chapter of Acts the record of the fulfilment of this word? Peter testifies that Jesus has been exalted to the right hand of God; and in proof of this points to the visible signs of the gift of the Holy Spirit. In these signs they could see the Son of man seated at the right hand of power; and this was the fulfilment of the prophecy of Joel, that the Lord would pour out his Spirit on all flesh. Christ reigns then as King, in that he sends his Spirit into the hearts of men; and this again is connected with the promise of the new covenant. The Son of man is the King in God's kingdom, as the dispenser of the Spirit, by which the law is to be written in men's hearts, and obedience to it secured.

The same thing appears from another point of view in his testimony before Pilate, as recorded by John. All the other evangelists tell us that, when brought before the Roman governor, Jesus declared himself to be the King of the Jews, and yet that Pilate pronounced him innocent of the charge of sedition. These statements imply that Jesus must have explained to Pilate that his claim was not a political one, and so that there must have been some such conversation as that recorded by John. There Jesus declares that he has come into the world to bear witness to the truth, and that his subjects are all they that are of the truth. Such is the nature of his kingdom. This harmonizes with the parable of the sower, in which the Son of man sows the word of the kingdom.

Thus Christ's kingly power is exercised by his Word and Spirit; and as these are the Word and Spirit of God, his reign is the reign of God. He continues to reign by these means, since he has left the world and gone to the Father; and if he appoints men as rulers under him in his kingdom, their only power is to teach what he has commanded, by the aid and blessing of his Spirit. There are indeed a number of parables in which Jesus speaks of himself as a householder or a king, leaving his disciples to carry on the affairs of his house in his absence till he shall come again; and in some of these he speaks of certain of his disciples as set over others as stewards. But it is ever indicated that all alike are his servants, and are to be called to account at the last for the use they make of the gifts and authority entrusted to them. It is also plainly said that the use they ought to make of them is to serve their brethren, in the spirit, and after the example, of their Master.

But while Jesus speaks of his kingdom as a present spiritual reality, he also warns the people that its appearance is not to be immediate (Luke xix. 11). He is to depart to receive his kingdom, as is described in the parable of the pounds; which seems to be the earliest clear intimation on record given by him of his departing and coming again.[1] But he has servants who work for him even in his absence, and are ready, unlike his fellow-citizens who hate him, to recognise him as king. "The Son of man coming in his kingdom" (Matt. xvi. 28) is equivalent to "the kingdom of God coming in power" (Mark ix. 1); and that was to be seen by some then living. Jesus undoubtedly refers to some outward manifestation of

---

[1] The words about the bridegroom being taken away (Matt. ix. 15; Mark ii. 20; Luke v. 35) are but vague, and have no definite historical reference; and the parable in Luke xii. 35-38 is given by Mark (xii. 33-37) as part of Jesus' prophetic discourse at the end of his ministry.

his royal authority, and most probably, as in his words before the Sanhedrin, to the outpouring of the Spirit, which was to be the proof of his exaltation, and to have visible evidences of its reality. The personal coming undoubtedly spoken of in Matt. xvi. 27 is not necessarily the same as that in ver. 28; the terms in which it is described are different in all the Gospels; and the solemn saying of ver. 28 may have been added, not so much to strengthen the warning of judgment, which was strong enough in itself, as to confirm the promise in ver. 25, that he that loseth his life for Christ's sake shall find it. This is sure, because even in the lifetime of some then present the Messianic kingdom shall be clearly seen to be established. In other sayings, however, Jesus passes over this nearer historical manifestation of his kingdom, and goes forward at once to its final appearance.[1]

The purpose of his coming again he declares to be to judge his people. The ideal or perfection of a kingdom of God such as Christ set up, is that all its members should be perfectly taught and guided by his Word and Spirit. This is not the case in any outward society on earth. But such a pure and perfect kingdom of God was foretold by many of the prophets, and they indicated that it was to be brought about by means of a judgment that should sift the people. Hence John the Baptist expected that the Messiah would undertake such a work at once in beginning the kingdom of God. But Jesus declared in many of his parables, that this sifting judgment was not to be till the end of the age.

[1] See Appendix, Note N.

This final judgment, however, is simply to be the completion of the work that Christ is carrying on now by his Word and Spirit and through the ministry of his servants. The exercise of discipline in the Church is, as Owen says, "an evidence and pledge of the future judgment,"[1] and Tertullian calls it *futuri judicii praejudicium.* Even the work of Jesus in his earthly ministry made a division among the people, and gathered to him those who were willing and prepared for a spiritual kingdom; and Jesus recognised this himself (Matt. xi. 25, xxii. 11-17), and as Messiah he pronounced the forgiveness of sins to those who believed (Matt. ix. 6).[2] He sometimes said emphatically, that he had come into the world for judgment (John ix. 39, xii. 31), and this effect of his work is also recognised in Luke ii. 34. Hence Ritschl thinks that this corresponded to the judgment foretold by the prophets.[3]

But, on the other hand, it must be considered that Jesus distinctly taught that his work in sowing the seed, however it might bring to light the different states of mind among the people, would not produce a perfectly pure society, and that there is to be a searching and final judgment at the end of the age; further, that except in the few places just quoted, he always speaks of judgment as future (John v. 28, 29, xii. 48), and declares that he came then not to judge the world, but to save it (John iii. 17, viii. 15, xii. 47). These sayings seem to show that in his view the judg-

---

[1] *Inquiry concerning Evangelical Churches,* Works, xv. p. 26.

[2] Cf. John v. 22, where judgment is described as a function of the Son of man.

[3] *Rechtfertigung und Versöhnung,* ii. 36-42.

ment announced by the prophets was, in its full and open realization, a thing of the future, to take place, not at the beginning, but at the end of the development of the Messianic kingdom.[1] Yet that is not a contradiction of Old Testament prophecy. For the final judgment is just the manifestation of the results of that process of sifting that the establishment of a spiritual kingdom necessarily implies. Christ's work of salvation does separate those who accept from those who reject it; and thus it virtually begins a judgment, that shall be made open and complete when his kingdom is perfected.

[1] So Weiss, *New Testament Theology*, p. 50. Dorner, *Glaubenslehre*, ii. 920, 929.

SUPPLEMENT TO LECTURE III.

THE KINGDOM OF GOD IN THE TEACHING OF THE APOSTLES.

IN the Epistles, the idea of the kingdom of God does not take such a commanding position, or occupy so large a space, as it does in the teaching of our Lord recorded by the synoptic evangelists. The different writers of the Epistles seem to have conceived the great blessing which Jesus brought to the world, and which they proclaimed, in different aspects, according to their turn of mind, and the different sorts of people to whom they had to proclaim it. Paul, having to meet the errors of Pharisaic self-righteousness, conceives the gospel mainly as the revelation of God's gift of righteousness; the Epistle to the Hebrews, addressed to those who clung to the old temple ordinances, speaks of the new covenant, with its better priesthood and freer access to God; Peter enlarges on the privileges and hopes of Christians as the spiritual people of God, to encourage them under trial and persecution; and John, in opposition to those who thought knowledge was everything, unfolds the contents of the gospel message as eternal life which was with the Father, and was manifested unto us. But though these conceptions of Christianity seem to be different from one another, and from the way in which Jesus is represented in the first three Gospels as describing his work; yet it will be found that they are all connected with the idea of the kingdom of God, and that this is the more general and comprehensive notion, of which they are but subordinate parts or aspects, and which in its totality includes them all. This is proved, not merely by the fact that we can by a process of abstraction and comparison reduce them all to aspects of the kingdom of God, while we cannot so reduce the kingdom of God under any of them; but by their being closely connected with it in Scripture, and by our finding in the Epistles the mention of the kingdom along with these more peculiar ideas of each of the apostles.

Thus the notion of covenant, which has such a leading place in the Epistle to the Hebrews, is in the Old Testament correlated to that of a kingdom of God. It was by a covenant that Israel was made God's peculiar people and kingdom of priests; and Jesus, while habitually speaking of the kingdom of God, described his death as the foundation of a new covenant. All that is said, then, in exposition of this idea in the Epistle to the Hebrews, is but an unfolding of one particular aspect of the kingdom of God; and in one place the very expression "kingdom" occurs (xii. 28), as describing in one great word the privileges and blessings of Christians. This seems to show not only that the writer's conception of Christianity as the new covenant is in fact a particular aspect of the kingdom of God, but also that this connection of the covenant with the kingdom was present to his mind, though on account of the state of mind of those whom he addressed, and probably also his own habitual mode of viewing the subject, he made the notion of the covenant more prominent. It is also doubtful whether he means by the expression (xii. 28), "receiving a kingdom that cannot be moved," to describe the kingdom as present, and not merely as future. Unquestionably, in the previous context he is speaking of the present privileges of Christians ("ye are come," etc., ver. 22). Believers are in some way brought into connection with the scenes and companies thus described. Yet as elsewhere the writer expressly says, "here we have no continuing city, but we look for one to come" (xiii. 14); and as even in the passage before us he calls that city "the heavenly Jerusalem," and in previous places speaks of the world to come (ii. 5, vi. 5); his real thought probably is, that we receive the kingdom now by that faith which is "the substance of things hoped for;" but that in actual enjoyment it is a thing of the future.

Very similar is the conception that we find in the first Epistle of Peter. While he is, as has been often remarked, very specially the apostle of hope, giving the first place in his thoughts to the heavenly inheritance, to the hope of which God has begotten us again by the resurrection of Jesus Christ (i. 3-5), and describes Christians as strangers and pilgrims in the earth (i. 1, 17, ii. 11, 12); yet at the same time he gives to the Christian community all the glorious attributes of Israel as the covenant people and kingdom of God (ii. 5, 9, 10), and his descriptions of their redemption by the blood of Christ (i. 18-20) are drawn from the passover at the Exodus, and those of their sanctification and blood-sprinkling (i. 2) from the covenant at

Sinai. The conception that is suggested to our mind by the whole strain of the Epistle is that of Christians as the people of God, redeemed by Jesus the Messiah, and journeying through the wilderness to the land of promise. This indeed answers to the radical idea of the kingdom of God in the Old Testament, but not to the complete realization of it as foretold by the prophets. That seems, in Peter's view, to be still a thing of the future, and in his encouragement to believers in affliction and persecution he falls back on the Old Testament thinking, as expressed in Ps. xxxiv. (1 Pet iii. 9-12), not representing affliction itself as a blessing so distinctly as Paul does. He does not so emphatically as Jesus describe the kingdom of God as a present reality and the sum of all blessings, though his thought moves in the same line as that on which our Lord's teaching proceeded. He has the conception of God as the Shepherd of souls (ii. 25), which is both an Old Testament idea, and one of Jesus' own, and he also represents God as Father, and his people as his children (i. 14, 17).

The Epistle of James is so entirely moral and practical, that it is only by incidental suggestions that we can gather from it anything like a connected system of doctrine. The expression kingdom of God occurs once in it (ii. 5); and then it is spoken of as a thing of the future. There is, however, hardly anything that can be regarded as distinctly expressing the characteristic ideas to which Jesus gave expression in the phrase.

Thus in the Epistles that represent the teaching of the original apostles, or were addressed especially to

Jews, we find that though the idea of the kingdom of God is not entirely absent, it is for the most part conceived as a thing of the future, of which believers in Jesus had indeed a sure hope and expectation, but not present enjoyment. This view was still that of the Old Testament and of John the Baptist; but did not come up to the full measure of the teaching of Jesus, which represented the kingdom of God as already present, in germ at least, and needing only to be developed, not to be introduced, in the future. The great difficulty in the way of the understanding and acceptance of this view was, that it implied a very spiritual conception of the nature of the kingdom of God, such as most men found it hard to apprehend.

During our Lord's earthly life, his disciples do not seem to have understood the spiritual nature of the kingdom of God which he proclaimed, any better than the mass of their countrymen. They did indeed cleave to him even after his refusal to be made a king by the Galilean populace had alienated many who had formerly regarded him as the Messiah: they did so from personal attachment to him, because his words were life to their souls; they saw him to be in a peculiar sense the Son of God, and he revealed God to them as a Father. But still they could not understand what he meant by speaking of dying and rising again; they thought that his kingdom was to be established immediately by some supernatural interposition, and they dreamt of earthly thrones being assigned to them in it. Hence, when Jesus suffered himself to be taken, and condemned, and crucified, their hopes were dashed to the ground.

They did not look for a resurrection, least of all such a resurrection as they afterwards believed and testified, and as is described in the Gospels. Yet the hints given as to the risen body of Jesus point to its being just such as he spoke of in his answer to the Sadducees about the resurrection, which had an important bearing on the question between Jesus and the Jews about the kingdom of God. It was not to be, as the Sadducees thought, a mere development of the hierarchy in this world, without any resurrection; nor yet, as the Pharisees imagined, an earthly sovereignty to be ushered in by a supernatural interposition of God and a resurrection of the pious dead to a life under earthly conditions in this world. The disciples saw Jesus alive again, and recognised him as the Master whom they had known, and who had been crucified; but he no longer lived among them under the same earthly conditions as before: he came and went mysteriously, and he ate with them apparently not so much to satisfy hunger as to convince them of his true humanity. They could not doubt that he had conquered death, and that thus his claim to be the Messiah was confirmed: he had entered into his glory, all power was given unto him, and he promised to be with them always. But there had been no such signs from heaven and world-convulsions as the Pharisees looked for; only they felt themselves to be new men, filled with hopes, and courage, and joy, such as they had never known before. Jesus had gone into heaven, and the Spirit of God came upon them manifesting itself in the usual way by ecstatic prophetic utterances. Hence they testified that even now Jesus was reigning; and while they still looked for him to come again when Israel should repent and all things be restored as the prophets had foretold (Acts iii. 19-21), they yet declared in the same breath that God had fulfilled his promise to Abraham, and sent his servant to bless them (*ib.* 26).

It is, however, worthy of observation that in the book of Acts the preaching of the original apostles, before the mission of Paul, is never described as proclaiming the reign of God, but that Paul's preaching is repeatedly described in that way (Acts xvii. 7, xix. 8, xx. 25, xxviii. 31). So also is that of Philip, the associate of Stephen (Acts viii. 12).

This seems to indicate that Paul, from the time of his conversion, saw more distinctly than the original disciples what was implied in the resurrection of Jesus. For it was the conviction of that great event that at once altered all his previous opinions. He had felt, more strongly than most others, the opposition between the recognition of Jesus as Messiah and all the received views of the Pharisees as to the kingdom of God; he was exceedingly zealous for the traditions of the fathers, and he saw that if Jesus were indeed the Messiah, these must be given up or altered: the teaching ascribed to Stephen was the natural consequence of belief in Jesus; and hence Saul consented to his death, and bitterly persecuted those who shared his faith. But when once he was convinced that Jesus was indeed risen, all this was altered. The Sanhedrin had been wrong in condemning Jesus, and therefore wrong also in that whole view of the kingdom of God that logically forced them to condemn him. It could not be by carefully observing the law and keeping up the hedge about it that the kingdom of God was to be hastened; it must be true, as Jesus proclaimed, that that kingdom was already come. Moreover, since he had risen, not to an earthly life, or to set up a worldly kingdom, but to bless his followers with inward peace and joy, and to enable them to meet death, as he had seen Stephen do, with calmness and hope, the kingdom must be inward and spiritual. Hence for Paul the glad tidings of the reign of God was the announcement that the Saviour promised of old had been raised up of the seed of David, and had been raised from the dead, and thus had established the reign of God.

This is the way in which the substance of the glad tidings, to the proclamation of which he was set apart, is set forth in Rom. i. 3, 4; and in a very similar strain he is represented as preaching at Antioch in Pisidia (Acts xiii. 32–39). Indeed, in the opening of most of his Epistles we can trace the idea of the kingdom of God in his thoughts, though it is sometimes so merged in the special subject of which in each case his heart was full, as not to be readily distinguishable. In the opening of the first to the Corinthians, he addresses them as a congregation of God called to be his holy ones, and to the fellowship of his Son Jesus Christ our Lord (i. 2, 9). In writing to the Galatians, he makes prominent the negative idea of deliverance from this present evil world. In the Epistle to the Ephesians, the idea of the Church, as the object of God's eternal love, is more prominent; but in the parallel one to the Colossians the kingdom of God's beloved Son is described as a present enjoyment of believers. In writing to the Christians of the Roman colony of Philippi, Paul enlarges on the heavenly citizenship of Christians; and to the Thessalonians he speaks of the kingdom of God in connection with their turning from idols to serve the living and true God.

But the notion of the kingdom of God appears more distinctly in the practical than in the doctrinal teaching of Paul. In Rom. xiv. 17 he uses the phrase "the kingdom of God" incidentally, as if referring to something which he did not need to explain; and says that it is "not eating and drinking, but righteousness, and peace, and joy in the Holy Spirit;" and he gives that as a reason for the lesson he is enforcing in the preceding sentences, that Christians ought not so to exercise their liberty in regard to meat and drink as to do moral harm to their brethren. The argument in vers. 4–12 shows that he viewed believers as servants of Christ, neither living nor dying for themselves, but being in life and death the Lord's, each one doing everything as to the Lord, and responsible to him alone; and he quotes a passage from one of the prophecies of the reign of Jehovah in proof of this (Isa. xlv. 23). The reign of God, then, is that dominion over men which Christ has acquired by dying and rising again (ver. 9), and it consists not in outward observances as to food and drink, but in righteousness, peace, and holy joy, *i.e.* in moral purity and love. Further, we may notice that the idea of Christians as one body under Christ, which underlies the exhortations here and onwards to the end of the Epistle, comes in as early as xii. 4, in the figure of the many members of the one body, which is a favourite one with Paul, and also in 1 Cor. xii.

We may say, therefore, that the notion of the kingdom of God, though it is expressly mentioned only in one place, underlies the whole of the practical part of the Epistle to the Romans, and is the presupposition of Paul's whole idea of Christian duty as there expressed. It does not hold such a leading place in the doctrinal part of the Epistle; though in v. 21 grace is spoken of as reigning, and in vi. 12, 13, which is however an exhortation, a reign of God over Christians is implied. But in his greater Epistles Paul views the salvation of Christ under the notion of the righteousness, rather than the kingdom, of God; though it is worthy of notice that the title Lord (κύριος), constantly given to Jesus, seems to rest upon a view of his work as being the establishment of the kingdom of God (cf. Rom. xiv. 9-12 with Phil. ii. 9-11). In 1 Cor. iv. 21, the kingdom of God is spoken of in the same sense as in Rom. xiv. 17, though with a reference to Paul's apostolic authority. Parallel, though somewhat more comprehensive, and approaching the use of the phrase in the Synoptic Gospels, is Col. iv. 11. When Paul uses it distinctively for the blessings brought by Christ, he generally speaks of it as a thing of the future. So 1 Cor. vi. 9, 10, xv. 50; Gal. v. 21; Eph. v. 5; 2 Thess. i. 5; 2 Tim. iv. 1, 18, and perhaps also 1 Thess. ii. 12, though this may possibly refer to the present. The only place where he certainly speaks of the kingdom as the sum of blessings, and also as present, is Col. i. 12, and there it is the kingdom of God's Son.

On the ground of 1 Cor. xv. 24-28, it is maintained by Weiss[1] and others, that Paul distinguished the king-

[1] *Bibl. Theol. des N.T.*, § 99, *n. c.*

dom of Christ, which he viewed as mediatorial, and having an end, from that of God, which he represented as future and eternal. That passage indeed speaks of the mediatorial reign of Christ as coming to an end; for in the light of ver. 28, where it is said that when all things shall have been subdued to him, the Son also shall be subject to the Father, ver. 24 must be understood of such a giving up of the kingdom that Christ shall cease to reign, and not merely of his restoring the kingdom to God in such a sense that he may continue to be king with God. The passage rather teaches, that when Christ in his royal power has put down all opposing powers, there shall cease to be any mediatorial reign, and God's dominion shall be direct over all, because in all. This is true; and it suggests important thoughts as to Paul's conception of Christ's kingship and mediatorial office in general. But it would not be safe to conclude from this, that wherever Paul speaks of the kingdom of God he refers to this final consummation, and distinguishes it from the kingdom of Christ as that which is now present. He seems to use the two phrases synonymously, and sometimes, as in Eph. v. 5, combines them.[1] Christ is now raised above all principality and power; but the kingdom that he exercises may be truly called God's

---

[1] According to the grammatical rule for the use of the article, τοῦ Χριστοῦ καὶ Θεοῦ should denote only one person, and be rendered, "of Christ and God," *i.e.* of him who is Christ and God. It is exactly parallel to τῷ Θεῷ καὶ πατρί (ver. 20); and there is no exegetical reason why it should be interpreted differently. If it be understood of one person, the passage speaks of the kingdom of Christ, probably though not quite necessarily, as a thing of the future; and in any case, it is very improbable that Paul would have written so, if he had uniformly distinguished between the kingdom of Christ as present, and that of God as future.

kingdom, since he reigns in God's name, and God reigns through him; only whereas God's reign is now mediated through Christ, at the last it shall be direct and immediate. Or, to put it otherwise, the future kingdom of God shall be the revelation of that kingdom of Christ which is real, though unseen, now. It is a Pauline idea, that the final judgment is to be a manifestation of what is real, though only perceived by faith now. In the passage, 2 Cor. iii. 1–v. 10, he represents Christians as having already life, righteousness, the glory of God; but these are not manifest as yet, but are concealed by our mortal bodies and the things of earth, and are to be revealed at last (iv. 10, 11, v. 10). Closely connected with this is the idea of the day of judgment as "the manifestation of the righteous judgment of God" (Rom. ii. 5; 1 Cor. iii. 12–15); of the final end for which all creation longs as the revealing of the sons of God (Rom. viii. 18, 19). So also he speaks of the appearing of the glory of our great God and Saviour Jesus Christ (Tit. ii. 13), and of the appearing of Christ in connection with his kingdom (2 Tim. iv. 1).

What hinders the manifestation of the kingdom and glory of God, is partly the unbelief of men, who are blinded by the god of this age (2 Cor. iv. 3, 4), and partly the fact that the whole creation has been made subject to vanity (Rom. viii. 20). Both these shall be done away when Christ has subdued all his enemies; then consequently shall be the manifestation of the kingdom in its full glory, and then, as God shall be all in all, manifestly reigning entirely in all hearts, the reign as mediated by Christ may be said to have come to an end.

As to the precise meaning of the Son's being subject to him that subjected all things under him, it is wisest not to affirm anything with confidence, since it is one of those ideas which occur only in a single passage, and on which, therefore, it is not safe to build a doctrinal conclusion. But the views given generally in Paul's writings serve to show that the contrast in his mind between the present and the future was not of two different kingdoms, the one of Christ, and the other of God, but rather between the spiritual reality and the outward manifestation of the kingdom, which is essentially one and the same, and is both God's and Christ's.

The fact that the idea of the kingdom of God, which is the leading thought in the teaching of Jesus according to the synoptic evangelists, is so much less prominent in the Epistles and in the discourses of the fourth Gospel, has been generally recognised by modern theologians, though in earlier times it attracted little or no attention. An explanation of it has been sought in two different and indeed opposite ways, some regarding it as an indication of advance in the conception of Christian truth, and others again seeing in it a proof that the apostles did not fully apprehend or retain the great ideas of the Master.

The former view is, that the notion of the kingdom of God is not the highest and most adequate representation of the salvation brought by Christ, but one borrowed from the Old Testament, and used by our Lord in his earlier discourses, because best adapted to the prevalent ideas and expectations of the Jewish people. In his later communications, however, with his own disciples, he chose rather to express the truth as to our relation to God through him by means of personal ideas and relations, such as life, fellowship, fatherhood, and the like; and these have been more fully developed by the apostles, especially by John. On this view, the conception of the kingdom of God is a merely transitional one, that was used mainly for historical and pedagogic reasons, but designed to give place to those expressions of vital union and relation that are truer representations of the reality.[1]

This view, however, can hardly be borne out historically. According to the representations of the synoptists, Jesus used the phrase "the kingdom of God," not only in his earlier teaching of the people, but also in some of his latest conversations with his disciples, as in his prophetic discourse on the Mount of Olives (Matt. xxiv. 14, xxv. 1), and even at the Last Supper (Luke xxii. 16, 29, 30); and after his resurrection, it is still described as the theme of his instruction to them (Acts i. 3). According to these statements, Jesus did not lay aside in his later and more familiar teaching this notion of the kingdom, but still used it, at the very time when he gave those profound spiritual views that are contained in the closing discourses recorded by John. We should be obliged to suppose, if we are to carry out the view indicated by Newman Smyth, that the synoptic evangelists were less exact in representing the real historical form of our Lord's teaching than the fourth Gospel. Now, though there might be no doctrinal objection to such an assumption, yet it is, on historical grounds, as a

[1] See Newman Smyth, *The Religious Feeling*, pp. 124, 125.

matter of fact extremely improbable, since all the circumstances of the case, and all the available evidence, external and internal, rather point to the conclusion, that the synoptists have more exactly portrayed the outward form and manner of Christ's teaching, however truly and profoundly John has expressed its spirit and higher side. Further, we must observe that the idea of the kingdom of God is very prominent in the Apocalypse; if, then, John had gathered from the later discourses of Jesus that that idea was to be left behind or laid aside in favour of more adequate conceptions, we can hardly conceive him to have written a book so full of it, and should be almost forced to the opinion that the Apocalypse was not written by the apostle, but by another John. This is indeed quite possible, but it is hardly safe to adopt a view that requires it as a necessary assumption on *à priori* grounds. In a word, this theory cannot be maintained without ascribing such an exclusive and determining authority to the Gospel and Epistles of John, historically as well as doctrinally, as cannot be verified by the known facts of the case, and endangering the trustworthiness of the synoptic representations.

However true it is that the idea of vital and spiritual union to Christ and God, as developed by Paul and John, is an advance on the merely external and legal relations which predominate in earlier and Old Testament modes of thought; this is not to be interpreted as if the notion of the kingdom of God was left behind as a merely outward one; we must rather recognise that the gospel proclaimed by Christ has elevated the theocratic idea to a truly spiritual one, as we find that in our

Lord's teaching it is viewed as a vital growth in the parables of the sower and the seed, and is connected with the fatherhood of God in the Lord's prayer.

The other explanation of the comparatively little prominence of the kingdom of God in the Epistles, is of an opposite nature, and supposes that it marks, not an advance in the development of doctrine, but rather a falling back, or failure to apprehend the full depth and height of the thought of Jesus. So Ritschl,[1] after a full and elaborate discussion of the question, comes to the conclusion " that the writers of the New Testament Epistles, while they care for the moral health of the congregations of the Christian religion, use for this end all possible relations of the idea of the moral kingdom of God, yet have not kept in view the essential destination of the religious congregations to the realization of the moral kingdom of God, and in this respect have failed to reach the high level of Christ's circle of thoughts."

A somewhat similar view is taken by Krauss,[2] who thinks that our Lord's idea of the kingdom of God as a spiritual and unseen fellowship of men with God and with one another, gives place in the Epistles to the notion of the Church as a religious society, which as such must be outward and visible, and the kingdom of God, in Christ's sense, is spoken of mainly as a thing of the future. This he believes to have been inevitable, because for Christ indeed the reign of God was perfectly realized in his own person as a present fact; but by the apostles it could only be grasped by faith in him,

---

[1] *Rechtf. u. Versöhnung*, ii. 292-300.
[2] *Dogma von der unsichtbaren Kirche*, p. 172.

and so was thought of by them mainly as a thing to be realized in the future, when he should appear again, and be with his people in person.

In favour of this explanation there is this to be said, that the process to which it ascribes the difference between the conception of the Epistles and that of Jesus' own teaching, is one which we know as a fact to have taken place in the age after that of the apostles. The Church very soon ceased to understand the real meaning of the Pauline doctrines, and in the writings of even the best of the Fathers, we find an external, shallow, distorted conception of Christianity taking the place of the profound, spiritual, and far-reaching ideas of the New Testament. It might seem, indeed, that to recognise traces of this process in the writings of the apostles who enjoyed the special enlightenment of the Holy Spirit, is somewhat dangerous, and may impair the regard we ought to have for the New Testament writings as the authoritative exposition of the principles of Christianity. But clearly the question is one of fact, and if we keep to what are the facts of the case, we shall not be led to any conclusion at variance with scriptural views of the authority of the apostolic writings. It is not the case, nor is it supposed by Ritschl or Krauss, that the Epistles contradict the teaching of Jesus, or give any view of Christianity that is inconsistent with his representations of the kingdom of God. If they for the most part conceive of Christians as a church or religious society, this is a notion that Jesus himself had taught them; and the other more comprehensive notion of the kingdom of God is not altogether absent from their minds, nor is it conceived in a way essentially different from that in which Jesus put it, though it is less prominent in their teaching. We must consider, also, that the form and selection of the truths insisted on by the apostles in their Epistles, was in large measure determined by the occasion of their writing, and more particularly by the great controversies they had to carry on in defence of the gospel, Paul against Judaic legalism, and John against incipient Gnosticism. Though they were taught by the Spirit to understand the truth more fully than they could know it during the earthly ministry of their Lord, they never could come to apprehend it as fully as it was in the mind of the Lord himself; and his words are still the most pregnant and comprehensive. "We know in part, and we prophesy in part," says Paul, even of himself and his brethren, who were under the teaching and inspiration of the Spirit. But in Christ are hid all the treasures of wisdom and knowledge: he has a perfect comprehension of the truth of God, and his words, spoken out of that perfect knowledge of the whole, are more full and adequate than any of his disciples'. Now the kingdom of God seems to be the most comprehensive idea in Christ's teaching; and the fact that the knowledge and prophecy of the apostles, though unfolding in many ways the import of Christ's words and work to meet the wants of the Church, were yet only in part, may sufficiently explain the less prominence they give to this great theme.

In the Apocalypse, the name and notion of the kingdom of God, or of Christ, occur very frequently; and it may indeed be said to be the main purpose of the book to exhibit the opposition of the kingdom of

God and the powers of evil in the world, and the final victory of the former. While it is much occupied with the future, and describes with great fulness and pictorial vividness the glory of God's eternal reign in the New Jerusalem, it also recognises his kingdom as a present reality, and founds all its representations not less on the teaching of Jesus in the synoptic Gospels than on Old Testament prophecy.

At the very outset, Christ is called "the ruler of the kings of the earth," ὁ ἄρχων τῶν βασιλέων τῆς γῆς (i. 5), a title taken from Ps. lxxxix. 27, indicating the Messiah's kingdom. Parallel to this is the ascription to him of the divine title, "King of kings and Lord of lords" (xvii. 14, xix. 16), as the guarantee of his victory, taken from Deut. x. 17, Dan. ii. 47; and this parallelism shows the identity in the Apocalypse of the kingdom of Christ and the kingdom of God. This kingdom is represented as having various successive stages. When Christ's birth is mentioned (xii. 5), it is said he "is to rule all the nations with a rod of iron," with reference to the prophecy of Ps. ii. 7; and that same reign is mentioned as still future, when he is described as appearing as a warrior after the fall of Babylon (xix. 15). To this final establishment of the kingdom at the second advent, the prophecies of Ps. ii. and Dan. vii. are applied in i. 7 and xix. 11–16. But the kingdom of God and of Christ is not entirely relegated to the future advent of Christ. His personal exaltation is described as his being caught up unto God and to his throne (xii. 5), and made to sit on it, and receiving authority over the nations (ii. 26, 27, iii. 21); and the reign of God is represented as come when

Christ is exalted, and Satan, as the accuser of the brethren, is cast down from heaven (xii. 10), though there is still a conflict to be waged on earth. While this is still going on, the Lamb in heaven is represented as the shepherd of the saved (vii. 17, xiv. 1-5), *i.e.* their leader and king. One other epoch at which the kingdom of God is celebrated in triumphal songs as having come, is after the seventh trumpet (xi. 15-18), at the close of the first of the two great series of visions, into which the book obviously falls. Whether the two series of visions are to be regarded as parallel representations of the same things from different points of view, or as representing distinct objects, makes little difference in the application of this passage; for even if the latter view be correct, the song of triumph seems to go forward by anticipation to the final victory, and so this coming of the reign of God is not really different from that described in ch. xix. Thus, in relation to the person of Christ, the kingdom has two great epochs, his exaltation to heaven, and his second advent from heaven.

In relation to Christians, it is said that they are made by him "a kingdom to be priests unto his God and Father" (i. 6), the idea being taken, as in 1 Peter, from the fundamental theocratic passage (Ex. xix. 3-6). They enjoy the blessedness of his reign over them as his own purchased people, and this blessing they have even now in the midst of tribulation (i. 9). In ch. v. 10 the same idea is expressed, and conjoined with that of those who are Christ's kingdom themselves, reigning as kings on the earth. A share in Christ's royal power is promised to those that overcome (ii. 26, 27, iii. 21), as a future privilege, as in Luke xxii. 29, 30; Matt. xix. 28; 1 Cor. vi. 2, 3; but in Rev. v. 10 the correct reading seems to be the present tense. It is not necessary to give this a future meaning; it may be taken as indicating the same gradual advance in the reign of Christians, that we have seen to be represented in that of Christ himself. Christians reign in proportion as Christ himself does; and just as Christ's kingdom is represented, both as already come with his exaltation, and as yet to come in the end of the world; so his people are described in one place as already reigning on the earth, while after the overthrow of the beast and the false prophet, it is said of the souls of the martyrs, "they lived and reigned with Christ a thousand years" (xx. 4). This millennial reign certainly describes a triumph of Christ's kingdom in this world before the great change that is to introduce the new heavens and the new earth. The description given of it is very brief and general: no outward glories or earthly enjoyments are spoken of; the bright colours of perfect blessedness are reserved for the description of the New Jerusalem,[1] which is undoubtedly heavenly, not of this earth; and so vague is the picture of the millennium, that good authorities are divided on the question whether Christ is represented as personally reigning on earth, and even whether the martyrs who reign with him, do so in earth or in heaven. The vision may be regarded as giving assurance of an earthly consummation of the kingdom of God previous to its ultimate consummation in heaven; but beyond that we cannot go. It is in a manner parallel to

[1] See Appendix, Note O.

Paul's idea of a kingdom of Christ, which he is in the end to deliver up to God: only it describes a period of triumph for that kingdom when it is to have perfect rest for a thousand years; whereas Paul seems to represent it as given up to God immediately on its triumph being complete. Yet the two representations agree in this, that the end of the reign of Christ is the general resurrection, when the last enemy, death, shall be for ever abolished. The thousand years of the Apocalypse are doubtless to be understood symbolically, like the other numbers in that book, as denoting a great though limited time, proving the completeness of the victory by which it is obtained. That victory is the destruction of the beast and the false prophet, and the binding of Satan in the abyss. Now the beast and the false prophet are undoubtedly symbols of earthly antichristian powers, probably one or other of them identical with the man of sin, described by Paul in 2 Thess. ii. Whether their fall is past or future need not be here inquired; for in any case the destruction of such earthly powers describes a historical event in the course of the world's progress, not a cosmical change which shall bring its history to an end. The millennial reign, then, would seem to denote simply the triumph of Christianity in the world, and it is distinctly depicted as being neither absolutely complete nor final. It may not even point to any one definite and precise period of triumph, but may indicate in general the times of success and victory that Christ's cause is to have in the course of the world's history as foretastes of its final and everlasting triumph.

LECTURE IV.

DOCTRINAL IDEA OF THE KINGDOM OF GOD.

LUKE XVII. 20, 21.—"And being asked by the Pharisees when the kingdom of God cometh, he answered them and said, The kingdom of God cometh not with observation : neither shall they say, Lo, here ! or, there ; for lo ! the kingdom of God is within you."

LECTURE IV.

DOCTRINAL IDEA OF THE KINGDOM OF GOD.

IF there is good reason to believe that when our Lord spoke of the kingdom of God he was not merely accommodating to current language an idea that might more adequately be expressed otherwise, but giving the most appropriate utterance to his meaning, inasmuch as his work was really the accomplishment of what had been foretold by the prophets, though in a far higher form than they clearly saw, and in a way quite different from the expectations of the time; then this notion is one that deserves and demands careful study, in order that we may have a clear and correct understanding of what it means.

To form a definite and precise conception of the kingdom of God as Jesus proclaimed it, is, however, far from being an easy task, though it is one that must be at least approximately performed, in order to have any clear ideas on the subject. The difficulty arises partly from the comprehensiveness of the term which our Lord used. It may be said to include the whole of Christianity, all that Jesus came to set up on earth. The kingdom of God is spoken of by him as the entire theme of his preaching, and of that of his disciples; and whether he speaks of blessings, duties, ordinances, dealings of providence, history, or judgment, all alike are connected in some way with the kingdom of God. It is viewed at different times in very various aspects; and we have to remember that the same phrase denotes, according to the connections in which it stands, the royalty, the reign, or the realm of God. The difficulty of defining it is further increased by the fact that it is a living and growing thing, not a mere stationary and lifeless institution. As life itself is so hard to define, so are all things that have life. They cannot be fastened down to one particular shape or phase, for in virtue of the principle of growth and development in them, they are ever changing, and their forms are free and elastic, not to be trimmed into mechanical or mathematical regularity. The kingdom of God is a thing of this sort, a seed or plant that appears in different forms at successive stages of its history. Hence a definition that might exactly apply to it at one stage might be quite unsuitable at another: we must seek to discover what are the elements that are common to it in all its outward forms.

Yet these very sources of difficulty may indicate in general where the definition is to be sought. If it denotes comprehensively all that Jesus came to set up, it must be distinctively Christian in its character. We have not here to do with those more general senses in which God may be spoken of as a king, and is so described in some places of Scripture. As upholding and governing all things by his providence, God may be appropriately conceived as a universal king; and more particularly, as exercising a moral government over his intelligent creatures, he may be compared to a righteous ruler among men. But it is neither God's general providence nor his moral government that Jesus means when he speaks of the kingdom of God, but a sway that God exercises by that grace which he came to reveal and to bring to men.

Then, further, since the kingdom of God is a living and growing thing, it denotes Christianity not as a mere system of doctrine or outward institution, but as an actual salvation, a new life. It is not merely a sect holding certain beliefs taught by Jesus, nor a society instituted by him and governed by laws of his appointment; it is a body pervaded by new spiritual life, or that spiritual life itself pervading and transforming the life of men. Such are the general conditions that must be fulfilled by any definition of the kingdom of God that would be true to our Lord's conception of it. It appears from a general survey of his teaching about it, that the kingdom is distinctively and comprehensively Christian, and that it refers to Christianity in its living and practical aspect.

Most of our Lord's sayings describe what belongs to the kingdom, rather than what it is in itself, since they were designed for the practical purpose of bringing men into the kingdom, and not for helping us to define its nature. But there are some that indicate more directly what it is, and from these a definition may most properly be formed. Such are the following passages:—

(1.) Matt. vi. 10 compared with Luke xi. 2. The fact that in the Lord's Prayer as given by Luke the petition, "Thy will be done on earth as it is in heaven," is, according to the best authorities, omitted, seems to show that petition to be an explanation or expansion of the preceding one, so that the prayer in the shorter form would contain the same meaning, only not so fully expressed, as in the longer form. According to this explanation, then, the kingdom or reign of God would consist in his will being done on earth as it is in heaven: and that the will of God here meant is that expressed in the law of righteousness and love, appears from the whole tenor of the preceding chapter of Matthew.

(2.) Matt. xii. 28; Luke xi. 13. "If I by the Spirit of God cast out demons, then is the kingdom of God come upon you." This saying shows that the kingdom of God is brought near by the Spirit of God as a power working on the side of moral goodness, casting out the spirit of Satan as the leader and representative of moral evil. With these may be compared the Joannine sayings about the new birth of the Spirit as necessary for entering the kingdom of God (John iii. 3–8).

(3.) Luke xvii. 20, 21 shows that the reign of God was even in the days of Jesus a present reality of an inward and spiritual nature.[1]

Along with these particular utterances, we must take with us the general truth embodied in our Lord's teaching as a whole, that the kingdom of God is essentially and inseparably connected with his own person as the Son of man.

From the materials already gathered, looked at from the points of view indicated by these sayings, which approach the nearest to giving us an idea of the essential nature of the kingdom of God, we may now, with a view to clearness of thought, endeavour to frame a definition of it as conceived by Christ. Various

[1] See Appendix, Note P.

definitions have indeed been given already by eminent theologians, and sometimes in the symbolical books of the several Churches,[1] but these are so diverse, and some of them so open to criticism on various grounds, that there seems to be room and need for proposing another, that may bring out simply and precisely the essential elements in the notion of the kingdom of God. The following may be taken as a basis at least for an exposition of the idea:—The gathering together of men, under God's eternal law of righteous love, by the vital power of his redeeming love in Jesus Christ, brought to bear upon them through the Holy Spirit.

The definition must clearly be verified by a careful examination of each part of it, to see whether each is well founded in the teaching of Christ, and whether any important part of his teaching about the kingdom of God is omitted. As we proceed with this examination, we shall have the opportunity of comparing our definition with some of the others that have been given in regard to the points in which they differ.

1. By taking as the generic notion of the kingdom of God "a gathering together," we can retain the comprehensive sense of the Greek word $\beta\alpha\sigma\iota\lambda\epsilon\iota\alpha$, as meaning both reign or exercise of kingly power, and realm or subjects of such power; for gathering together may denote either the act or the result, the process by which men are brought together and kept together, i.e. kingly power or reign, or the society formed by that process, i.e. kingdom or realm. It is important to recognise the former element in the definition, not only

[1] See Appendix, Note Q.

because the scriptural term includes it, but also because some modern views of the kingdom of God are seriously defective in this respect.

One of these is that of Maurice, who in some respects makes admirable use of the notion of the kingdom of God in the exposition of Scripture and for practical purposes, contrasting it as he does with the world-kingdom in its various forms. But he regards the kingdom of God as a spiritual constitution really embracing all men by nature whether they know it or not, and only revealed, not actually founded, by the coming and work, the life and death, of Christ. He maintained this on the ground of a mystical philosophy, according to which mankind was created in Christ the Son of God, and he is in them all, though not known or recognised by many until he is revealed in them, when they come to see their real position as sons of God, and giving up the attempt to live in selfish isolation, are willing to live as God's children in that spiritual constitution or kingdom in which they have all along been. Neither the work of Christ nor the conversion of men makes any real change in their relation to God; the one is but the revelation, and the other the recognition, of the essential relation of sonship in which all men ever are, because really and mystically in God's Son. Maurice did not deal much in precise definitions; but if this view of the kingdom of God was to be formulated, it would have to be described, not as a gathering together of men, but as the revelation of the essential oneness of men with Christ.

It would be out of place to enter here into an

examination of this theory as a whole; but I cannot but think that no view does justice to the sayings of Jesus about the kingdom of God which does not regard it as something that he not merely announced as already existing and only needing to be revealed, but actually brought near and established among men. The same remark applies to views sometimes indicated or implied, though seldom explicitly stated, identifying the kingdom of God with his government and training men by moral and spiritual laws.

In the sense of the realm or society gathered together by Christ as the kingdom of God, our definition corresponds, in its generic part, to that of the Church in all its various forms; for all the different theological schools agree in defining the Church generically as a collection of men (*cœtus hominum*), however they vary as to its specific difference.

This means that Jesus' ideal is a social one; his aim is not merely to elevate and sanctify individuals, but to unite them into a community, to renovate society, and indeed ultimately humanity itself. This is indicated by the name kingdom of God, and is proved by all the considerations that show that the name is not a mere figure of speech, but the appropriate designation of a great reality. It is a society bound together by certain laws, and ruled by a power which guides the action of the parts and of the whole to an end that is adequate and good. What Jesus has originated and brought into the world is not simply a healing of the moral diseases and satisfying the spiritual wants of individuals, but a gathering of them together into one body or community. The ideal of Christianity is a society, a city, a country, a congregation, a people of God. There is not one of the New Testament writers in which this does not appear in one form or other; and the very variety of the forms in which it is clothed by the different apostles brings out more strikingly the identity of the general notion underlying all these various forms. Only, as we shall afterwards see, it is a gathering together of men by spiritual means and powers, and therefore it is not a society in the sense in which that term is applied to those outward and visible combinations into which bodies of men form themselves under various influences and for various purposes. Hence it is described as a heavenly country, the Jerusalem that is above, the city that is to come. What form it shall assume when its principle of union is fully operative and its gathering together of men has been accomplished and made manifest, doth not yet appear; but meanwhile the kingdom of God is a society only in the sense in which Protestants describe the Church catholic as such, *i.e.* the sense in which the Romans spoke of *societas generis humani*, not as being one polity under one government, but as being spiritually one, having the same objects and the same principles, the same supports and the same enemies.[1]

But here the question may naturally arise, Is the notion of the kingdom of God really different from that of the Church of Christ? Are these not just different names for the same thing? So it has often been assumed, and the terms have been used as synonyms, and discussions about the kingdom of God or of Christ have often passed on, without explanation or argument

---

[1] See Arnold's *Life and Correspondence*, Letter xxii.

for their identity, to conclusions about the Church.¹ This has been very generally done, though in many different ways, from the time of Augustine until recently. Of late, however, the notions of the Church and the kingdom of God have been not only distinguished, but by some entirely separated from each other; and it has been held to be of great doctrinal importance to maintain the distinction. It is necessary therefore to consider in what way these terms are related to each other in the New Testament, how far they are distinct in meaning, and what is the real distinction between them.²

The name *church* is in Jesus' teaching simply a historical designation, not a theological idea, as the name *kingdom of God* is. It is not, as he uses it, a thought that stands in direct connection with the great general principles of religion, and from which practical consequences are deduced; it is simply the name of the association of his disciples for the purpose of carrying out his mission. The idea, which may be conveyed by his use of the name, that his followers are the true people of God, as Israel was of old, is not made prominent by Jesus, though it was afterwards emphasized by the apostles. That idea, in our Lord's teaching, appears more in his sayings about his people being elected of God, than in the two places (Matt. xvi. 18, xviii. 17) where alone he speaks of the Church, in both of which, too, he seems to mean the outward visible society of his disciples. In the same merely historical

---

[1] Such a transition is made both in Whately's and Maurice's works on *The Kingdom of Christ*.
[2] See Appendix, Note R.

way the Church is spoken of in the Acts, the Catholic Epistles, the Revelation, and the earlier Epistles of Paul; and it is only in his later Epistles, especially those to the Ephesians and Colossians, that it appears as a doctrinal idea, being conceived as the company of the elect forming the body of Christ.

Shall we say, then, that according to the teaching of Christ, the Church is essentially an external society, and that the notion of an invisible Church involves a contradiction; that what is meant to be expressed by it is the kingdom of God, and that the true distinction is not between the Church visible and invisible, but between the Church, which is essentially visible, and the kingdom of God, which is spiritual? So many modern writers say, *e.g.* Schleiermacher, Schweizer, Ebrard.

But it is undeniable that Paul, in his later Epistles at least, speaks of the Church in a way that can only be understood, if he means by it the body of those who are truly believers in Christ; and unless the authority of these Epistles is to be rejected, these statements fully warrant the idea of the Church invisible as held by Protestants.

Besides, the notion of the Church as an external society cannot stand by itself except on the hierarchical theory of its constitution, which is opposed to the whole tone and spirit of New Testament teaching. If Jesus appointed the apostles as the heads of an ecclesiastical hierarchy that was to be the essential element in the Church he founded; then we can maintain the idea of a visible Church without any recognition of a Church invisible; and that is the Roman Catholic theory.

But if that is not what Christ instituted; then the visible Church of professing Christians must presuppose a body of true Christians, the Church invisible: and to say that this is not the Church but the kingdom of God, is either to introduce needless confusion, or to make the distinction one of two different bodies, and not merely two different aspects of the same body. If the kingdom of God is the thing meant by the invisible Church, then the manifestation of that kingdom is the visible Church; but if the manifestation of God's reign over men includes more than falls within the functions of the Church as an external society, then there must be a similar difference between the kingdom itself and the Church invisible.

The relation between the notion of the Church invisible and that of the kingdom of God may be seen, by considering wherein they agree, and wherein they differ. They agree in respect of the persons included in them. The subjects of Christ's kingdom are the same who are members of the Church invisible. This appears exegetically even from the Old Testament, where "the congregation of the Lord" and the "kingdom of priests" denote the same people, and also from the passages in the New Testament where those Old Testament expressions are used. So the theological definitions agree in describing each not only as a company of men, but in its component parts as the same company. Both, too, regard them as gathered together in Christ by God's redeeming love. But the notion of the Church contemplates them solely in their relation to God, whether as chosen by him as the objects of his love, or as trusting in him in response to that love, or as his saints or holy ones; whereas the teaching of Jesus about the kingdom of God describes them as united under that law of love which is the fulfilment of all righteousness in all the relations of society. Thus it describes them by those qualities in which they are in this life but imperfectly conformed to what they ought to be. Christians form the Church invisible in virtue of those things in which they are complete at once in Christ, their election of God, their justification by faith, their consecration to God as his saints: they form the kingdom of God in virtue of that in which they are not perfect at first, their doing the will of God, in loving him supremely, and their neighbour as themselves. Hence, while the notion of the Church invisible is essential to some aspects of Christian doctrine, that of the kingdom of God is more directly applicable to Christian duty, and this may be one reason why the latter is more prominent in the teaching of Jesus, and the former in that of Paul. When the task of Christian life is contemplated from the standpoint of the Church, it must be expressed somewhat in this way, that we are to aim at making the actual as like the ideal as possible, the Church visible as like as may be to the Church invisible, one, holy, catholic, apostolic. That is true; and that representation may be made to indicate all the duties of Christians as members of the Church or religious society instituted by Christ. But then it only includes their duties as members of a religious society, and not as members of the family, the State, and other lawful and divinely sanctioned societies; and so either the ideal is too narrow, or the Church must be made to dominate over all other societies. The notion of the kingdom of God, however, in the sense of Jesus, is wide enough to include all the relations of life, and the promotion of it is an adequate expression of the task of Christian life.

Thus there seems to be room and need in theology both for the notion of the Church and for that of the kingdom of God. They are not identical, as was assumed in former times; nor can either supersede the other, as some in modern times are disposed to discard the doctrine of the Church invisible for that of the kingdom. Both have a solid foundation in the New Testament; but as the one is a religious and the other a moral notion, the doctrine of the Church invisible is necessary in speculative theology to preserve its truly Christian character; while the idea of the kingdom of God has its chief value and use as affording an adequate category under which to unfold the body of Christian duty.

Both the Church and the kingdom of God are represented in the New Testament as having a twofold aspect, external and internal, visible and invisible. In regard to the Church, this has often been pointed out; and in regard to the kingdom of God it appears in the parables of the tares and the draw net. The distinction is not that the Church is external, and the kingdom of God spiritual, for each has both characters; but that the Church describes the disciples of Christ in their character as a religious society, the kingdom of God as a moral society. The special functions of the Church are the exercises of worship, and have to do with the relation of men to God; those of the kingdom of God are the fulfilment of the law of love, the doing of the will of God in all departments and relations of human life.

If this be so, then that clause of our definition is justified which describes the gathering that forms the kingdom as "under God's eternal law of righteous love," that being a brief expression for the moral law as fully unfolded in the teaching and life of Jesus. This element in the idea is overlooked in the Reformation definitions, but it is contained in one form or other in the modern German ones. By this clause we distinguish the kingdom of God from the Church, which is described in harmony with New Testament teaching by qualities that refer to man's religious relation to God, not to their moral duties one to another, whether it be defined as the company of believers, or the communion of saints, or the number of the elect, or the multitude of those who profess the true religion.

This may seem to be too narrow a definition of the Church, and to countenance the pernicious idea that Christianity has only to do with religious exercises in the limited sense of that term, and not with the whole of human life. It might perhaps do so, if we do not keep distinctly in view what Christian worship really is, and if we forget that the Church, though not identical with the kingdom of God, stands in a very close and organic relation to it. But if we bear these two things in mind the danger may be obviated.

First be it understood that Christian worship, for which the Church is united, is not a mere performance of external rites and ceremonies, but the offering up spiritual sacrifices, presenting our bodies a living sacrifice, offering through Christ the fruit of our lips, giving thanks to God's name, and doing good and communicating, visiting the fatherless and widows in their affliction, and keeping oneself unspotted from the world. Such is the worship that the Church is called to offer to God; and when we speak of it as a society for worship, we mean to include all that. This covers the whole life of a Christian; nothing is excluded as secular, all is truly sacred. The Church is a religious society in this comprehensive sense, uniting her members in a worship that is thus not merely ritual but moral, only not making them a political society, or calling them to redress social wrongs, or to create a perfect republic.

But, secondly, the worship, which is the function of the Church, naturally tends to produce and grow into that perfect ideal which is the kingdom of God. Its ordinances of worship are means of growth in righteousness and Christian perfection, and prepare its members for the fuller and wider life of what is to be, not merely the Church but the City of God. The Church, though only a religious society, has the hope and promise of developing and expanding into a more adequate form. But the people of God must be content to exist meanwhile as a Church, without attempting to set up a theocracy, until the time come for the perfect kingdom of God. In this, as well as in our Lord's own person, was verified the parable of the corn of wheat falling into the ground and dying. The people of God must cease to exist as a body politic, if they were to be a source of life to the world. The Jews would not understand or submit to this. They wished to retain their national life; they put Jesus to death, just because his work seemed to endanger this. But had it been possible to have set up the kingdom of God in the form of a State, it could not have become universal, it must have excluded other States, and so been like a seed remaining whole and self-contained, having life, but not developing and spreading it, or like the leaven, separate and apart from the meal. Only by the breaking up of the national form, and by coming to exist simply as a religious community, could the Israel of God penetrate all nations with its life.

This, put in more general terms, simply means, that before men's relation to one another can be put right, their relation to God must be rectified; before there can be a perfect commonwealth, there must be a religious society of men reconciled to God. Because the Church of Christ is such a society, it is fitted to be a preparation for the kingdom of God, the Church visible being the school in which the children of God are trained in those religious exercises that tend to perfect their moral character, and the Church invisible the germ that is to develop at last into the full and perfect moral society which is the kingdom of God.

2. This leads us to another aspect of this society. Having seen how it is to be distinguished, but not separated, from the Church of Christ, we must now consider its specific religious character as distinguished from merely secular notions of the community of mankind.

For the idea of the Christian commonwealth includes also this in it, that it is a community or communion not merely of men with men, but of men with God, a polity in which God and men are both included as members. This appears in all the Biblical representations of it. If it is presented in the synoptic Gospels as a kingdom, it is the kingdom of God; if, according to Paul, it consists of righteousness, and peace, and joy, it is righteousness before God, peace with God, joy in God; if, in the Epistle to the Hebrews, it is viewed as a covenant, it is a covenant with God; if by John it is conceived as eternal life, that life is in Christ and in God. Thus God is, if we may so say, an integral part of the commonwealth that Jesus proclaimed and founded on the earth. It is not merely a state in which men are united in the relations of citizenship for the realization of righteousness: it is a society in which God and men are united as members of one organic whole; it unites men one to another by uniting them to God.[1] No doubt it is a community in which God is the Lord and King, and men the subjects; but still they are not mere slaves or vassals, but fellow-workers with God for an end that they have in common; they are dependent on him not as on a Being who is out of the community to which they belong, but as on one who is within it, as its Head and King. For the idea of a kingdom of God is a community not merely ruled by God as standing outside and above it, but as its Head and Chief, in fellowship with the members, and uniting them with him in aiming at common ends. A body politic is such in virtue of the common good being the end of all its members; and if such a community of

[1] Cf. the Stoic doctrine, *Mundum regi numine deorum eumque esse quasi communem urbem et civitatem hominum et deorum.*—Cicero, *De Fin.* iii. 19 seq.

men with God is possible, it must be because there is an end that is common to both.

We may regard the reign of God as consisting in his will being done; and if that is to be not merely the dominion of a master over slaves, but of a king over citizens, the will that is to be done must be one that men can make their own without deviating from their true and highest good. This is so if the will of God is conceived as coinciding with the moral law, or rule of duty given in the moral nature of man. Now so indeed it is, according to the teaching of Jesus. He sums up all the law in the two great commandments, in the golden rule, in the precept of brotherly love after his example; and he represents this righteousness as the highest good of man. In thus fulfilling the law men are perfect as God their Father in heaven, and become his sons (Matt. v. 45, 48). The end of this divine commonwealth, then, is the perfection of man's being in his moral likeness to God; and this is an end in which God's glory and man's highest good coincide, and is therefore common to both.

Yet this point of view is not obtained, as it was by the Stoics, by overlooking or extenuating the infinite distance between God and man. It was comparatively easy for the Stoics to speak of a society of men with gods, for they held that a good man was equal to the gods, and only surpassed by them in that they being immortal are longer good.[1] But the religion of the Bible knows no such high thoughts of men or mean thoughts of God. It recognises the infinite greatness and holiness of God, and the entire dependence of man

[1] Seneca, *De Providentia*, c. i.

on him for godliness as well as for life. The divine commonwealth, then, is not a society to which men raise themselves by virtue, but one which is founded by God's voluntary and gracious condescension. There was such condescension even in admitting unfallen man to such a fellowship with him that he might hope for eternal life as the reward of his obedience; and much more is the grace of God to be recognised in founding a kingdom for guilty and helpless sinners. That a creature should have been made capable of having a common end with God is much; but that sinful creatures should be brought into such a position is far more. Yet this is the teaching of the gospel. The kingdom of God is for sinners, the poor in spirit, those hungering and thirsting for righteousness. By such God's will is to be done; and in the doing of it they are to be truly blessed, and his name is to be glorified. Thus the kingdom of God is to be realized; and it is to be a kingdom or fellowship embracing all men, a universal society. In this respect it agrees with the Stoic ideal, though differing, as we have seen, in its religious presuppositions. The Stoics recognised the brotherhood of all men, and made that the foundation of justice and civil society. Such, said Chrysippus, is the nature of man, that there is, as it were, a civil law uniting him with the whole human race, forming bonds of justice between man and man. All the lower animals were made for the sake of men and gods, but the ultimate end of these is their own commonwealth and society.[1] This Stoic idea is the more important because the principles of that philosophy had great influence in

---

[1] Cicero, *De Finibus*, iii. 20, v. 23.

forming the system of Roman law, Stoicism being in general the philosophy that was most congenial to the best minds in the Roman Empire, and the great lawyers in particular being adherents of it. That system of law probably owes to the Stoic idea of the society of the human race its cosmopolitan character, which was attempted to be realized in a universal empire.

3. But though the Stoic philosophy might be the basis of a system of jurisprudence, it did not and could not establish a universal society, much less a kingdom of God. In point of fact, it was Christianity that made the idea of human brotherhood a reality, though Stoicism had been before it in giving currency to cosmopolitan thoughts and phrases. It was the religion of Jesus that first really united men as such in a bond of brotherhood. Nor was this a mere accident. That the philosophy of the Porch could have made the equal rights of all men as certain to the general mind as the redeeming work of Christ makes it to all who believe on him, must appear very doubtful when we consider Aristotle's argument, that if there be any men as inferior to others as the body is to the soul, or beasts to man, such are by nature slaves for whom it is best to be governed as such.[1] But even if it can be shown that any such hypothesis is impossible, still there would be needed some power or motive by which men might be brought into and kept in a cosmopolitan society.[2] Such a power Stoicism did not provide, perhaps did not even seek; and the system of law that

---

[1] Aristotle's *Politica*, i. 2.
[2] See Ritschl, *Unterricht in der Christlichen Religion*, § 8.

was founded upon it in the Roman Empire avowedly rested on material force for its maintenance. The art of government was that which the Romans recognised as their special function; and in their more worthy conceptions of it, it was government by law and justice; still at the best it was to be enforced by the might of empire and the force of war.

> "Tu regere imperio populos Romane memento,
> Hæ tibi erunt artes, pacisque imponere morem,
> Parcere subjectis, et debellare superbos."

Now we need not and do not deny that good laws and government have done much to check certain forms of moral evil, and to encourage and cultivate certain virtues. To the influence of society and civil law are due the order and peace that distinguish civilised nations from barbarians. By stigmatizing and punishing theft, murder, violence, and other offences as crimes, civil society has not only checked them outwardly by restraining the overt act, but has succeeded, in the mass of the community, in overcoming the desires that lead to such offences, and made it natural and easy for men to resist temptations to them. But the range is limited within which this can be done. The influence of civil government can only be negative; it may repress, and even eradicate, crime, but it cannot produce positive virtue; and there are many vices that it cannot even negatively check, since they could not be inquired into and punished without danger of tyranny. And it cannot of itself lead to a universal brotherhood of men, for its power is limited by the bounds of the State. It may foster public spirit within the limits of the people, but that could not be a cosmopolitan philanthropic sentiment unless all the world were in one State.

On these principles a universal commonwealth must be a universal empire, and that means a universal despotism. Mankind are so divided by nature into different races, inhabiting different countries, and living under different circumstances, that no one form of civil government can be equally suited or beneficial to them all: and hence if their unity is sought to be achieved by bringing them all into one universal State; some peoples, if not all, must be under a government that is not the best suited for them, and that they would not spontaneously choose. So it has proved in point of fact in history. Neither in its pagan form nor in its Christian medieval form, did the Roman Empire give a civil government that all the nations under its rule could accept as suitable. To some portion or other of its subjects, if not to all, it was felt as a foreign yoke, that either crushed the spirit out of the people, or was cast off when they asserted their freedom and nationality. The Roman jurists may have laid the foundation of a universal law, but they have not been able to maintain a universal State; and it is recognised by modern thinkers that this failure was not merely due to the imperfection and incomplete development of mankind, but is inevitable, from the natural diversities and separation of nations, so that the ideal of a reign of justice and peace on earth must be sought, not in a universal State, but in a world-wide federation of States.[1] The only universal society possible, in consistency with true ideas of human freedom and morality,

---

[1] See Kant, *Zum ewigen Frieden*. Rothe, *Theol. Ethik*, § 444.

is not a political but a religious one, and that must form the bond of union among States.[1]

If Stoicism had not any motive principle to realize its cosmopolitan ideal, and could only borrow the secular arm of imperial power; there was another philosophical system that professed to possess a power of its own, which if applied would lead to a commonwealth in which righteousness would reign. That was Platonism, which proceeded on the principle that no man is willingly evil, and that virtue consists essentially in knowledge. Hence education was the means by which philosophers of this school sought to realize their ideal. Wisdom, in their view, was the secret of virtue and happiness, and the teaching of wisdom will bring about these ends. This philosophy, however, has an essentially aristocratic character, and fails to reach the cosmopolitan idea of the brotherhood of all men as such. The Platonic republic is composed of distinct classes, sharply marked out from one another; and philosophers of this school habitually looked with contempt on Christianity because it welcomed as its converts men of all classes, even the most degraded and vicious, and treated them all as brethren. But this is the peculiar excellence of the gospel of Christ, and that which commended it in early times to many who had tried to find satisfaction in Platonism and other forms of philosophy, but found that they offered their highest good only to select souls, capable by nature of the contemplation of ideas, and trained by discipline to perfect wisdom.[2]

[1] Rothe, *Theol. Ethik*, § 438, 9.
[2] See Justin Martyr, *Dial. cum Tryph.*, c. 4, 8.

In order, then, to understand the notion of the kingdom of God as realized in Christianity, we have to consider, not merely that it is a society of men with God, extending to all mankind, and embracing men as such, but also to inquire what is the power by which this society is brought and kept together; or, in other words, by which God's will is done. It is not the power of physical force, either natural, as in the Roman Empire, or supernatural, as most of the Jews expected in the establishment of an earthly kingdom of God; it is not that of wisdom and education, which the Platonic philosophers generally looked to as able to bring about a golden age; yet it has proved more mighty than either. It has made the spirit of humanity, regard for man as such, the common property of civilised mankind; it has by slow degrees abolished slavery, emancipated and elevated woman, withdrawn public toleration from vice and cruelty, and introduced philanthropic and benevolent institutions as part of the ordinary necessaries of society.

This power, as expressed in our definition, is a vital one; it is the energy, not of force or of teaching, but of life. This is implied in all the parables in which Jesus compares the kingdom of God to seed, and its progress to the growth of the seed; also in his declaration that true goodness must be from within, not from without, which he illustrates again by the metaphor of the tree and its fruit; and in his assertion of the need of being converted and becoming as little children, as well as in the more express statements in the fourth Gospel, of the necessity of being begotten again, receiving eternal life through faith in him, and being in him as branches in the vine.

All these sayings prove that Jesus looked for the success of his work and the realization of the kingdom of God to a new principle of action in the hearts of men. It was something more than a knowledge of new truth working on men by moral suasion, as for instance bringing more powerful motives of hope or fear to bear on them; it was a new inclination, a new love, a new passion possessing their souls, call it enthusiasm of humanity, or call it more adequately love to God and man. This made the cold affectionate, the selfish loving, the worldly godly; this made one publican forsake all and follow Jesus, and another resolve to give the half of his goods to the poor, and restore fourfold his ill-gotten gain; this was nothing less than getting a new heart, a new life; and it was this principle of godly unselfish life that was to secure the doing of God's will in his kingdom.

4. What that principle is in itself, is not clearly brought out in Jesus' ordinary teaching, as recorded in the synoptic Gospels; and this is not unnatural and need not surprise us, because that teaching was entirely practical, intended to lead the common people of Galilee to the actual possession of that new life through faith in him. For that purpose it was not needful that they should be made to understand the nature and working of the principle of this life, but only that they should be brought under its influence, and led to yield themselves to it. The physician, in his practical work among patients ignorant of medicine, does not attempt to explain the scientific nature and properties of his

remedies, though he may do so when he has to prescribe for a man of education and understanding. So Jesus, when he met with those who had some knowledge of Scripture and acquaintance with divine things, could describe the nature of the new life more directly than in his ordinary teaching; and John has largely occupied his Gospel with such discourses as those with Nicodemus, with the scribes in the temple at Jerusalem and synagogue at Nazareth, and with the disciples in the last hours of fellowship with them, recorded too after a long lifetime of Christian experience had matured his thoughts of them.

From the parable of the sower we learn that the principle of the new life is in the word of the kingdom proclaimed by Jesus, but that it needs to be received by faith, and kept in an honest and good heart. Jesus also teaches that the reception of the word in faith is due to the Father being pleased to reveal to babes the things hidden from the wise and prudent (Matt. xi. 25; xvi. 17); and that in coming to Christ men must not only humble themselves as little children (Matt. xviii. 3, 4), but deny themselves, and be willing to lose their very life that they may find it in him (Matt. xvi. 24, 25). These things are not presented in the synoptic Gospels as theoretic truths; they are only indicated or implied in the course of practical exhortations; but the principles thus indicated as underlying these practical exhortations are just those that are expressed theologically in the doctrines of the birth of the Spirit, of spiritual feeding on Christ as the bread of life, and of eternal life in union with him, contained in the fourth Gospel. From it we learn more distinctly to speak of the principle of new life as the Holy Spirit, which the Father gives to them that ask him, to them that believe on Jesus; and this is entirely in accordance with the Old Testament prophecies of the moral renewal of the people in the last days. The Holy Spirit is described as the gift of God's fatherly love (Luke xi. 13); it is the Spirit of our Father (Matt. x. 20), and works by awakening love in our hearts when we apprehend our full forgiveness by God (Luke vii. 41–50; Matt. xviii. 23–35); so that we may well express it, as in our definition, as the vital power of God's love. Jesus spoke of God in a far more gracious way than he was commonly thought of then; he described him as bountiful, merciful, gracious, loving; and what was far more, he manifested God's character in his own. From his life of untiring, wise, and holy beneficence, self-denying and self-sacrificing, men learned to know and to feel what God is, and to believe that he was personally seeking them, and yearning over them with all a Father's tenderness and love.

5. But we must recognise more than this. If Jesus' work were only to reveal God as the Father of mercies and God of all grace, there would be nothing in it essentially different from that of the prophets of Israel in former times. It would indeed be true that he has made a fuller and more affecting discovery of the divine character, and that he was in his own person and life a perfect image of that character; so he might be recognised as in degree indefinitely superior to all the prophets; but still, if that were all, he would only be, as Nicodemus acknowledged him, a teacher sent from God, and we should have no explanation why

his person as the Son of man is so essential to the kingdom of God. In order to that, we must regard him as coming, not merely to teach and show that God is love, but to do a great act of salvation in which the love of God is exercised towards men. Not by mere manifestation, but by actual exercise, does the love of God become the vital power of his kingdom; and that is in Jesus Christ. This is indicated by Jesus Christ when he says "the Son of man," *i.e.* the king and representative of God's kingdom, "came to minister and to give his life a ransom for many" (Matt. xx. 28; Mark x. 45); and this is expressed in our definition that God's love, whose vital power establishes and maintains his kingdom, is his redeeming love in Jesus Christ. It is love not merely showing kindness and bestowing favours, but delivering men from bondage by a ransom. The bondage is that of sin, and the deliverance is effected by Christ's death as the objective ground of forgiveness. This appears from the sayings of our Lord on this subject recorded in the synoptic Gospels.

One of the most distinct and at the same time best authenticated of these is to be found in his words at the institution of the Lord's Supper: "This (cup) is my blood of the covenant which is shed for many unto remission of sins" (Matt. xxvi. 28). The kingdom of God in Israel had been founded by sacrifice; it was based on the deliverance of the people from Egypt by means of the passover, and it was ratified by a covenant-sacrifice. The reason of this undoubtedly was that the people needed to be cleansed from sin in order to enter into covenant with the holy God; and Jesus, adopting almost the very words used in that covenant rite, declares that his blood, which is about to be shed, is the blood of the covenant, and is shed in order to the forgiveness of sins. This plainly means that his death on the cross is the ground on which the sins of his people are forgiven, and they brought into covenant with God ; and a comparison of his previous statement, that he came to give his life a ransom instead of many, shows that his life is given for their life, or in other words, that his death comes in place of theirs.

The same thing is taught in the discourse recorded in John x. 1-18, in which Jesus speaks of himself as the Good Shepherd, and declares that as such he lays down his life for the sheep. In this parable the sheep are viewed as being in danger of perishing from the attack of the wolf; the hireling fleeth, but the good shepherd saves them by laying down his own life. Here also we may see a reference to the kingdom of God, for the flock under its shepherd is one of the most familiar figures for the kingdom in the Old Testament. It is important also to study this discourse in John x. in its historical connection with the preceding narrative in chap. ix. The Sanhedrin had excommunicated the blind man whom Jesus had healed, because he confessed him to be the Messiah ; but Jesus, in spite of that, had sought him out and received him ; and the discourse has reference to this. Jesus claims to be the head of the kingdom, the true shepherd of Israel, on the ground that he has entered legitimately. Though he may seem to them to be breaking over the fences by receiving that man whom they had cast out, he is not really doing so ; he is himself the door, as well as the shepherd; and all who ever came claiming supreme authority are thieves and robbers. He proves himself to be the shepherd by the fact that the sheep hear his voice and follow him; and they do so because he lays down his life for them. Here we see that the redeeming love of Jesus is the power that draws men to him, and unites them in the kingdom of God. So he said later, in connection with the overthrow of the kingdom of this world and the casting out of its prince, " I, if I be lifted up from the earth, will draw all men unto me" (John xii. 31, 32).

Thus it appears that only by his death could Jesus found the kingdom of God, because that was the greatest act of love to men. But it was the greatest act of love only because at the dearest cost it secured the greatest blessing to them, the forgiveness of their sins, or the possibility of fellowship with God, notwithstanding the consciousness of sin, and without weakening the feeling of its evil. That Christ really bestowed this blessing on men is not merely stated in one or two of his sayings; it appears from the most striking facts of his ministry. He received sinners; he gave them peace and joy; yet he never led any of them to think more lightly of sin, or to be less sensible of its evil. What was the secret of this? Was it not that he invited men to fellowship with himself, who was perfectly pure, and felt sin as the greatest evil? None who really came to him could love sin, or make light of it. His whole demeanour showed that all the sin around him was a burden and a grief to him. When assured by him of forgiveness, men might be sure of it, since none ever hated sin or saw its evil as he did; and they could not think lightly of it, since he manifestly was deeply grieved by it. It was just because he had such a perfect hatred of sin, and would make no compromise with it, that his career on earth must end in rejection, condemnation, and death. Now he calls his disciples to follow him in this career. Only if they are willing to deny themselves, and take up the cross, and follow him, can they be his disciples.

Hence we learn that if from one point of view it is true that he died that we might have life, from another it is equally true that he died that we might die too. Life through death is the law for us as well as for him; only his life through death must come first, and make ours possible. His blood was shed on behalf of many ($\dot{v}\pi\grave{\epsilon}\rho$ $\pi o\lambda\lambda\hat{\omega}\nu$), i.e. not merely in their stead, but as their representative in the covenant. His saying, that he gave his life a ransom instead of many ($\dot{a}\nu\tau\grave{\iota}$ $\pi o\lambda\lambda\hat{\omega}\nu$), may best be interpreted as meaning, not precisely that his life was instead of theirs, but that his giving his life a ransom was instead of their doing so.[1] What a sinner, feeling the evil of sin, and yet longing to have fellowship with the holy God, would desire to do, is to make amends for his sin; and many are the ways in which men have striven to do so, by penances, and mortifications, and self-inflicted sufferings. But all in vain. No man can do this for himself; for the wages of sin is death, and he cannot give his life a ransom. The Son of man came to do that for us, that we might be able to give up our lives in him, and so might have forgiveness. When we are converted and become as little children,

---

[1] This construction is, I think, established by the acute reasoning of Ritschl (*Rechtfertigung u. Versöhnung*), but it does not prove the general theory for which he contends.

we give up our old life, deny ourselves, that we may have our life in Christ.

This idea, that the disciples' self-denial and beginning a new life is after the pattern and in the power of Jesus' own death, is expressed by him in various places and ways. It is indicated when he speaks of his suffering and death as a baptism (Luke xii. 50; Mark x. 38, 39). The word is used doubtless with reference to the idea of immersion, and shows that the suffering that was before him would be, as it were, a flood with its waves and billows going over him; but there is surely an allusion also to the use of baptism as a sacred rite, symbolizing the end of an old and the beginning of a new life. His death was that even for him; and therefore our fellowship in his death and rising again is so for us.

This point, that the kingdom of God is established by the power of redeeming love, is so important that it may be well to show the truth of it by another line of evidence. Some modern writers, who have done much to bring out the meaning of the kingdom of God, have thought it possible by means of it to dispense with the doctrine of the vicarious atonement of Christ; but if we examine the use which they thus make of it, we shall find that it will not really serve their purpose, unless it involves a true redemption.

The book entitled *Ecce Homo* powerfully and beautifully shows wherein the peculiar value of the work of Christ consisted, not so much in that he taught a higher morality than was before known, but that he made it a power over men, and secured its actual observance in a way that had never been done by any other teacher; and that he did this by founding a universal society, whose law was to be active brotherly love; that he called such love into being by evoking an enthusiasm of humanity, and did so by his own character and life. He was a perfect man, and he brought his followers under a sense of infinite obligation to him. True; but is it possible that he could have done so unless he were more than man, and unless the sense of infinite obligation were produced by his bestowing the highest blessing, peace with God, at the cost of the actual sacrifice of himself?

Again, this writer recognises one of the great means by which Christ sought and accomplished the moral restoration of men from sin to holiness; and that was by bringing them under the strongest motives of love and gratitude, to live a life of holiness. In respect of this, he showed himself in a true and spiritual sense a king, setting up on earth a new society or fellowship of men, and binding them to himself and to the law of the kingdom by the strongest and most efficacious of all ties. But there is another part of Christ's work, another element of his power, that must be acknowledged also; and that is partly, though not fully, recognised in *Ecce Homo*, especially in the following passage (p. 232) in reference to the conversion of Zaccheus: "This great but simple achievement he gained power to perform, not through reflection and reasoning, not through the eloquence of a preacher, not through supernatural terrors, but through the cordial restoring influence of mercy. It was mercy, which is not pity, a thing comparatively weak and vulgar, but pity and resentment blended at the highest power of

P

each, the most powerful restorative agent known in the medicine of the soul; it was mercy that revealed itself in Christ's words, the pity slightly veiled under royal grace, the resentment altogether unexpressed, yet not concealed, because already too surely divined and anticipated by the roused conscience of the criminal. And mercy, more powerful than justice, redeemed the criminal while it judged him, increased his shame tenfold, but increased in the same proportion the wish and courage to amend." The writer appears just to catch a glimpse of this idea, and then lose sight of it again; for as he goes on, after describing as a parallel case that of the abandoned woman in Simon's house, to speak of the power by which such conversions were wrought, he says no more of the restorative influence of mercy, but merely speaks in general about enthusiasm.

What is indicated in that passage contains in germ the main ideas of the priesthood and atonement of Christ; and the same element of mercy might have been recognised in many other narratives of Jesus' dealing with sinners. Now, in the exercise of mercy he acted as a priest, reconciling men to God, and enabling them to draw near to him and enjoy his favour. It is this part of Christ's work that is the foundation and means of the others. By it mainly, and in the first place, he founded the kingdom of God.

This brings us back to the point that we reached before, when considering the relation of the Church to the kingdom of God, that the latter, or moral society of men, can be established and realized only through the former, or religious society. We can now see the meaning and truth of this more clearly than before;

and we shall do so if we look at the use that Ritschl makes of the connection of the Church with the kingdom of God. This is another of the attempts to do justice to the peculiar and unique relation of Christ to the kingdom of God without acknowledging a vicarious redemption.

Ritschl's view in substance is that Christ guarantees the establishment of the kingdom of God, inasmuch as he has founded the Christian Church, which is the religious community enjoying the blessings of the kingdom, and working for its realization as their highest end. The Church is that community in which alone men can have reconciliation to God and freedom from the sense of guilt, and so be able to act from motives of love, and realize that community of perfect love that is the kingdom of God; and since Christ by his life and work on earth has founded the Church, he has in this way secured the realization of the kingdom of God. He has done this, however, not by the vicarious endurance of the punishment due to sinful men, but by his perfect fulfilment in loving word and deed of the work of his calling, which was the highest conceivable; and by his perseverance in it in spite of all opposition, and patient endurance of all suffering even unto death.

In this way Ritschl thinks he can assert a unique and essential importance of Christ for salvation, without admitting the juridical ideas implied in the evangelical doctrine of the atonement. But I think it will appear, if we probe these statements a little, that they are either vague and indefinite phrases, or if they express actual realities, imply a view of Christ's work not essentially different from that which he rejects.

When he attaches so much importance to Christ's founding the Church, he cannot mean by that the mere work of gathering men together into an external religious society by teaching and persuasion, in the way in which an ordinary man with new views and powerful influence might form a sect or party. No Church formed merely in that way could secure the reign of God, *i.e.* the obedience of the law of love. Even though the teaching by which he gathered them be the exhibition of the kingdom of God in all its greatness and blessedness, mere teaching would not gather a company of pure and ardent seekers after that kingdom; and so far as it did so, it would be the truth taught, and not the society formed by it, that would really be the means of bringing in the kingdom.

If, again, Christ be conceived as founding the Church, not merely by teaching, but by a supernatural spiritual influence on the souls of men, then indeed the Church would no longer be a merely external or accidental society; and this influence would secure that it led to the realization of the perfect fellowship of love. But on that view Christ's person would be merely of indirect importance; the really essential thing would be the spiritual influence that he used to found the Church; and the Church too would be unnecessary, since that spiritual influence might secure at once and directly the love which is the spirit of the kingdom.

If the kingdom of God, or perfect moral society, can only be established by means of the Church, *i.e.* the religious society founded by Christ, that must be because men need to be reconciled to God before they can serve him and work for his great end; and if the Church that Christ has founded does secure the realization of the kingdom of God, it must be not merely a sect formed by a teacher, nor a mystical body formed by a spiritual influence, but a company of men reconciled to God, and enabled to worship him without fear or evil conscience. If Christ, by his work on earth, made such a Church possible and actual, then indeed he stands in an essential relation to it, and through it to the kingdom of God. This seems to be really what Ritschl means; at least it is the only sense in which his statements are true and adequate to his object.

But if Christ did this, and did it as Ritschl says he did his work, by his own perfect and unbroken fulfilling of his calling, in spite of all opposition and suffering; must he not have acted as our high priest, in the sense in which that office is explained and illustrated in the Epistle to the Hebrews, *i.e.* as our brother who has taken our nature and sympathizes with us, our forerunner, surety, representative? He forms a brotherhood of men reconciled to God, by calling them to himself and inviting them to come to God with him and in his name, as he himself draws near to God with unshaken filial confidence, even when wearing their nature, sharing all their sorrows, and bearing the utmost consequences of their sins. Can he be conceived as enabling them in fellowship with him to come to God without fear, unless he has put himself under that burden of sin that prevents their coming to God without him? If it is because of their evil conscience that they cannot approach God without him, they need him, not only to teach them and to show them an example, but to deliver them from that evil conscience, and he does so by offering himself without spot to God. This, and nothing less than this, is required by Ritschl's view of the work of Christ, if it is to be indeed a reality; and this is the essential point in the doctrine of vicarious atonement, it is Christ's suffering for sins, the just on behalf of the unjust, that he might bring us to God. Substitution may seem to some a harsh word; it is an inadequate expression, and when taken alone may even be misleading; but the representation of many by one, of the people by their king and high priest, of believing sinners by the incarnate Son of God, is the more true and comprehensive idea; and that is necessarily implied in any view that makes Christ's person and work essential to the kingdom of God. I contend, therefore, that what Ritschl truly and powerfully sets forth of the work of Christ as the founder of the Church, and the bearing of that on our forgiveness, so far from enabling him to dispense with the Catholic doctrine of the atonement, really implies and carries with it the essential principle of that doctrine.[1]

This element in the idea of the kingdom of God, that it is founded by a true redemption of sinners by Christ, is one that is absent in most of the modern German definitions; it is expressed most distinctly in that of Luther, but implied in all those that identify it with the Church, though when it is distinguished from that, this point needs to be more distinctly brought out. For this is at bottom what makes the Christian kingdom of God to be what it is. The kingdom of God in the Old Testament was, as we have seen, in substance God's special revelation of law to Israel. What law could do

[1] See Appendix, Note S.

it did, and no more. If there has been in Christianity a realization to any degree of righteousness and brotherly love, and if there is a hope of that being one day perfect and universal; it is because in the fulness of time God sending his own Son in the likeness of sinful flesh and for sin has condemned sin in the flesh, that the righteousness of the law might be fulfilled in us, who walk not after the flesh but after the Spirit.

LECTURE V.

ATTEMPTS TO REALIZE THE KINGDOM OF GOD
IN THE PAST.

MATT. xiii. 24, 25.—"The kingdom of heaven is likened unto a man that sowed good seed in his field : but while men slept, his enemy came and sowed tares also among the wheat, and went away. But when the blade sprang up, and brought forth fruit, then appeared the tares also."

LECTURE V.

ATTEMPTS TO REALIZE THE KINGDOM OF GOD IN THE PAST.

I PROPOSE now, in order to illustrate the nature of the Christian kingdom of God, to consider the chief forms in which men have attempted to realize it on earth. My object is not to trace the history of the kingdom of God: that includes the whole history of the Christian Church in the widest sense. Neither is it to trace the history of the notion of the kingdom of God as a part of the history of doctrines. I wish to consider only the attempts made on a large scale to make the ideal of God's kingdom a present reality, and to explain the views held about it only so far as is needful for the understanding of the institutions actually set up or proposed as its accomplishment. Such explanation is chiefly necessary in the earliest period of the Church's history, when no attempt at setting up the kingdom could be made, though views were gradually formed about it, which had a great influence on the way in which the task was gone about, when it became possible to attempt it.

The kingdom of God continued to be a familiar phrase in the mouths of Christians after the apostolic age, and to some extent a leading idea in their minds, though it was somewhat variously applied, and seldom in so comprehensive a way as by Christ himself.[1]

It was a part of the Church's faith that continually appears as a powerful practical motive to a Christian life, that Christ is to come again to reign, and that this, which is called indiscriminately the kingdom of God and of Christ, will perfect the happiness of his followers. This kingdom in the future is variously described, and sometimes it is connected with the idea of a reign of Christ in the present, or at least held along with that; but it is seldom absent, and is the form in which the belief in Christ as a king most generally expresses itself in the early Christian ages. In itself it is undoubtedly a biblical and Christian idea, derived from the representations of the New Testament, and expressing that aspect of the kingdom of God that is specially prominent in the apostolic Epistles. In the sufferings of the age of persecution it was natural that Christians should look with special interest and attention to the final triumph of their Lord, of which their faith was assured, and pass over in their thoughts from the present affliction to the glory of the kingdom that was to be perfected when their Lord should come again. It was also inevitable, as Dorner[2] acutely points out, that in endeavouring to understand the elements of their Christian faith in intellectual conceptions, they should look first at Christianity in its final and perfect development as foretold in prophecy, where they could perceive its different parts as they were to be unfolded in the perfect flower, while they might not so easily

---

[1] See Appendix, Note T.
[2] *Doctrine of the Person of Christ*, vol. i. p. 145, E. T.

see them as wrapt together in the swelling and hopeful bud in their present experience. Even yet we can best understand some parts of Christian experience by considering them first in their ideal and destined perfection, rather than in the confused and imperfect forms in which they actually appear.

But this natural and inevitable tendency brought with it certain dangers. Since the prophetic descriptions of the future of God's kingdom are generally couched in the language of poetry and figurative allusions, there was a possibility of taking these too literally, and so forming earthly and sensual conceptions of the future blessedness of the saints. This actually took place to some extent from the very first, and the error has frequently reappeared in later ages. It is an error, however, that is so obvious to any spiritually-minded man, and is so distinctly condemned by some plain and emphatic statements of Scripture, that it may be said to carry with it its own antidote, and therefore to be comparatively harmless. It can hardly ever exist without being seen, and it always provokes a decided protest and strong reaction.

There was, however, another error apt to rise in connection with the tendency to look mainly to the future consummation of Christianity, less glaring, and therefore more insidious, but not less dangerous to the genuine spirit of the gospel. That was a failure to connect the future blessings of the kingdom of God with the present experience of Christians. A most characteristic feature of our Lord's teaching was that he habitually spoke of the kingdom of God as present as well as future. It had already come, and was within men; and though it was indeed to have a future manifestation and triumph, that was but the development and full maturity of the seed now sown by the Son of man. The same connection of the future with the present appears also, though not quite so conspicuously, in the apostolic Epistles; and even in later times its importance was seen in relation to some doctrines. Thus, in regard to the person of Christ, his divine glory was first clearly perceived in his exaltation; but it was seen that, in order to avoid the heathen notion of an apotheosis, regarding Christ as only a deified man, the glory to which he has been raised must be regarded as really his from the beginning, and only veiled or laid aside during his earthly life.

But a similar connection was not always observed in the views taken of the kingdom of Christ or of God, *i.e.* the salvation that Jesus has brought. That was thrown entirely into the future; and even when it was not conceived in an earthly or sensual form, it was disjoined from the present. Christians were looking for the kingdom of God as that was predicted by Christ, and by the prophets and apostles; but meanwhile they were afflicted and desolate, not having received their consolation. That joy in a salvation and kingdom already theirs, that is expressed in the beatitudes of the Sermon on the Mount, and in many a glowing passage in Paul's writings, was too much lost sight of, or at least it was forgotten that in this we have the earnest and first-fruits of the perfect kingdom, and that our hope of the future rests upon our being in the kingdom of God now. This was the same tendency that had appeared in Judaism, when the theology of the scribes succeeded the living faith of the prophets; and it led to results similar to those that were seen in Pharisaism. A kingdom that was conceived as entirely future, and not as the development and manifestation of a living power working in the present, could only be brought in by purely supernatural means, by an abrupt catastrophe, a coming of Christ that should introduce a new order of things, as by a sudden revolution. A future kingdom to be thus brought in must either be simply waited for in passive expectation, or if it is to be brought into any connection with the present life and work of Christians at all, it can only be by the assumption that their present faithfulness and obedience to Christ, as their Lord and Saviour, will secure their interest in his future kingdom. They cannot be regarded as really helping on that kingdom, or working for it now; but if they are faithful and diligent, then God will, by a purely supernatural act, bring in the millennial kingdom. This co-operated with other tendencies to lead to a spirit of legalism, akin to that which arose in connection with similar views of the kingdom among the Pharisees. Christianity, instead of being viewed as the fulfilment of the promises and actual realization of the kingdom of God, was conceived merely as a new law, the observance of which would lead to the enjoyment of a kingdom still entirely future.

This tendency, however, was latent at first, and indeed was counteracted by the healthy Christian consciousness that already, through faith in Christ, there was enjoyed a new and blessed life, and that this was a social life uniting believers together in a community of brotherly love and fellowship. Though the name of the kingdom of God is not generally given to the Christian community, yet it is habitually regarded as a spiritual commonwealth (πολιτεία), in which all members are fellow-citizens, and to which all men are invited. This is just, in fact, the idea of a cosmopolitan society of brotherly love; and as it is always viewed by Christians as held together by regard to God as revealed in Christ, it really corresponds to the kingdom of God in some of the aspects in which Jesus spoke of it. This comes out most clearly and beautifully in a passage in the Epistle to Diognetus (chaps. v. and vii.), but the same thing in substance appears more or less distinctly in the writings of most of the Christian apologists. Justin Martyr, along with the chiliastic view of the kingdom of God as future, also speaks of Christ reigning even now, sending forth his word of calling and repentance as the rod of his power according to Ps. cx. (*Dial. with Trypho*, c. 83); and Athenagoras speaks of God as the supreme Lord and king who is recognised and obeyed by Christians in the law of brotherly love to all men (*Leg.* c. xviii., xxxii.).

A similar view of the Christian community comes out in those writings that have for their object to inculcate unity and concord among Christians, such as Clement's Epistle to the Church at Corinth, and the Ignatian Epistles. While the kingdom of God is spoken of as future, the Church is described as a brotherhood or commonwealth, in which all the members are under law to God and Christ, and bound to one another by mutual duties of love.

In these various modes of representation, which are

rather hinted than directly expressed, we may trace the germs of two or three different views of the kingdom of God, which afterwards became more developed and had great practical effects.

One was that the kingdom of God or of Christ is yet to come, being conceived in the form of a thousand years' reign; by some in a more gross and material way, by others more spiritually. Such was the view of Papias, Barnabas, Justin, Irenæus, Tertullian.

Another was that God rules Christians even now through Christ, as a spiritual kingdom or city, so that the kingdom of God is already present. This was combined with the other view by most of the earliest Fathers; but it was not made at all prominent till the Alexandrian teachers raised a protest against the extravagances of chiliasm. Clement of Alexandria writes very nobly and eloquently of the kingdom of God, describing Christ as gathering the bloodless host of peace by his blood and by his word, and assigning to them the kingdom of heaven (*Coh. ad Gentes*, c. xi.), and he connects the idea of the kingdom with that of the family of God, speaking much and beautifully of God's fatherhood, and fatherly love to men. At the same time Clement distinctly teaches that we are the children of God, not by nature, but by adoption, of his own goodness and rich mercy to us (*Strom.* ii. c. 17). Accordingly, all that he says in so many places of the fatherly discipline and chastisement of God, inflicting punishment for the good of his children, may be taken as describing the blessedness of the kingdom of God. His conception of it is ever a spiritual one, as a present blessing enjoyed by Christians, though he is influenced

Q

by Platonism to ascribe to enlightenment and teaching more power than they really have, and to present Christ too much only as a teacher, and not also as a Redeemer. He views the kingdom of God as the state of enlightenment, training, and discipline under which Christians are, and speaks in Platonic language of the heavenly city, or ideal State, for which they are being prepared. This teaching seems more exactly to agree with our Lord's conception of the kingdom of God than anything that we find so fully expanded in the writings of the early Fathers.

But meanwhile there was also being developed among Christians the thought and the reality of the Catholic Church, and that came to supersede or be identified with the kingdom of God. The notion of the Church as the mystical body of Christ consisting of all those who are spiritually united to him in faith and love is, as already said, contained in Paul's later Epistles. That which constituted the oneness of Christians in the apostolic age, was simply their common loyalty to Jesus, whom they all by the Holy Spirit called Lord. Soon, however, it began to be seen that this implied also agreement in certain fundamental religious beliefs, and the necessity of maintaining these against insidious errors led to a more complete organization and closer association of the Christian congregations than they had at first. Thus in the second century the unity of the Church came to be regarded as of primary importance, and to be made to consist in outward organization. The one body for which Christ gave himself, and in which alone were the blessings of salvation to be found, was identified with the outwardly organized community of Christians. At first this did not cause much difficulty, because as long as to be a Christian implied self-denial and sacrifice in joining a despised and persecuted sect, the outward profession corresponded tolerably well to the reality, and the external society of Christians was, as compared with the heathen world around, believing, loving, and holy. So the writers who regarded the kingdom of God as a present reality might identify it with the Church of which Paul spoke so much in his later Epistles, and might apply both ideas in a general way to the actual society of Christians.

But with the period of comparative rest and prosperity which Christians enjoyed in the former half of the third century, a change of circumstances came. There was a general relaxation of Christian earnestness and moral strictness; men could more easily join the Church from mixed motives; and when the fierce persecution under Decius arose, many were found unable to stand the test of martyrdom, and lapsed from their faith. It was becoming apparent that the outward body of Christians did not correspond to that Church that is described as the body of Christ, in all of whose members he dwells by his Spirit. This difficulty might be met in three different ways, and, in fact, was attempted to be dealt with in each of them by different parties.

One way was to endeavour, by increased strictness of discipline, to restore to the actual Church that purity which she seemed in danger of losing. This was a very natural effort of earnest Christians in a time of moral laxity, even apart from any doctrine or theory of the Church; and there was a series of attempts to give effect to it. The Shepherd of Hermas has this for its main object. It describes the Church as in a state of moral degeneracy; and seeks by a series of visions, commands, and parables, of an allegorical nature, to awaken Christians to greater moral earnestness, and to establish in the Church a more strict and perfect discipline; so that the actual Christian community might possess the moral purity of the ideal. The same effort was carried farther and to greater strictness of discipline by the Montanists, and was continued afterwards by the Novatianists and Donatists. As it appears in Montanism, we may see the connection of this movement with the chiliastic view of the kingdom of God. The Montanists held very strongly the conviction, which was at first common to all Christians, that the return of the Lord and the establishment of his kingdom in glory were close at hand. The Church was to be revived and prepared for that by the voice of the Spirit speaking through inspired men and women, and rousing the brethren to a more rigid and heroic contention against evil. No restoration on a second repentance was to be allowed to those who fell into sin after baptism. Such might, and would if they repented, be forgiven by God and received into his kingdom; but they should never be restored to the Church, which must thus be kept pure. This system maintained the purity of the Church at the expense of its catholicity, for it frankly allowed that it did not comprise all who should be saved. Such a view was possible only on the assumption that the coming of the Lord would be very soon, so that the anomalous state of things which the Montanist discipline necessarily brought about would be merely provisional and of short duration. It could not be borne in continuance, that men who might be forgiven by God, and heirs of his kingdom, should be excluded from the Church of Christ. The process of time, as it disappointed the expectations of the speedy advent of Christ, practically confuted this system; and those who would still carry out the principle of making the outward Church perfectly pure, were obliged to maintain also that it included all the saved, as the Donatists seem to have done.

A second course possible in the circumstances was to maintain as the primary principle the unity or uniqueness of the Church as an outward society out of which is no salvation. This principle was strongly maintained by Cyprian against the Novatianists, and by Augustine against the Donatists. Neither of these sects, nor the Montanist before them, was at first regarded as heretical; but as the Church in general did not adopt their strict views in regard to discipline, they were forced in order to carry them out to form separate communions. If this were to be allowed, clearly the outward unity of the Church would be given up. It was not merely that there might be different rules of discipline in different local churches; but after the schism of Novatian, there was in the same place bishop against bishop, and altar against altar. Against this Cyprian most earnestly set himself. He felt and confessed as strongly as possible the degeneracy of the Church's moral state before the Decian persecution, and speaks strongly of the guilt of the lapsed, and of the impropriety of restoring them to Church fellowship without distinct and manifest evidence of repentance (*de Lapsis*). But he declares that the guilt of schism is as great as that of apostasy, or even greater, and that at all hazards the unity of the Church is to be preserved. That unity is in his view secured by the regular succession of bishops, *i.e.* by outward organization (*de Unitate Ecclesiæ*). This necessarily implied that the external organized Church, the community ruled by the one harmonious episcopate, was the body of Christ, the mother of all believers, out of which was no salvation. The holiness of the Church could only be an approximate quality, unless it could be supposed that the episcopal organization had the power either of infallibly securing or magically producing holiness in its members, which was not held at that time. Cyprian does not identify the Church with the kingdom of God. He still regards the kingdom as future and heavenly; but the Church is the only way of access to it. His teaching, however, marks this momentous step in the history of Christian doctrine; that at the time when the discrepancy between the outward body of Christians and the people who were truly sanctified had become apparent, the outward Church as organized in the episcopal system of those days[1] was decided to be the true body of Christ.

The third possible course to be taken, in view of the state of things that appeared in the third century, was to make a distinction between the outward community of Christians and those who are really united by a

---

[1] I follow the general usage of historians in speaking of the church government of that time as episcopal; but I think the advocates of Presbytery have made out that it was not a diocesan, but a parochial episcopacy, the bishop, priests, and deacons corresponding to the minister, elders, and deacons of Presbyterian congregations.

living faith to Christ; and maintaining the teaching of Christ, that the kingdom of God is spiritual, to acknowledge that the true body of Christ cannot be infallibly recognised by any outward marks, and to regard the external Christian society as but an approximate representation of the true Church. This was the view afterwards taken by the Protestants, and expressed in the distinction of the Church invisible and visible, but anticipations of it are found in some of the Donatists, especially in the grammarian Tichonius. He laid down seven rules for the elucidation of obscure and difficult passages of Scripture; and the second of these was " On the twofold body of the Lord" (*de Domini corpore bipartito*), which requires the reader to be attentive when the Scripture speaks really of others from those of whom it seems to speak, *i.e.* appearing to describe those outwardly connected with Christ, really speaks of those truly one with him. Tichonius was a Donatist, but differed from the others of those opinions, and was censured by his bishop Parmenianus, because he held the Church to be diffused over all the earth, and not restricted to the Donatist communion; and thus he occupied a sort of intermediate position between the Catholics and the most of the Donatists. This seems to be indicated in his distinction of the twofold body of Christ. Augustine, criticizing his rules, says that this is indeed true, but wrongly expressed, for he should rather have spoken of the true and the pretended or mixed body of Christ.[1]

Augustine did not identify the external Church with the true body of Christ, but recognised that there were

[1] *De Doctr. Christiana*, iii. 32.

many hypocrites in it. These, he says, are not to be considered even now as members of Christ, though they partake of the sacraments of the Church. But, on the other hand, he held that no one could be saved who had not Christ as his head, and no one has Christ as his head who is not in his body the Church. Thus the true body of Christ is restricted within the limits of the outward Christian society; and though not every one who is baptized is saved, none is saved who is not baptized. With this view, the only distinction that he needed to recognise was that of those who are truly members of Christ inwardly as well as outwardly, and those who are so only outwardly and in pretence. But Tichonius seems to have recognised the true spiritual body of Christ as existing in different outward communions, Catholic and Donatist; and therefore it was not enough for him to speak of a true and false body of Christ, as if all his true members must be in one outward communion. So he spoke of a twofold body of Christ, thereby anticipating or feeling after the later developed Protestant doctrine of the Church invisible.

This view, however, gained at that time little countenance; and under the influence of Augustine, the Catholic doctrine triumphed over that of the Donatists, as it had previously overcome the kindred systems of Montanism and Novatianism. Thus the Catholic doctrine of the Church was carried to its completion, and at the same time came to exercise a momentous influence on the conception of the kingdom of God. As we have seen, the Montanist and other anti-Catholic movements were obliged to lay great stress on the second coming and future reign of Christ;

and so in proportion as those tendencies were overcome, these prophetic ideas became of less importance and interest. When at the same time the authority of the bishops as ministers of Christ and rulers of his Church came to be emphasized as the bond of unity, a different view of the future kingdom inevitably arose. The healthy Christian instinct regarded the promised glory, not as a sudden magical transformation, but as the perfect development of blessings already realized; when, therefore, the present privilege of the Church came to be regarded as consisting in its being under the government of Christ's ministers, the future glory of the kingdom naturally came to be conceived in an ecclesiastical or political form. Then, when in the fourth century the Roman power ceased to persecute the Church, and became Christian, and afterwards the Western Empire was seen falling before the barbarians, while the Catholic Church with its ecclesiastical organism was flourishing; it was not unnatural that men should think that this was the establishment of the kingdom of God on the earth, and the overthrow of the last great heathen empire.

The great exponent of this view is Augustine; and he gave the idea of the kingdom of God a shape which long possessed the minds of men, and found embodiment in the medieval system of the Papacy.[1] Meanwhile the acceptance of Christianity by Constantine, and his victories over Maxentius and Licinius, opened up the possibility of the current theories of the kingdom of God being translated into fact. As long as the Christian Church was poor and powerless, unauthorized by law, and if not persecuted, at best only ignored by

[1] See Appendix, Note U.

the Empire in intervals of its long conflict with the new religion; there could be no attempt to set up an outward kingdom of God. If it was conceived as an earthly sovereignty, it could only be regarded as a thing of the future, to be established by some mighty act of divine power; and so it was conceived by the Chiliasts, whose hopes were set on the end of the present age and the reign of Christ and his saints in a new earth. If, on the other hand, the idea was entertained of a kingdom of God, which had already come and was a present reality, that could only be conceived as a spiritual thing, a reign in and over the hearts of believers; and so it was generally viewed by the Alexandrian Fathers. These two accordingly were the only alternative views in the days of the suffering Church. But as the ecclesiastical hierarchy was developed, and the idea of the Catholic Church formed, another notion of the kingdom was being prepared, and was ready to step forth on the stage of history when the empire became Christian. Now it was possible to regard the reign of God as actually come already, and yet to conceive it as not merely invisible and spiritual, but an outward and visible dominion. Now the will and law of God could be done, not merely by patient and heroic endurance, but by public law and observance; now an outward order could be established that would realize the kingdom of God. The sovereign of the world was now a worshipper of God and Christ; was not that the fulfilment of the Apocalyptic cry, "The kingdom of the world is become the kingdom of our Lord and of his Christ"? (Rev. xi. 15).

Now for the first time it became a practical question what the duty of a Christian king is, and what his rule has to do for the kingdom of God; and as this question has not even yet been answered in a way satisfactory to all, we cannot wonder that in those days when it was new, and some practical solution had to be found without delay, much confusion arose, and many rash experiments were made. Neander[1] has pointed out, that in the policy of Constantine there were three different systems, alternating and crossing one another: that of simply tolerating the Church; that of recognising it as the theocracy, which he was bound to support and to follow; and that of taking his place as himself a bishop in outward things, and practically ruling as a theocratic sovereign through the Church. Had the first policy been consistently carried out, the only difference that the conversion of the empire would have made would be that Christians would now be secured from persecution; the positive reign of God could only be conceived in such ways as were possible before. But the general opinion was, that a sovereign who believed in God and Christ must reign for them, and the only question was how. Had the Church been perfectly united under the organized hierarchy that was afterwards formed, it might have successfully asserted its claim to be the kingdom of God, and kept the emperor in the position of its loyal son and defender. But this ecclesiastico-theocratic idea was not yet fully developed; and, moreover, there were beside the Catholic, Novatian and Donatist communions claiming to be the true Church of Christ.

[1] *Kirchengeschichte*, i. p. 483, ed. 1856.

If Constantine was to do more than tolerate, he must decide between these rival claims; and as he had thus to determine theological questions, he was forced practically into the position of an overseer, *i.e.* bishop of the Church. Thus the third of the above-mentioned policies, the politico-theocratic, as we may call it, ultimately became that of Constantine and his successors; and the Eastern Church never got above the position thus assigned to it. In this system there is a kingdom of God; the empire is Christian; the emperor fills a sacred office; he judges on his own responsibility what is the will and law of God, and enforces that in his law and government. His episcopate in the Church is indeed only external, not implying spiritual duties or powers, but by means of it he has, directly or indirectly, a practical control over the Church. This system might be tolerable under Constantine, whose views were generally in agreement with the majority of the Church; but when, under his successors, it became the means of forcing Arianism on the Church, its dangers began to be felt, and the glowing expectations of a Christian state, that Eusebius of Cæsarea had entertained, was rudely dispelled. The necessity was seen of asserting and maintaining the Church's independence of State control; and among many prelates who purchased Court favour by unworthy complaisance, a series of great and heroic bishops—Athanasius, Lucifer of Cagliari, Eusebius of Vercelli, Chrysostom, Ambrose, Augustine—raised the dignity of their office, and vindicated the freedom of the Church.

But as Augustine's view of the Church being exclusively the kingdom of God, and the State the kingdom of this world, became general, it was impossible to maintain the independence of the Church without asserting also its supremacy over the State. That the kingdom of God ought to rule on earth, is to a Christian a self-evident proposition; and if Providence had given Christians the opportunity of establishing this rule, they ought certainly to do all in their power to bring it about. But now the idea had come to prevail, that the kingdom that Christ had instituted was the society of believers organized into a body by the government of bishops and synods with the power of the keys of the kingdom of heaven: hence the aim of those who would labour for the kingdom must be to make this hierarchy not only free from constraint or control, but supreme over all other powers. On the other hand, if the State be outside of the kingdom of God, and civil government be only an earthly institution, aiming at mere earthly ends and using earthly means, how can it be in any way christianized, or made to promote the spiritual aims of the kingdom of God, except by being guided blindly by the Church, which is the kingdom, and used by her as a means for her own high ends? Earthly rulers must learn from the teachers of the Church how God would have them to use their authority, and ought to use it in accordance with their instructions.

There can be no doubt that on the whole the things for which the Church contended in this hierarchical way were for the most part truly Christian objects. What she aimed at was in itself the carrying out of the precepts of Jesus as they were understood by the Church; and though doubtless in some respects they were misunderstood by her, yet they were not then understood better by others; indeed, the Church had mainly to contend with those who did not even attempt to carry out Christian precepts, but struggled only for their own interests. On the whole, the power of the Church and her prelates was exercised against impurity and inhumanity, and in defence of the weak and oppressed against the strong. This appears in their opposition to the licentious and cruel shows of the theatre and arena, in Ambrose's excommunication of Theodosius for the massacre at Thessalonica, and in the long-continued efforts of the Church for the amelioration, and finally for the abolition, of slavery. These proceeded on the conviction of the dignity and value of all human beings alike as redeemed by Christ; and the general nature of all the social objects for which the Church exerted her authority shows an appreciation of the moral character of Christ's kingdom as one of purity, equity, and mercy. No doubt she strove also for the maintenance of orthodoxy, and the forcible suppression of heresy; and in the end this aim came to be preferred to the others; but the leaven of intolerance was only beginning to work, and was comparatively slight in the fifth and sixth centuries. We can well understand how earnest Christians in those days thought themselves to be advancing the kingdom of God in the only way that was open to them, by labouring for the promotion of the Church's power, and the increase of the dignity and authority of her prelates. In so far as their efforts secured the spread of righteousness, and peace, and joy in the Holy Ghost, they were really building up the true kingdom of God, though, in consequence of the distorted way in which that kingdom had come to be conceived, they were also erecting what proved a monstrous travesty of it, the earthly and worldly dominion of the Papacy.

But the mistake of identifying the outward organized Church with the kingdom of God had other and more far-reaching consequences than even this. It affected men's whole conceptions of Christian life and duty, falling in as it did with other tendencies in the same direction that prevailed then and for ages after. If the Church alone is the kingdom of God; then, since Christ speaks of that kingdom as the highest aim of man, and represents it as comprehending all that he has to do, all Christian duty and activity must take the form of service of the Church, and what cannot be brought into that category must be rejected as forming no proper part of the life-work of a disciple of Jesus. He is to seek first the kingdom of God, and to live for it, casting aside as a hindrance what lies outside of it; and that meant, on the theory then current, whatever is not in some way or other a service of the Church. Thus the ethics of the Church came to take a purely negative attitude towards the State and natural social life, and to assume a one-sided theological character. A man was not held to be serving the kingdom of God when discharging the duties of a parent, a statesman, a handicraftsman; these and all such occupations were secular, belonging to that world (*sæculum*) which is alien and opposite to the kingdom of God; he is only living for it in so far as he renounces all these. This ideal was first sought in the cells of hermits or convents of monks, which were called heavenly commonwealths (οὐράνια πολιτεύματα), where men might live the angelic life (ὁ τῶν ἀγγέλων βίος); and afterwards it was attempted to make the whole Church conform to this ideal, or at least form a means towards it. The Church, as the kingdom of God, must on the one hand be as much as possible separate from the world, and on the other hand must rule over the world as completely as possible. It has often been pointed out, that the elements of asceticism on the one hand, and priestly ascendency on the other, are closely associated. Both grew together in the history of the Church, and both are connected with the ecclesiastical view that came to be taken of the kingdom of God.

It followed from this view also, that an undue place must be given to the outward ordinances of the Church, and a magical efficacy ascribed to them. For the kingdom of God, as set forth in the New Testament, is not only the aim of Christian virtue, but the sum of Christian blessedness. It is the substance of the glad tidings of Christ, and believers must needs look in it for those spiritual blessings that their souls need, such as forgiveness of sins, assurance of God's love, peace of conscience, sanctification, comfort in affliction, and hope in death. Anything that does not provide for men these blessings, whatever it may be called, is not for them the kingdom of God in any practical and valuable sense. When, therefore, the kingdom of God is identified with the outward Catholic Church; these blessings must be sought in it, and must be regarded as coming to men through its organization and ordinances. The baptism of water is identified with the washing away of sins and the new birth of the Holy Spirit; the divine life thus communicated is to be nourished by a bodily receiving of Christ in the Lord's Supper; the assurance of God's favour, and the support of his grace, is given to believers through the blessing of the priest or bishop; and the backslider is absolved from guilt, and assured of an entrance into heaven by the power of the keys in the hands of the Church and her officers. The Christian salvation in all its parts is indeed conceived as coming from God of his grace; this was the great truth that Augustine vindicated against the Pelagians. But then this truth was conjoined with and vitiated by the mistake that that salvation must come through the ordinances of the Church; and thus the Christian system was made to assume a magical form, and all that genuine Christian feeling which recognises that salvation must come by the grace of God was directed to the support of a superstitious sacramental system.

The development of ideas by which the hierarchical system was evolved from the notion of the Church being the kingdom of God, was accompanied by another tendency, which more and more connected that kingdom with the Empire of Rome. The reign of the imperial city had come to exert a sort of fascination over the minds of men. It was the realization of the philosophic ideas of a universal State, the representative of order and justice, civilisation and peace. Even Augustine is not free from the influence of the comманding and majestic imagination of the Roman Empire. Hence the importance in his eyes of the question he discusses in his *City of God* as of fundamental apologetic moment, a question that is apt to seem to us of a very secondary interest and value.

R

Virgil, the great singer of Rome, whose consummate epic really celebrates not Æneas, but the Roman people, was a favourite and much-quoted poet with him; and he makes it a main task of his work to explain on Christian principles the rise and dominion of Rome. In this respect also Augustinian ideas bore fruit with his successors in the teaching and defence of the Church, especially the bishops of Rome. Leo I., in his sermon on the martyrdom of Peter and Paul, argues that Rome had been raised in divine providence to the empire of the world, in order by uniting mankind under one government, to facilitate the spread of Christianity; and that Peter, the prince of the apostles, and Paul, the teacher of the Gentiles, were led to it as the place from which the light of the true religion might most easily be everywhere diffused, and thus the city that had been the capital of the world became the capital of the kingdom of God. It is needless here to trace the well-known train of circumstances by which the bishops of Rome gradually acquired a predominant power and authority in the Church, the result of which was, that Rome became the seat of ecclesiastical, as it had formerly been of political, empire. The more the kingdom of God came to be conceived as an external hierarchy, the more necessary it was that it should have a regular organization, and that the bonds that united its different parts should be drawn closely and firmly together. Gregory I., who has been called the first real Pope, was in theology a disciple of Augustine, and spoke of the Church as the city of God (*civitas Dei laborans in terris, regnatura in cælo*). In his time we find that this idea of the kingdom of God led to increased missionary enterprises, and to efforts to enforce uniformity of rules and observances, and to bring formerly independent Churches, as the Celtic, into subjection to the authority of Rome. About the same time too, most of the barbarian peoples, who had destroyed the Roman Empire, accepted Christianity, some at first in the Arian form, but ultimately in that of the Catholic Church. Then began to appear the idea of a new world rising out of the ruins of the old, a world that should be from the first not pagan, as the old world had been, but Christian. Thus the way was prepared for a fresh phase in the attempts to realize the kingdom of God on earth, the holy Roman Empire, which began with the coronation of Charles the Great by Pope Leo III. on Christmas day 800, and was permanently established by that of Otto the Great in 962.

The new Empire was a theocracy; the earthly power of the king was consecrated by the bishop's anointing; the old rite by which the kings of Israel were marked as inspired by God was applied to make the earthly kingdom a heavenly one. The chief who had been made king by elevation on his soldiers' shields was now made the Lord's anointed, head of the Christian world. Thus it has been truly said: " Charles' imperial power was to him the kingship or highest magisterial office, as, though in itself belonging to the kingdom of this world, expressly taken up as an element in the kingdom of God, and thereby hallowed. By his coronation as emperor, he believed himself to have received, not in the first place new powers, but new duties, to conduct his kingdom as essentially Christian, and therefore in the interests of Christianity, *i.e.* as then understood, of the Church, to rule his people as a Christian people."[1] The Emperors, however, were also conceived to be universal sovereigns. The Christian idea of the kingdom of God as world-wide, embracing all men without distinction, was strangely blended with the old Roman notion of a universal Empire, and afterwards at least, also with the universalism which the Roman jurists had derived from the Stoics. As the Catholic Church was one through all the world, the Empire was this one body in its earthly aspect, and the emperor its temporal head, consecrated as Christian by the coronation of the Pope, the spiritual head of Christendom. The Roman Empire had been raised by Divine Providence to be a protection and support to the Christian Church; it had itself become Christian; and the King who was chosen to rule it received in his coronation at Rome a religious and sacred character. The ceremony was not a mere spectacle, but essential to the office, and was of an ecclesiastical and almost sacramental character; the Emperor is said to be ordained or consecrated, just as might be said of a priest or bishop; he was actually made a deacon, and received the communion in both kinds as a cleric.[2]

Such in general was the medieval view of the kingdom of God. But this general scheme was held in two forms, between which took place the gigantic conflicts of that time. On the one hand, the papal theory applied to it the principle of Augustine, that civil government belongs to the world as distinct from the city of God; and deduced from that the

[1] Rothe, *Vorlesungen über Kirchengeschichte*, ii. p. 194.
[2] See Bryce's *Holy Roman Empire*.

inference that the imperial power is only holy in so far as it is not only consecrated, but ruled and directed by the Church, through her head the Pope. The successor of Peter, as the Vicar of Christ, has not only the keys of heaven, but the two swords of Peter, and he only delegates to the Emperor the civil sword; he gives him the crown, and is as the sun, the greater light, while the emperor, as only the ruler of this world, is but as the moon, the lesser light, deriving all his splendour from him. This was the doctrine to the practical establishment of which Hildebrand and Innocent III. devoted their great ability and indomitable perseverance and courage. The Empire might seem a superfluity on this theory, since the Popes could rule directly the several sovereigns of Europe, and the unity of the Church under its single spiritual head at Rome might sufficiently maintain the oneness of Christendom as the kingdom of God. But whatever may be said in theory, without the Empire the Papacy never could have attained in practice the temporal sway it had in the twelfth century. The kings of France and England were able to resist the claims of the Popes; and so also might the Hohenstaufens have done had they been only German kings, and not burdened also with the crowns of Italy and Rome, the latter of which was regarded as the crown of the whole world. These involved them in enterprises foreign to their nation and beyond their strength.

But over against this papal theory of the kingdom of God there was another, held by the great German emperors, and afterwards by the civilians, when the study of the Roman jurisprudence was revived. According to it, the Empire was indeed hallowed by the papal consecration, and might be admitted to be inferior in dignity to the Papacy, but was not subject to its authority. The Emperor, as well as the Pope, was God's vicar on earth, inferior no doubt, as having to do with worldly things only, but reigning over these by a divine right, and responsible only to God. Much earlier than Charlemagne the Old Testament theocratic idea of kings being the vicegerents of God[1] had come into currency; and the sacredness that attached to each sovereign in his own kingdom belonged all the more to the Emperor as suzerain of them all, and lord of all Christendom. The Emperor was to do justice to all in the name of God, as is truly described in Carlyle's vivid picture of Frederick Barbarossa.[2]

While the Empire and the Papacy had such fierce and obstinate conflicts, both were aiming at the realization of the kingdom of God in earth as that is described in Scripture. In the scriptural arguments on both sides there was much fanciful allegorizing and arbitrary twisting of texts; but in the main both had a true ideal, a state of universal and lasting peace, which could

---

[1] A Council at Toledo in 693 ordained: "Post Deum regibus, utpote jure vicario ab eo præelectis, fidem promissam quemque inviolabili cordis intentione servare."—Neander, *Kirchengeschichte*, ii. 52.

[2] *History of Frederick II. of Prussia*, i. 99. "A magnificent magnanimous man, holding the reins of the world not quite in the imaginary sense, scourging anarchy down, and urging noble effort up, really on a grand scale, a terror to evil-doers and a praise to well-doers in this world, probably beyond what was ever seen since. Whom also we salute across the centuries, as a choice beneficence of heaven. Encamped on the plain of Roncaglia when he entered Italy, as he too often had occasion to do, his shield was hung out on a high mast over his tent, and it meant in those old days, Ho, every one that has suffered wrong, here is a kaiser come to judge you as he shall answer it to his Master! And men gathered round him and actually found some justice, if they could discern it when found."

only be secured by righteousness, established and enforced by the authority and will of God. The ideal is one to which the modern world has come no nearer even yet; the utmost that can be said is, that there is some tolerable approach to it in the internal order of individual States in the civilised world; but the attainment of international peace or international justice is still a problem of the future. That this end was really the aim of the Papacy in its best representatives we need not doubt. The time of its highest power was preceded by a period of deep moral corruption and degradation, and was brought about by a reformatory movement, of which Hildebrand was the moving spirit. He desired in the first place to purify the Church from the abuses of simony and profligacy, then to assert its independence of the civil power, and then to make it a universal theocracy; and whatever ambition and arrogance there was in his way of pursuing these aims, we need not doubt the sincerity of his last words: "I have loved justice and hated iniquity, therefore I die in exile." The lines on which he worked for his end were those that had long before been laid down and recognised as principles, the identification of the visible Church with the kingdom of God, the reign of God in it by bishops, the separation of the clergy from the people by a strict ascetic life, the use of force to maintain the truth and coerce heretics; these ideas, which had been more or less distinctly sanctioned by Augustine, now bore fruit, and were carried to their practical consequences in the medieval Papacy.

Our object does not require us to trace the often-told history of the conflict between the Papacy and the

Empire, but only to note how far it illustrates the views of the kingdom of God sought to be realized on each side. The successive failure of both to gain their end permanently shows the very same causes in operation that led to the fall of the theocracy in Israel. The victory that Hildebrand gained over Henry IV., when he constrained him to wait as a penitent in the snow at Canossa, was partly due to the intellectual and moral superiority of the inexorable Pontiff to the unstable King, but it was not achieved without the temporal aid of the faithful Countess Matilda: the power of the great Frederick Barbarossa was broken, not by any superior spiritual power in the Church, but by the alliance of the Italian cities, who defeated him at Legnano, having been enlisted, not by principle, but only by political circumstances, on the side of the Pope: and Frederick II., the last Emperor who could resist the Popes, was foiled, not merely by ecclesiastical arms, but by political combinations. The victory of the Papacy was not gained by moral firmness and endurance, like that of the early Church over the persecuting Empire, but to a large extent at least by carnal weapons and worldly policy. Hence it needed to be supported by similar means, and in order to maintain their spiritual reign, the Popes became temporal sovereigns.[1] They were thus involved in all the vicissitudes to which temporal power is liable, and to which it was specially exposed in those unsettled and lawless days; and this may help to explain the strange circumstance, that the heyday of the Popes' power in the

---

[1] Such ideas were expressed by the Abbot Joachim. See Neander, *Kirchengeschichte*, ii. 453.

thirteenth century was so speedily followed by their lowest humiliation in their exile at Avignon in the fourteenth. They were unable to maintain that theocracy which they had succeeded in rearing, because they had made the kingdom of God a kingdom of this world, and it was therefore necessarily subject to the changes of all things of this world. It could not be eternal; it was not even long-lived. Had the hierarchy, as ministers of Christ, moved the consciences and won the affection and confidence of the people, they might have acquired a power, strong, beneficent, and lasting, which might have been considered a reign of God in Christ's sense; in so far as any of them did so anywhere, they did establish God's kingdom; but for the most part, and especially at the head of the hierarchy, they did not look to any such means; and so, whatever they desired, they failed, even when they had most power, to establish a reign of righteousness and peace; and they soon lost the power which they gained by worldly means, and used in a worldly way.

This failure of the papal system led to a revival of the imperialist theory, though the Empire as a fact could never more be made anything like the universal Christian monarchy which it was in idea. But when men were longing for the kingdom of God, and feeling that it ought to be established in the earth, since the nations were now Christian; deeply sensible of the evils of the time, lawlessness, cruelty, deceit, and vice of all kinds, and finding that the Popes who claimed to be the vicars of Christ, even when they had asserted their power over kings and emperors, had not brought in a reign of justice and peace; they looked to the notion of a universal government in the name of God and according to his will; and that they could only conceive as a monarchy in the only empire that had ever established a universal system of law. The hope of the world must still lie, they thought, in the Roman Empire, its Emperor raised above all national kings and princes, and able as God's vicegerent to do justice to all, and enforce peace among all. The great exponent of this idea is Dante, in whom we see the curious combination of different elements in the theory; the abstract theoretical argument, that universal peace requires a universal government, and that this must be a monarchy as the most perfect representation of the rule of the one God; the Augustinian idea, that the Romans had obtained universal dominion on account of their virtue, and had been raised in Providence to promote the spread of the gospel; the reverence for Virgil as the poet of Rome; the medieval assumption that the kingdom of the Franks is the Roman Empire; the feeling that the Church had been corrupted by the donation of Constantine, which is undoubtedly accepted as a fact, and that the Popes had illegally grasped the civil sword in addition to the spiritual. Dante recognises the distinction between the Church and the State, and accepts the identification of the latter with the world as distinct from the kingdom of Christ, which is not of this world; but he argues from these premises that the State must be independent in its own lower sphere; though owing reverence and honour to the Church. "Man's nature is twofold, corruptible and incorruptible, he has therefore two ends, active virtue on earth, and the enjoyment of the sight of God hereafter; the one to be attained by practice conformed to the precepts of philosophy, the other by the theological virtues. Hence two guides are needed, the Pontiff and the Emperor, the latter of whom, in order that he may direct mankind in accordance with the teachings of philosophy, must preserve universal peace in the world. Thus are the two powers equally ordained of God, and the Emperor, though supreme in all that pertains to the secular world, is in some things dependent on the Pontiff, since earthly happiness is subordinate to eternal."[1]

But this theory, though widely prevalent among the jurists of the fourteenth and fifteenth centuries, was never carried into effect; the nearest approach to it was the attempted reformation of the Church by the Council of Constance, when the Emperor Sigismund appeared as the temporal head of Christendom, and called Popes and heretics alike to the bar of the Council. That might seem to offer promise of the realization of the ideas of Dante, and might have done so under a wise and strong Emperor. But Sigismund had nought of the genius of the Swabian Kaisers; and he who broke his safe-conduct to Huss was a miserable representative of justice. Besides, there were other ideas and tendencies rising that made this form of conceiving the kingdom of God an impracticable dream. The medieval attempt to carry out Augustine's notion of the city of God had proved a failure in both its forms, the papal and the imperial; and though the holy Roman Empire lingered out a nominal existence for four centuries longer, already it was neither holy, nor Roman, nor an Empire.

Already, indeed, long before history had finally condemned the medieval theory of the kingdom of God,

[1] Bryce's *Holy Roman Empire*, p. 268.

there had been significant and even prophetic voices raised against it. The corruption of the Church, the worldliness, pride, and greed of its rich and powerful ecclesiastics, the externalizing of Christianity by making it a system of ritual observances, and the inconsistency of all this with the teaching and spirit of Christ, were keenly felt by many earnest souls, and led to protests, efforts, and hopes for a reformation, and a restoration of Christianity to its primitive purity. And as the corruptions of the time seemed to consist at bottom of worldliness, and to be due to the Church having gained so large a share in the good things of the world; a return to the poverty and humility of apostolic times seemed a natural remedy. But these ideas very naturally led to an overthrow of the foundation of the then current view of the kingdom of God, which was the doctrine of Augustine, that the reign of Christ began with the establishment of the visible Church, with its episcopal government. That idea was natural enough then; but now the very thing that had been held to be the setting up of Christ's reign on earth, came to appear as the source and beginning of the Church's gross corruption. The millennium cannot have begun, as was thought: the papal or imperial system is not the kingdom of God, rather should we see in it the usurpation of Antichrist. The thousand years' reign of Christ and his saints is yet to come, and must be looked for in a future period of the Church's history.

These views were most distinctly expressed by the Abbot Joachim, but were bitterly denounced by many as heretical. They were, in one point of view, a revival of the chiliasm that had prevailed in the ancient Church, but with important differences. There appears nothing of a sensuous nature about Joachim's views of the millennium; on the contrary, sensuality is one of the evils against which he most strongly contends; his notion of the perfect state of the Church is open to criticism rather as unduly and one-sidedly spiritualizing it. He distinguished three great stages of divine revelation,—the age of the Father, when God is revealed as Creator, the object of fear and reverence; the age of the Son, when God is revealed as incarnate in Christ, opening up the treasures of wisdom and knowledge; and the age of the Spirit, which is still future, when God shall be revealed through love directly to the soul of every man, when there should be no need of teachers or pastors, since all should know God in mystic contemplation. In this conception of the reign of God as inward, consisting in the influence of his Spirit on the hearts and lives of men, Joachim seems to have come nearer Christ's true meaning than the current idea of its being a kingdom maintained by law and force.

But the weakness of all millennial theories is, to disjoin the future from the present, and regard the promised reign of Christ as to be accomplished in a future period, by means of manifestations totally different from those of which we have experience now. These may be variously conceived, sometimes in gross material forms of chiliasm, as mere miraculous power, sometimes, in the more refined forms that the system has assumed in modern times, as the personal presence and influence of Christ: in Joachim's view, it was by a new dispensation of the Spirit that the great change was to be effected. This he separated so sharply from the dispensations of the Father and of the Son, that he was accused in his own day of perverting the doctrine of the Trinity in the direction of Tritheism; and in later times he has been thought to have been indifferent to historical Christianity altogether, and to have taught a kind of Pantheism, quite independent of the facts of Christ's incarnation and sacrifice. These charges are probably unfounded as regards Joachim's personal opinions and teaching, though they indicate the dangerous tendencies of some of his speculations. His failure to connect the future reign of God with the present also prevented his teaching having any great practical effect in the reformation of the Church. It awakened a sense of the evils of the existing state of religion, and called forth hopes and longings for a better state in the future; but as that was looked for in a new and more perfect dispensation, there was no present relief for the troubled soul, and nothing to do but to wait and watch for the coming of the better day. It may indeed be said, that St. Francis and the Franciscan order of contemplative and preaching friars were a result of Joachim's ideas, as they were supposed to have been predicted by him; and so his teaching may be regarded as having had this practical result in the way of reformation. But the Franciscans embodied very little of Joachim's reformatory ideas; and instead of helping forward his view of the kingdom of God, became devoted supporters of the Papacy, those of them who maintained their original principle of real poverty being condemned and persecuted as heretics.

These protests against the medieval theory of the

kingdom of God as realized in the external organization of the Church under the Papacy are interesting, as showing how genuine Christian feeling rebelled against it when its consequences were fully seen. But no thorough and radical reformation could be effected, until there was recognised a present kingdom of God of a spiritual nature. Men might point to a millennial reign of Christ as a thing of the future, and even of a near future, for which preparations might already be made; but if, in the meantime, they could speak of no other kingdom of God than the Church of professing Christians, that would still hold the chief place in their faith and allegiance. The truly reformatory teaching, that which has been proved by history to have had the power to elevate and liberate men's religious ideas, and to give purity and power to their Christian life, has been that which distinguished the true Church of Christ from its appearance to the judgment of charity, and so represented it, that the blessings of the spiritual kingdom of God could be enjoyed in it here and now. The former of these was done by Wycliffe, John Huss, and other precursors of the Reformation, who distinguished the true Church invisible from the outwardly professing Church visible; the latter was done by Luther and the other Reformers properly so called, who proclaimed the doctrine of justification by faith alone. The former may seem to have a more direct connection with our subject than the other; but without the latter the true Christian idea of the kingdom of God cannot be understood or realized.

Wycliffe's reformatory influence was derived mainly from two prominent parts of his teaching, the authority of Scripture as superior to all speculations and traditions of men, and the spiritual nature of the Church, as opposed to the external Catholic view of it. The former was the more far-reaching in its consequences, though in itself it was but general and indefinite, and without the latter it could not have free scope; for however the authority of Scripture may be asserted, if the Church which is the body and kingdom of Christ be identified with an external society, it will naturally claim the right of interpreting Scripture for individuals. Wycliffe, by means of the doctrine of predestination, which he maintained so strongly, broke through this theory of the Church; and so he defines the Church militant as "the body of the predestinate, while it is here journeying to its home."[1] He denied the divine right of the hierarchy of his day, recognizing that in the apostolic Church there were only two kinds of ministers, presbyters and deacons, and that bishops and presbyters were originally the same. He inveighed against the worldly power and wealth of the clergy, which he regarded as a mark of Antichrist, and held that preaching the gospel is the most essential function of the ministry. The saying ascribed to Augustine, that the Popes and clergy are vicars of Christ, and kings vicars of God, he interpreted as meaning that while civil rulers are armed with power by God for restraining rebellion and crime, the ministers of the Church are to be followers of Christ in his humiliation, imitating his poverty, his meekness, his diligence and labour.

In these views we have really the beginning of a new era. We have an express assertion of what has been

[1] Corpus prædestinatorum dum hic viat in patriam.

called the formal principle of Protestantism, the sole authority of Scripture, with the practical application of that principle in the translation of the New Testament into the language of the people; and though we do not find so full and clear an expression of the material principle of the Reformation, justification by faith, yet Wycliffe's teaching about the Church as the body of true Christians, brought men into direct relation with God in their religious life, and so contained the germ at least of what was brought out with so much power by Luther.

The same view of the Church was held by Matthias von Janow, who was the teacher of John Huss, and was proclaimed with clearness and energy by the latter. Huss, I think, was the first to express clearly the idea, that as there may be those in the Church visible who are not members of the Church invisible, so there may be members of the Church invisible who are not in the visible. He says there is a fourfold " relation of men in this life to the holy mother the Church; some are in the Church both in name and in reality, as the predestinate who are Catholics obeying Christ; some neither in reality nor in name, as pagans foreknown [but not predestinate]; some only in name, as foreknown hypocrites; and some in reality, though they seem to be outside, as predestinate Christians, whom the satraps of Antichrist seem in the face of the Church to condemn."[1] Similar doctrine was taught by John of Wesel and John Wessel; the former, however, still

---

[1] "Quadruplex habitudo viatorum ad sanctam matrem ecclesiam: quidam sunt in ecclesia et nomine et re, ut prædestinati obedientes Christo Catholici; quidam nec re nec nomine, ut præsciti pagani; quidam

represents the invisible Church as included within the visible; the latter more nearly approaches Huss' position. This doctrine of the true Church being the spiritual body of Christ, even in the form that included it within the outward Church, was condemned by the Council of Constance, and was one of those for which Huss was led to the stake. It was on this point that Luther first came into direct collision with the express doctrine of the Church of Rome.

But before the Reformation produced a radical change in the religious conception of the kingdom of God, we may trace the beginning of another line of thought, independent yet closely akin in some respects to it, a kind of speculation that has led to many noteworthy results which have been combined in various ways with the theological and ecclesiastical theories. The last great conflict of the Empire with the Papacy, that of the fourteenth and fifteenth centuries, was carried on, not so much by arms, as in the days of the Hohenstaufens, as by literary controversy; and the most formidable opponents of the papal claims were not the mail-clad knights who used to follow the imperial standard through the Tyrolese passes into Italy, but the men of learning and letters, such as Dante, Marsilius of Padua, John Gerson, and William of Ockham. It was in this age that the universities arose, and they speedily became an intellectual power and bond of unity in the civilised world, just as the Church represented its religious, and the Empire its political one-

nomine tantum, ut præsciti hypocritæ ; et quidam re, licet videantur esse foris, ut prædestinati Christiani quos Antichristi satrapæ videntur in facie ecclesiæ condemnare." Quoted by Münchmeyer, *das Dogma von der sichtbaren u. unsichtbaren Kirche*, p. 16.

ness. Since the great and all-absorbing question of the day was that between the claims of Pope and Cæsar, men's minds were led in the direction of political discussion and speculation, to determine what was the right relation of the rival powers, what the foundation of each, what the principles on which mankind ought to be governed, and what the best way of securing the ends of government. Thus ideal states came to be conceived and sketched, at first, as in Dante's *de Monarchia*, in the medieval method and spirit, and then on other principles at once more ancient and more modern. With the revival of learning and the sense of the power of intellect and education, there awoke again in Europe the conception of the Greek philosophers, that knowledge and culture might be the true bond of society, and the means of bringing it to a perfect development.

Now began that remarkable class of literary works in which political and social ideals are presented in the form of imaginary commonwealths, of which More's *Utopia* is the best known and of most interest to us. These are attempts to conceive a perfect state of society, and thus in fact deal with the same subject as Christ spoke of when he described the kingdom of God. They do not draw their ideals from Scripture, or profess to be attempts to unfold its teaching, but are independent efforts, on the basis of reason and experience, to conceive the nature and conditions of a perfect state of society. Most of them were the work of sincere believers in Christianity, and more or less pervaded with Christian principles; but they did not, like the medieval theories, start from these as their basis, or undertake to develope and apply the principles of Christianity. They took up the problem in its more general aspect, as it had been treated by the ancient Greek statesmen and philosophers, and some of the principles that had been advocated by them, but had been lost sight of since the rise of the holy Roman Empire, now reappeared. Chief among these are two, which have become leading ideas in certain influential schools in modern times; that of liberty, which was especially derived from the Athenian statesmen and poets; and that of education, which is to be traced up to Plato, whose republic gave the suggestion and pattern to these imaginary States.

Liberty and learning were the watchwords of the humanists in their conflict against authority and prescription; and the struggle for these two objects was then a common one, since the authority that claimed to be divine had come to ally itself with falsehood and ignorance. But in the army of progress there were combined two different principles or tendencies, which have only in recent times appeared in their distinctness and separation, or even antagonism. These are the same as we before observed in the difference between the liberal democracy of Athens and the ideal republic of Plato; in the former of which freedom, and in the latter education was the ruling principle. In More's *Utopia* we see the two principles side by side. The Utopian commonwealth rests upon community of goods, the absence of money, the education of its citizens; yet in many respects, and particularly in religion, it allows personal freedom of choice and action within certain limits; and More indicates that he does not approve of community of goods, though he has described it as existing in

Utopia. We must always remember that the method of conveying political ideas in the description of imaginary commonwealths was chosen, because it was the only safe way in which many opinions that were then considered heretical could be published, and that for the same reason things were introduced into those descriptions which the writers did not mean seriously to recommend. Still the inconsistencies that we see in the *Utopia* are doubtless partly due to the fact, that the two principles of freedom and education, which were both dear to the author, are in one respect very opposite in their tendency, the one leading to individualism, and the other to socialism or collectivism. These two tendencies are becoming more and more distinct in the present day, since the ideas of the humanists came to the front again in the eighteenth century. But in the sixteenth, they did not get beyond the stage of literary discussion and philosophical speculation; and the practical movements of the time were connected rather with the religious beliefs that produced the Reformation.

The result of the medieval attempts to realize the kingdom of God had been that. Christendom was sent back to the position of Judaism, and made an external and worldly theocracy, which had come to be regarded, not as a preparatory and temporary state of things leading on to a better reign of God, but as the final and highest ideal to be attained. What was needed therefore was just the republication of the teaching of Jesus and his apostles about the kingdom of God; nothing more, but also nothing less. The recovery of this original Christian teaching, after it had been so long buried in ignorance and overlaid with superstition, was made possible by the preservation of an authentic record of it in the New Testament, and from that pure well of divine truth the Reformers drew their reformatory ideas. The central truth of the gospel, forgiveness of sins by God's free grace, irrespective of any merit or works of men, but to be received by faith alone, was what Luther, Zwingli, and their associates proclaimed in opposition to the ecclesiastical doctrines of salvation by human merits and outward rites, which had grown up under the shadow of the external theocracy. This evangelical doctrine very directly led to a new conception of the Church, such as had been held before by Wycliffe and Huss. In those three great writings in which Luther first positively unfolded his teaching, his *Address to the Emperor and Christian Nobility of the German Nation*, his treatise on *The Babylonian Captivity of the Church*, and that on *The Freedom of a Christian Man*, he developes in different aspects the thought of the universal priesthood of believers, which he bases on the passage in 1 Pet. ii. 5-10, where the spiritual theocracy of the New Testament is described in contrast with the outward theocracy of the Old. Not ecclesiastics alone, but all Christians have liberty and dominion over all things as kings and priests, in virtue of faith; while, on the other hand, they are servants of all, in virtue of love, which is the fruit and effect of faith.[1] In these ideas the outline is drawn of a Christian commonwealth or kingdom of God, founded on the gospel as set forth in the New Testament, and freed from the intrusion of that notion of ecclesiastical organization that had led to

---

[1] See Dorner, *Geschichte der Protestantischen Theologie*, pp. 93-108, for an analysis of these three works in their relation and importance.

such fatal corruptions in the Middle Ages. But as yet Luther had done nothing towards the actual realization of such an ideal. He was simply a teacher, and had no authority or rule either in Church or State. He unfolded the teaching of Scripture, and appealed to those who had the rule to amend the abuses which he pointed out. He appealed first to the Pope and bishops, then, these failing, to the Emperor and civil authorities; but to both alike in vain. Instead of prevailing on the authorities, either in Church or State, to undertake a reformation of the commonwealth, Luther was excommunicated by the Pope, and put under the ban of the Empire. At this point of his career he was withdrawn alike from danger and from public activity by his seclusion in the Wartburg. Nothing had as yet been done in the direction of reformation beyond teaching; and though both Luther, with his friends at Wittenberg, and Zwingli, with his at Zurich, had for some years boldly and clearly proclaimed evangelical doctrines, which implied a breach with the medieval theory of the kingdom of God, and a return to the New Testament conception of it, neither the Saxon nor the Swiss Reformers had as yet taken any direct steps to a reform of the institutions of the Church.

In fact, the first attempt to carry out a new conception of the kingdom of God was made in a different line, and by men of a different spirit from Luther and Zwingli, by the enthusiasts who are known under the general name of Anabaptists, Thomas Munzer, Storch, and their associates. They held in common with Wycliffe, Huss, Luther, and Zwingli, that the Church is not the body of those under ecclesiastical government, but the community of saints; but there they differed from these Reformers in assuming that these could be outwardly known. None but genuine saints are to be admitted to Christian fellowship, and thus the Church is to be made identical with the spiritual kingdom of God. So far their view was a revival of Donatism, but it also included Montanistic elements, for they made prominent the direct teaching of the Spirit, and depreciated the Word and external means of grace. Conversion, according to them, was to be effected by a sudden, absolutely supernatural work of God overpowering the soul, which must passively wait for it and yield to it. They looked for the teaching of the Spirit, apart from the Word, by immediate suggestions and inspirations; and those who received such were regarded as heavenly prophets, or even incarnations of deity. As the Church, in their view, must be perfectly pure, consisting only of those who have come under the direct influence of the Spirit of God, there was no room in it for infants, and they could see no propriety or use in infant baptism.

But while their idea of the Church as a community of true saints, ruled and guided by inspired prophets, was apparently diametrically opposed to the medieval idea of it as an organized hierarchy, they agreed in regarding it as an external society, and their views of its relation to the State were identical with those of the Middle Ages. The State was for them too the world, which was to be subject to the Church as the kingdom of God. Munzer applied to the civil rulers and princes of the earth the divine oracle in Hos. xiii. 11: "I gave thee a king in mine anger, and took him away in my wrath;"[1]

[1] See Dorner, *op. cit.* p. 132.

and they all held that Christians should not take any part in civil government, but that the saints as such were to rule the world. Clearly, however, there had never as yet been any such kingdom of the saints on earth, it must be a thing of the future, hence they were led to a revival also of the chiliastic views of the ancient Montanists, and to even more gross and carnal conceptions. The thousand years' reign of the saints was approaching, and it was to be ushered in by great and terrible judgments, which are to make a visible separation of mankind, so that all the ungodly shall be destroyed, and all the saints gathered into a perfect kingdom, to reign on the earth. They applied to this all the apocalyptic images of the coming judgment, taking them in their most literal senses, and the sayings of John the Baptist, about Christ coming with his fan in his hand, to purge his floor, to gather the wheat into his garner, and burn up the chaff with unquenchable fire, omitting to take into account Christ's own teaching about the inward nature and gradual growth of his kingdom. From all this there resulted something like a reproduction of the fanatical Jewish ideas of an earthly kingdom of Messiah, to be established by a sudden miraculous interposition from heaven, in the overthrow of the kingdoms of this world, and the dominion of the chosen people of God.

But the Anabaptists went a step farther than the Chiliasts in the ancient Church; for they held that the coming of the reign of the saints was not merely to be waited and hoped for, but to be hastened by human efforts; and as they looked for it as an external reign of power, they were led to assume that it might be advanced by force and violence.[1] Thus they stood in the same relation to the older Chiliasts, such as the Montanists, as the Zealots among the Jews did to the Pharisees. The rising of the peasants in Germany in 1526, against the oppressions and hardships to which they were subjected, had at first a merely political character; but in Saxony, where most of the people had received Luther's teaching, it assumed a religious aspect, and Thomas Munzer put himself at its head. This seemed an opportunity for asserting the rights of the Christian people, and establishing, in place of the old despotism, a Christian commonwealth in which all should be equal, and have all things in common.[2] This movement, indeed, to which Luther was strongly opposed, was speedily put down, and its enthusiastic leader slain; but the same fanaticism broke out later in the Rhineland and Low Countries, when the Anabaptists got possession of the city of Münster, and actually succeeded for a time in erecting their kingdom of the saints there. The magistrates were deposed, and the inspired prophet assumed supreme power, at length also the name and insignia of a king; all were equal; all goods were common; and all partook of common meals. The government was held to be a theocracy, in which God reigned through inspired prophets; but it was disgraced by legalizing polygamy, and by sensual excesses under the name of Christian liberty. These enthusiasts hoped that friends would come to their help from elsewhere, especially from the Netherlands,

---

[1] See Dorner, *Glaubenslehre*, ii. p. 937.
[2] See Robertson's *Charles V.*, Book IV. Mosheim's *Church History*, Cent. xvi. sec. i. chap. 2. Beard, *The Reformation*, p. 199 ff.

and that from Münster, as from a New Zion, the millennial reign of Christ might be extended around; but in this they were disappointed, they could not resist the forces sent against them, and their theocracy was extinguished in blood.[1]

No similar attempt has ever since been made to carry out such chiliastic ideas of the kingdom of God. The tenets of those enthusiasts have been by their successors freed from the taint of licentiousness and violence, and held with various modifications by a number of later sects, most completely perhaps by the Mennonites and Quakers, who assert an inner light or direct teaching of the Spirit, reject all outward ordinances, and regard civil government as essentially unchristian. But the Baptists and, to a less extent, the Independents of later times retain portions of the original Anabaptist theory, and even the Polish Antitrinitarians were historically allied to them. It is quite true, as Dorner[2] argues, that this whole mystical and fanatical movement is not properly a fruit of the Reformation, but is due to the Catholic notion of the State as essentially worldly, and to pre-Reformation mysticism; but we cannot but recognise on the other hand, with Rothe, that from Anabaptism historically start all the sects of the Reformation, which afterwards came to assume a thoroughly Protestant type.[3]

In contrast with the carnal and earthly theocracy of the Anabaptists, Luther's idea of the kingdom of God was thoroughly spiritual. The definition and explanations in his Larger Catechism make it plain that for

---

[1] See Robertson's *Charles V.*, Book V.
[2] *Geschichte der Protestantischen Theologie*, pp. 115, 116.
[3] Rothe, *Vorlesungen über Kirchengeschichte*, ii. 418.

him the kingdom of God is his sanctifying power in our hearts and lives, exerted through the Word which reveals Christ's work as our Redeemer, and by the Spirit who brings home to our consciences and hearts this gracious revelation of Christ's redeeming love. Luther lays great stress on the assertion that the Holy Spirit works only with and through the Word, as distinguishing his doctrine from that of Munzer and the enthusiasts; and he says that their pretence to a direct teaching of the Spirit separate from and above the Word, is just the same as the claim of the Pope to have all the laws in the shrine of his heart.[1] This position is of fundamental importance for Luther's whole doctrine of the means of grace. It is to be observed, however, that what he means by the word of God in this connection is not simply the books of Holy Scripture as such, but the gospel or revelation of God's free forgiveness which is contained in them, and is also contained and sealed in the sacraments. He always conjoins the sacraments with the word; and when he asserts their necessity, it is as objective testimonies of the grace of God in opposition to the arbitrary subjectivism of the enthusiasts. The gospel and sacraments, then, are the outward means by which God reigns, and his kingdom is extended; the Holy Spirit working along with them and by their means in men's hearts, and so producing truly Christian life and conduct. The ministry of word and sacraments is the power of the keys, which Christ has given to his Church, *i.e.* to the whole body of believing men, the community of saints. The exercise of this power is to be committed

[1] See *Schmalkald Articles*, Part III. art. 8.

to those who are qualified to use it, having the graces and gifts needed for preaching and applying the gospel. They need no other consecration than the call of the people, however other arrangements may be submitted to for the sake of order. Holding, as against the enthusiasts, that the members of the true Church cannot be certainly known, Luther refrained from any such attempt as they made to set up an outward kingdom of God, and even from giving the Church any external organization, beyond the maintenance of the ministerial office on the principles above stated. He also differed widely from them in his view of the State. Civil government was in his eyes, not a thing profane and worldly, to be superseded by a theocracy, but a divine institution, profitable for the community and lawful for Christians to hold. As the kingdom of God includes all Christians, laymen as well as clergy, and does not require them to go out of the world; and as the reign of God consists in all of them being governed by his Word and Spirit: so magistrates, princes, and kings were to be thus governed. They are not, as on the Roman Catholic view, to take their direction from the clergy and carry out blindly what these declare to be the divine law; they are to hear the word of God for themselves, and obey it on their own responsibility. But they have only to do with outward things, and have only material weapons. The ministry of the word and sacraments does touch the consciences and hearts of men; with that the civil ruler may not interfere; he must not attempt to constrain the conscience. He may indeed and should promote the gospel, and prevent false teaching, but no one must be put to death for his opinion. In this respect Luther was more advanced than any other of the Reformers. Also, he holds that the end of civil government is only earthly peace, while the end of the Church is eternal peace.[1]

Luther's great power lay in his firm grasp of the principles of the gospel, and application of these to personal experience and Christian life; he had less capacity for ecclesiastical organization, and the work of that sort that had to be done fell mostly to Melanchthon. Luther was the less careful about details of that kind, because his spiritual conception of the Church and kingdom of God showed him that any attempt to realize it in an actual society was vain; hence he was willing to accept such arrangements as seemed practicable as temporary expedients, provided only they did not contradict any of the essential principles of Christianity. The full realization, or as he calls it revelation,[2] of the kingdom of God was to be a thing of the future, not indeed abruptly separated from the present, but to be laboured and prepared for by the ministry of the word and sacraments; and the arrangements that may be made for that now are but temporary expedients, adopted to make the best of existing circumstances, and having no inherent sanctity about them. It has been strikingly said by one of themselves: "For the Lutheran the ecclesiastical constitution is nothing more than a camp which the Church militant pitches for herself on the battlefield, a tent which she erects for one or two

---

[1] See Augsburg Conf. c. xxviii., and quotation in Dorner, *Gesch. d. Prot. Theol.* p. 264.
[2] Larger Catechism.

nights during her pilgrimage to the city of God. We need not wonder, then, that not too much care is given to the matter."[1] Thus as the bishops would do nothing for reformation, but simply opposed it, Luther fell back upon the princes who favoured his cause, and gave them an episcopal authority in the Church. This he was the more easily led to do, because he held that much of the power of the bishops belonged to them, not by divine right as ministers of the gospel, but by human law as princes; and to this he reckoned their jurisdiction in matrimonial causes, tithes, church property, and the like.[2] These the magistrate was entitled and bound to assume to himself. Even what was called the greater excommunication as then in use, Luther held to be, not a spiritual, but a civil act, though he expressly claims for the ministry of the word the lesser excommunication, or right of excluding the unworthy from the Lord's table. But the practical result was, especially when Luther's free and spiritual teaching became hardened with a dogmatic and sacramental system, that the civil power gained complete control of ecclesiastical affairs, and no independent Church life was developed in the Lutheran communions.

Zwingli agreed with Luther and his precursors, Wycliffe and Huss, in holding the Church to be, not the ecclesiastical organization, but the company of the elect; and he was also at one with the Saxon Reformer in opposing the attempts of the Anabaptists to make a pure Church and realize a theocracy on the earth. He drew even

---

[1] K. H. von Scheele, *Theologische Symbolik*, quoted in *Theologische Literaturzeitung*, 1883, No. 15, where a similar sentiment is cited from Oehler.
[2] Augsburg Conf. c. xxviii.

more sharply than Luther the distinction between the Church of the true children of God, which is invisible, because none but themselves can certainly know who these are, and the Church which is visible, consisting of those who have given their names to Christ, among whom may be many ungodly, as tares among the wheat. In this Church visible there are two functions necessary, prophecy or the preaching of the word of God, and discipline, by which the ungodly, who care not for the spiritual ministry of the word, are to be restrained. The former belongs to the preachers of the gospel, the latter to the magistrate; and magistracy is as necessary for the Church as the ministry of the word. This separation of the preaching of the gospel from the exercise of discipline, giving the one to the ministers and the other to the magistrates, was logically connected with Zwingli's defective doctrine of the sacraments. He would hardly recognise them as means of grace at all, but regarded them as mere signs or badges of Christian profession. Hence he could not, like Luther, see in the administration of them, as well as in the preaching of the word, the wielding of the sword of the Spirit, by which the kingdom of God is to be extended; and thus he might regard them as mere external things, the control of which might be left to the Christian magistrate, as a means of maintaining outward order in the Church. It is to be observed also, that the magistracy, with which he had to do, was not a sovereign State, but only a municipal authority. Neither the separate cantons nor the Swiss Confederacy were then in law sovereign States, but only portions of the Empire. They had asserted their freedom from the domination of the Hapsburgs as archdukes of Austria; but they did not deny their authority as emperors, and Zwingli addresses Charles V. as his sovereign. It was not therefore to the State in the strict sense of that term that he gave the right of Christian discipline, but to the representatives of a Christian municipality. But, indeed, the political relations of that day were so confused, and the variance between the legal theory and the actual facts so great and perplexing, that for a time no clear view of the relation of Church and State could easily be attained; and the result was that practically, both in Germany and German Switzerland, though in different ways, the State gained an undue control over the regulation of ecclesiastical affairs. Luther's ideal was more in accordance with the New Testament than Zwingli's; but the evil effects of the power given by the latter to the magistracy were ere long arrested and corrected by the teaching and work of Calvin, which led the most of the Reformed Churches to pursue a different ideal in their efforts to realize a Christian State or kingdom of God.

Calvin makes considerable use in his theology of the idea of the kingdom of God, and his view of it is in substance the same as that of Luther. He describes the original state of man in innocence as a reign of God (*regnum Dei*), which was lost by the Fall (*Inst.* II. ii. 12); he speaks of the promises of the kingdom of God in the prophets as the most convincing proof that hope and salvation are to be sought for man in Christ alone (*Inst.* II. vi. 3); and in describing the offices of Christ, he explains that his kingdom is spiritual, maintained by the power of the Holy Spirit, and securing for us spiritual and heavenly blessings (*Inst.* II. xv. 3–5). In other places he speaks of the reign of Christ as exercised by the Word as well as by the Spirit, and his general descriptions of it, in his expositions of the Lord's Prayer for instance, are not unlike Luther's, though not quite so simple and vivid in their expression. The Genevan Reformer was at one with Luther and Zwingli also in opposing the fanatical attempts of the Anabaptists to set up an outward kingdom of God in the world, and in recognising the legitimacy and authority of civil government. But he avoided the consequence to which they were led, Luther by expediency, and Zwingli by defective doctrine, of surrendering the discipline of the Church to the control of the civil magistrate. He attached importance, not only to the sacraments as means of grace along with the word, but to the ecclesiastical discipline that regulates their administration, and he contended so earnestly for the Church's freedom in the use of it, that he risked the whole Reformation at Geneva on this point. His ideal was that Church and State should be independent, each acting on its own responsibility, and both co-operating for the promotion of the cause of Christ. In some respects the arrangements actually made at Geneva did not correspond to the doctrine laid down in his *Institution;* and the latter must be taken as expressing what he desired, the former what he was able to obtain or was willing to allow. The other Reformed Churches followed his theoretic principles rather than his practical example, and these formed the ideal that the most spiritual and earnest Protestants strove to realize in the age that succeeded his.

The office of the civil magistrate, according to Calvin, has to do with the things of this world, and is needful because the kingdom of God as yet gives only a foretaste and earnest of its perfection in the heavenly state. Till then earthly government is necessary for the maintenance of justice, order, and peace; and Christians may lawfully accept and discharge the functions of magistracy; and are bound to be subject to the magistrate, whoever he may be, and whether the form of government be in itself or in the circumstances the best or not. The magistrate is the deputy or minister of God, from whom he derives authority to wield the sword, and to whom he is responsible. He ought to foster and defend the outward worship of God, the sacred teaching of piety, and the good state of the Church, to repress idolatry, blasphemy, and public offences against religion.[1]

The practical issue of Calvin's teaching was, that in the countries where the Reformed religion was adopted, the kingdom of God was sought to be realized in an alliance of Church and State in such a way as to secure, more or less perfectly, their mutual independence and harmonious working. In Geneva, in Holland, and in Scotland this was carried out with a large amount of success. In France the State remained Catholic, and the Reformed Church never gained more than toleration, guaranteed by the Edict of Nantes in 1598.[2] In England the clergy surrendered the independence of

[1] *Inst.* IV. xx. 2, 3. It is to be observed that the positive services to religion as assigned to the magistrate are not mentioned in earlier editions of the *Institutio*.

[2] It may be noted, however, that the theory of the relation of Church and State held by the French jurists and ecclesiastics who maintained the Gallican liberties was substantially the same as that of the Reformed Church.

the Church to the king, and it was never regained, though the more advanced Reformers and early Puritans would have liked to obtain a system like Calvin's. The peculiar form which this system assumed in Scotland, that of successive Covenants, in which the Church and nation entered into solemn religious vows and engagements, not only to one another, but to God, illustrates its character, and the circle of biblical ideas on which it rested. For in Scripture the notion of a divine covenant is correlative to that of the kingdom of God. Israel was God's kingdom, because of the covenant between him and them made on Sinai, and renewed at times of revival and reformation in later ages. But this covenanting attempt to realize the kingdom of God had in several respects an Old Testament character. It failed to do justice to the spirituality and extent of the New Testament idea of the kingdom of God, and had not entirely got quit of the effects of identifying it with the Church. Then the men of that day were too much inclined to look for express Scripture precept for everything they did, seeking for guidance in the letter, and not trusting enough the spirit of biblical teaching. This led them to go almost exclusively to the Old Testament for their laws and examples, for it is only in it that we have an example of a nation embracing the true religion. Thus they were misled into the attempt to make the Church and the nation conterminous. They recognised, indeed, the distinction of the two, and the possibility that they might not coincide, but their aim was that all citizens should belong to the true Reformed Church, and that no other form of religion should be publicly professed or practised.

This Old Testament tendency also confirmed them in the retention of the error, which has been the source of so much evil, that external force may be used in the support of religious truth and for the repression of error.

A crisis came in the history of this attempt to realize the kingdom of God at the time of the English civil war in the seventeenth century, when it seemed to be about to succeed in England as well as in Scotland. The oppressions of Erastian prelacy and arbitrary government were broken, and the English nation united in a Solemn League and Covenant, religious as well as civil, with the Church and nation of Scotland. The aim of the Presbyterians was to have a Church thoroughly reformed and in agreement with the sister Reformed Churches, independent of State control, yet in alliance with the civil power, so that both should work together for the promotion of godliness and morality in the land. For this ideal they laboured hard and prayed earnestly, and were content to spend and be spent to the utmost. Our Scottish forefathers were faithful to the Covenant, which was the symbol and means of this, through good report and bad report. They fought for it, with Cromwell and against Cromwell; they argued, and wrote, and testified for it; and when nothing more was left to be done, they suffered deprivation, and banishment, and torture, and death for this cause.

But they failed. The kingdom of God was not to be established in that form. Their defeat, too, came in the hour of their success, and from their own allies. It soon appeared that all the nation was not prepared to accept the Presbyterian ideal of the kingdom of God, but that many, who were not only to all appearance truly godly, but most zealous in opposing the oppressions of arbitrary power in Church and State, could not join in the form of doctrinal belief and Church government which the Presbyterians desired to see established; and more than that, that they were determined to assert their and their brethren's freedom. Had there been practical unanimity in the nation, even as much as there was in Scotland, the system of the Covenant might have succeeded for a time; but in the face of differences of opinion the element of intolerance, which was latent in it, was pushed to the front, and being too weak for the rising conviction in favour of freedom of conscience and speech, proved the ruin of the whole system. The defeat of the Presbyterians in their conflict with the Independents and sectaries in England practically showed the impossibility of constructing a kingdom of God in the form of a covenanted Church and nation. But their opponents were not adverse to the idea of a kingdom of God, very far from it, only they had different ideas of how it was to be realized. There were many in England at that time who had millenarian notions similar to those of the Anabaptists. Such were the Fifth Monarchy men, who dreamed that the time had come for setting up that kingdom of Christ, or of the saints, which was foretold in Daniel as to come after the fall of the four world-empires. Their views present no new feature of importance beyond those we have already noticed, and need not be more particularly discussed.

But a really new conception of the kingdom of God is to be traced in the views of the leading Puritans who were opposed to the Presbyterians, and these are interesting in themselves, and as forming a transition to more modern views. It has been truly said that "the constitutional and ecclesiastical problems which still, in one shape or another, beset us, started to the front, as subjects of national debate, in the years between the close of the civil war and the death of the king."[1] The Presbyterians were anxious to reform the Church of England more thoroughly, but they desired still to retain its national character. They would have a Church in alliance with the State, and embracing as far as possible all the people, not only preaching the gospel and dispensing the sacraments, but exercising discipline, and in all these functions aided and supported by the civil power. They expressed their willingness to make allowance for conscientious and well-disposed men who might not be able to conform to the order and government that was to be established in the Church; but they desired, in the first place, to have that order established, and they would not agree to a general or indiscriminate toleration for all sects and opinions. The Independents in the Westminster Assembly really held the same view. They desired to have congregational churches established and backed by the civil power, and a limited toleration extended to dissentients who did not deny certain fundamental doctrines. But when they found that Presbytery was the system preferred by the great majority of the ministers of England, they endeavoured to obstruct any such settlement, and made common cause with those who sought an entire and unlimited toleration.[2]

In the course of these discussions the best of the

[1] Green's *Short History of the English People*, chap. viii. § viii.
[2] See Appendix, Note V.

Independents were led to conceive of the Church or kingdom of God, which the State ought to aid and support, as being not any one organized body or collection of such bodies, but the whole of the godly in the nation, however they might differ in doctrinal or ecclesiastical views. This was the practical aim for which Cromwell contended, that godly men should not be excluded from the public service because they would not take the Covenant; and as the establishment sought by the Presbyterians was inconsistent with such religious liberty, he and his adherents opposed any Church discipline free from State control. Thus their system practically came to be very nearly akin to that of Zwingli, leaving only the function of preaching to the ministry, and putting Christian discipline into the hands of the magistrate. Only, since now the magistrate was not merely a municipal authority, as at Zurich, but very decidedly a sovereign power, and since the commanding personality was not, as then, the Reformer, but the Protector, the system now developed its real character as a political theocracy, the Church being merged in the State, and the kingdom of God conceived as a Christian State, in which the sovereign rules for God and Christ. The cosmopolitan character of the Christian kingdom of God also comes out here, for Cromwell's plans and ideas were not merely national and insular, but contemplated an alliance of the Protestant Powers as those on the side of God and godliness, and aggressions upon others. He desired to make acquisitions from Spain, which he regarded as the great anti-Christian power and chief enemy of England; and he made attempts in this direction in the West Indies and the Low Countries, the results of which were the conquest of Jamaica and of Dunkirk. Thus he sought to extend the power of England as a Christian nation, and rear an empire on the basis of his theocratic ideas. But it was the force of arms by which he proposed to achieve such a vast and comprehensive project. This is the dark side of the Puritan ideal. Not so was the people of England or the cause of Christ to be extended; but rather in the way of peaceful emigration and colonization. The English race has indeed expanded to an empire covering great parts of the world, and has carried with it to a large extent the Christian beliefs and principles with which it has been imbued. The earliest of these colonizing emigrants had the Puritan ideal in their minds, and sought to realize it in a new England across the Atlantic; and though it was not more successful there than in the old England in the precise form then aimed at, yet the spirit of the Puritans has largely influenced the great American commonwealth.

After all, this Puritan attempt to realize the kingdom of God was in some respects more spiritual, larger-hearted, and more liberal than any that had gone before it. The notion of identifying the kingdom with any outward Church organization is entirely got rid of, and it is regarded as comprising all the godly, and to be promoted by advancing what is their common interest. God's hand is recognised in history, and Cromwell regarded himself as having received a clear call to assume the supreme power, and use it for the advancement of God's cause. Yet this effort failed even more rapidly and conspicuously than any of the former. It failed because the power of the Protector was not based on the will of the people, but on mere force. However the army may have been a fair representative of all that was best in England, Cromwell never could gain any really popular and constitutional basis for his government. His Parliaments were either weeded of all opposing elements, or when their conduct did not agree with his views of his own calling and duty, were unceremoniously dissolved; and so his government, however beneficent, was a usurping despotism from first to last. Unless there could be some assurance that a heaven-directed leader would always be raised up when needed, there could be no permanence for such a government. Moreover, the idea of making true godliness the great recommendation to public employment, good and Christian as it might seem in theory, proved fatally mischievous in practice; for godliness can very easily be counterfeited, and so this acted as a premium to hypocrisy.

So it would seem, that the attempts in the past to realize the kingdom of God have been but a series of failures, each more disappointing than the preceding. Is this all that has come of Christ's work in proclaiming and establishing the kingdom of God? No, for the conscious efforts of men are only one side of the process by which it is to be realized. Through all these ages the good seed of the kingdom of God has been growing, though the tares have been growing along with it. The mistakes and faults of men have indeed tended to hinder that growth; but even the mistaken work of earnest and good men has done good; the failures in the past afford at least beacon warnings for the future; and the Lord of the kingdom is one who "shall not fail nor be discouraged till he has set judgment in the earth, and the isles shall wait for his law."

LECTURE VI.

THE KINGDOM OF GOD IN RELATION TO MODERN SOCIAL IDEALS.

MATT. vi. 10.—"Thy kingdom come. Thy will be done, as in heaven so on earth."

COL. iv. 11.—"Fellow-workers unto the kingdom of God."

REV. xi. 15.—"And there were great voices in heaven, and they said, The kingdom of the world is become the kingdom of our Lord and of his Christ, and he shall reign for ever and ever."

LECTURE VI.

THE KINGDOM OF GOD IN RELATION TO MODERN SOCIAL IDEALS.

THERE has been in most ages more or less in the aspirations and plans of earnest lovers of their fellows that is akin to the Christian idea of the kingdom of God, and more perhaps in the present day than at any former time. Even in the thoughts of those who stand aloof from religious ideas and influences, and do not accept Christianity, there is much that agrees, to a certain degree, with the Christian ideal. Thus, in regard to the end to be aimed at, most earnest thinkers will agree that the highest aim for mankind is a perfect society, not the mere perfection or happiness of the individual; and this harmonizes with what is implied in our Lord's making the kingdom of God, not our own salvation or perfection, our highest aim. Again, most people would agree that the ideal of a perfect society is one in which each member attains his own wellbeing in the very act of helping the others and the whole society to theirs, that is, where the mutual goodwill and good offices of all promote the good of the whole; and this is just the Christian doctrine of brotherly love, of Christ's disciples being members one of another, and thereby organic members of one great body.

That man's ideal is a social one, and that it is a state of universal brotherhood, are convictions almost universally felt in the present day; and they are really among the elements of which the great thought of the kingdom of God consists. It is still more universally admitted, that mankind is as yet very far indeed from that ideal, and that very great changes are needed in order that it may be attained. Some, who would not deny that this is the only worthy ideal, may think it unattainable, and in despair of its being reached sink into pessimism.

But among those who believe that the ideal is attainable, there are great differences of opinion as to the way and means in which it is to be sought and hoped for; and it is in reference to those that the Christian ideal may be compared with other views now current as to the improvement of mankind. The various opinions and schemes on this subject may be divided into three classes, according as they look for the realization of the ideal, either to human power, or to natural law, or to divine grace.

I. There are many schemes and theories which proceed upon the assumption that a perfect human society can be attained by human power, that term being taken in its widest sense, as including forms of government, legislation, organization, coercion, education, and in short all the ways in which men can determine the conduct and mould the character of their fellows. This idea is venerable for its antiquity; for it is that which has lain at the bottom of all the many attempts to produce a right state of society by laws and government. All the legislations, and systems of administration, and constitutions, and forms of government, and enforcements of conformity, and persecutions of error, have proceeded on the assumption that by such means men can be brought into and retained in a good social state. It is true the aims of many of the legislators and rulers in the past have been very low and selfish, and the social order they sought to secure very far from the ideal of modern enlightenment; still many of them have aimed at some not unworthy ideal, and some even at the highest. It has been attempted, and that throughout a long course of ages, to attain the Christian ideal by means of ecclesiastical organization and civil power.

The form in which this idea shows itself most actively in modern times is that of democratic socialism. Other forms of government have been tried as means of securing the perfection of society, despotism, constitutional monarchy, ecclesiastical hierarchy, aristocracy; all have proved failures, and do not commend themselves to the ideas of the present day; so that the experiment is not likely to be re-tried with any of them, but it may still be made with the sovereignty of the people. Socialism is just the old attempt to realize the perfect society by force of law and State power; only the power is to be vested not in any monarch by divine right, or heaven-born leader, or council of the wisest, but in the people itself as a whole. But the same tendency in principle is seen in many movements much less extreme than that. There has been a reaction from the individualism of a former age, when freedom from government interference was chiefly sought for, and *laissez faire* was the motto; the general conscience has become awake to a sense of responsibility for many of the evils of society, and appeal is made to government to prevent or cure them, which it can only do by placing restraints on individual liberty, and taking the management or regulation of various departments of social life out of the hands of the several members of society into those of the society as a whole. The poor law of this country implies a certain degree of socialism,[1] and so also does the provision of elementary education in part by rates and government grants. A system of entirely free education, such as is advocated by some, would be still more socialistic. Where the government is in the hands of the people, such proposals find the more favour, because there is less jealousy of their interfering with liberty than if they were the regulations of a sovereign or an aristocracy; and there is at the same time more confidence in the capacity of government for dealing with them. Men are not so sensible of the danger of giving too much power to government when it is popular as they would be if it were autocratic or aristocratic. Sanitary legislation, compulsory provisions against the spread of disease, restrictions on the hours and kind of labour, compulsory insurance, public provision or regulation of houses for the poor, and the like, are ways of government interference, adopted or proposed in modern times, all taking away so much from individual freedom and responsibility, and bringing various departments of social life under the control and protection of law. These are not all to be condemned simply because they are applications of socialistic principles: some of them may be necessary or justifiable

---

[1] See Fawcett's *Manual of Political Economy*, 6th edition, p. 297.

on account of special circumstances. But the unlimited yielding to this tendency, the notion that wherever there is an evil we may apply to the State to remedy it, would land us at last in thorough socialism. For that is just the thorough carrying out of the notion that the society is to order and determine all things, the individual nothing.

Martensen recognises three kinds of socialism—the imaginary socialism of Plato's republic, More's Utopia, and other unrealizable theories; the revolutionary socialism, which is akin to communism; and ethic or Christian socialism, which recognises individual rights of property, but also the duty of society to care for the individual as opposed to the principle of *laissez faire*.[1] But if this duty be recognised as one of perfect obligation, it must carry with it a right of control over the individual, and then the only question is how far it is to be carried. If it is the right and duty of the State to protect the individual absolutely to the utmost of its power from all that might injure him, then the State's function is identified with that of the family; and the State must have that entire control which parents have over their children under age. To this system of paternal government, it is an unanswerable objection that it is entirely destitute of that foundation in nature which parental authority has; since there is no form of government that has either that superiority

[1] Christian Ethics (Social). It is hardly correct to designate this form of socialism specially and exclusively Christian; for there is nothing in his description of it that necessarily implies Christianity; and on the other hand, both the others may be and have been Christian. Many of the imaginary republics were Christian, and one of them was almost exactly carried out by the Jesuits in Paraguay; while revolutionary socialism was set up by the Anabaptists in the sixteenth century.

in wisdom over its subjects that parents have over their children, or that natural affection that parents feel for their children. When something approaching to this has been found, as in the socialistic organization of the natives of Paraguay by the Jesuit fathers, the result has been to keep the community in a state of continual pupilage.

If on the other hand it be recognised, that the strict and proper function of civil society is, not to protect the individual from all evils, as for instance from natural calamities, or his own folly, but only from the injustice of others; then a definite line is drawn, and the freedom of the individual is guaranteed. The State may indeed, though existing primarily for that end, undertake more; but only on the condition that it can do each thing it undertakes satisfactorily, without so relieving the individual of responsibility as to paralyse his energy and power of development. What can be done in this way must be a question of detail and of circumstances in each case.[1]

Socialism, as a general system, is not necessarily antichristian, or even unchristian, though some forms of it are inconsistent with the principles of Christianity. That extreme form of communism which would abolish the family, is clearly so; for Christianity undoubtedly recognises marriage as a divine institution, indispensable for the maintenance of chastity as long as mankind lives in this world, and hallows it as a blessing to the Christian. The New Testament also recognises the rights of private property, though it is

---

[1] See Mr. Goschen's Lecture on *Laissez Faire and Government Interference*, Edinburgh, November 2, 1883.

not so clear that these are regarded as absolutely essential in the same way as marriage is. We might understand the various statements bearing on this subject as simply teaching the inviolability of private property in fact, and condemning any violent or unjust invasion of it, whether by individuals or the community, but not necessarily implying that private property is essential to society, or forbidding its abolition by legal and equitable means. The example of the primitive Church at Jerusalem has often been appealed to as favouring community of goods, though it was perfectly voluntary there, and not by compulsory law. It must also be observed, that there are different questions as to different kinds of property; some condemning as unjust and mischievous private property in land, others extending the condemnation to private property in capital, and private employment of labour; while others would abolish all private property whatever. On these points Scripture gives no decision; for the provisions of the Jewish law are acknowledged not to be binding as such, and the application of their principles to Christian communities is not clear. We are thrown back on the general principle that Christianity recognises nature as the work of God, and what is founded on it as according to his will; and so the question must be, what kind of property arises from the nature of man in relation to the world in which he has been placed. To what can an individual claim a right in natural justice and reason? The right of private property has often been extended too far, as over the persons of men in slavery, or as in the right of private jurisdiction and private war in the Middle

Ages; and it may be a fair question for a Christian, in regard to other kinds of property, whether they have a foundation on natural right; for in that case alone can Christianity regard them as essential to society.

The fact that the wealth of mankind is due partly to the productive power of nature, and partly to the employment of human labour and skill, seems to suggest that the former portion should not be appropriated to individuals, but held as a common possession, and the latter should be the private property of the individual whose labour and skill has gained it, and of those to whom he may give or leave it. But the combination of the two factors in almost every production, the division of labour, and the employment of machinery and capital in all advanced communities, make the question, what is due to nature and what to man, and of the latter what is due to each of many different workmen, a very complicated one, which it is the business of political economy to answer.

On the solution of this complicated problem, questions as to the legitimacy of different kinds of property seem to depend. The Bible indicates as a general principle, that a man has a right to the fruit of his labour (Gen. iii. 19; Ps. cxxviii. 2; Eph. iv. 18; 2 Thess. iii. 10, 12), and the study of human society seems to show that the recognition and securing of this is the best incitement to the energy and industry needed to make the earth yield her increase for the support and wellbeing of mankind.

There is no indication that Christ or his Apostles contemplated a state in this world in which private property should be abolished any more than marriage;

though doubtless they did not mean to approve all the kinds of private property then claimed. It is also an element in Christ's teaching, that property of every legitimate kind is a talent lent us by God, to be used for him and his cause, for the use of which we must give account (Matt. xxv. 14-30; Luke xvi. 1-13, xix. 11-27). Property therefore, according to Christianity, has its duties as well as its rights, and in any Christian State this must be recognised. But in these very parables the right use of earthly possessions is represented as the result of the kingdom of God, not the means of its establishment; and to suppose that the perfect moral society is to be attained by means of a rearrangement of the relations of private and common property, is to reverse the true order of things, and endeavour to change the tree by changing its fruit, instead of first making the tree good, that it may bear good fruit. All socialistic systems which endeavour to create the ideal community by law, must ultimately rest on force as the means of operation. Now this plan has been tried in many ways, and always found to fail; and it is not likely to be at all more successful in the modern democratic form than in that of the ancient States, or the external hierarchy and holy Roman Empire of the Middle Ages.

II. The class of views and schemes that look to the operation of natural laws for the perfection of mankind, is of much later origin than the former. It can hardly be traced back earlier than the beginning of the eighteenth century, when a reaction set in against the attempts to realize the kingdom of God by law and force, ecclesiastical or civil. The Catholic hierarchy had become a mere travesty of Christianity and an incubus on the spirit of man; the Protestant national churches had degenerated into schools of dogmatic theology, or institutes of ritualism; the Puritans had failed, as the Covenanters, and the Anabaptists, and the Romanists had failed before them: it appeared as if the more men strove to realize a divine ideal, the more intolerant and inhuman they became; and the only society in which all Christians could live together in peace seemed to be one which should recognise no religion at all. The most terrible evils had been wrought by over-government in Church and State, too minute definitions of doctrine, too precise rules for government and worship, too much interference of the State with the affairs of individuals. Freedom came to be desiderated in all these spheres. Might not things go better, if they were just left alone, and more scope given to the personal convictions of men and their efforts to carry them out?

At the same time the theological controversies of the previous age, and the variety of doctrinal systems maintained with rigid tenacity by different sects, led men who were in quest of something on which there might be the certainty of general acceptance, to turn away from Scripture entirely, as leading only to hopelessly disagreeing opinions, and to confine religion to the teaching of nature. Hence arose the system of Deism, regarding Christianity as a mere republication of the religion of nature, and as being as old as Creation.

This movement of thought was contemporaneous with the great onward rush of modern physical science, and its advance both in understanding the processes of nature, and making use of them for improving the condition of mankind. Nature, as studied by science and turned to account by art, seemed to present inexhaustible resources for the elevation and amelioration of human life; and if only men were allowed freely and fully to apply their minds to it, there would be found in it all that is needed for a perfect social state. It can tell us as much of God and divine things as we need to know; it may be trusted to guide and prompt each individual in his proper course; and if full liberty be allowed to all, the best condition of society in general will be attained. The freest possible discussion is the surest means to the discovery of truth; private enterprise, guided and watched by private interest, is the power most likely to carry out improvements in the best and most useful way; and the more strictly governments confine their operations to the necessary functions of protecting life and property, the happier will be the state of society. Such are the general principles of the philosophy of the eighteenth century, which are designated in German by the term *Aufklärung*, illumination or enlightenment. This philosophy looks for progress and ultimate perfection to the free and general diffusion of light. Nature, it says, will teach men, if they are only free to study and to follow it; truth will overcome error by its own inherent power; and the free co-operation and competition of individual interests and motives will work together for the good of the whole.

The rise and progress of this system of thought had the effect of throwing into the background the previously current ideas of the kingdom of God. The efforts so often and persistently made in various forms to realize that kingdom were discredited as mistaken and Utopian; and the kingdom of Christ either became a mere commonplace in orthodox theologies without any living power or influence, or was reduced in rationalist circles to the mere abstract impersonal notion of the reign of truth or virtue.[1] Even at an earlier period the Socinians and Arminians had been led by their system of doctrine to alter the nature of the kingdom of Christ as it had been generally understood. Their doctrine of free-will led them to deny that Christ reigns by the inward operation of his Spirit in the hearts of men, and to regard his kingdom as consisting merely in giving laws and enforcing them by rewards and punishments.[2] This was virtually to remove the kingdom of Christ from the special sphere of grace, and to make it really belong to the general providence or moral government of God, *i.e.* to the sphere of nature. The kingdom of Christ was not for them a kingdom of the saved, but one whose dignity and perfection were quite consistent with many of its subjects being finally lost. Against them the Calvinists maintained a more scriptural view; and the Lutheran theologians also never failed to distinguish Christ's kingdom of grace from that of nature or of power. When the kingdom of Christ was made to be a mere system of probationary government, it could not be regarded, as it is in the New Testament, as the highest good, and the idea failed to have any living power as an article of theology or principle of action.

---

[1] See Dorner, *Glaubenslehre*, ii. 95, 96.
[2] See De Moor, *Com. in Marckii Comp.* c. xx. § 34.

But the philosophical principles of the age of enlightenment were really working out a new conception of the ideal society, that was destined to exercise a real and powerful influence on thought and action. That philosophy as a whole was optimistic in character; it cherished confident hopes for the future of mankind. The age was proud of itself and its achievements as compared with the past, and full of the loftiest anticipations of the progress of enlightenment, culture, and virtue in the time to come. Now these hopes did not rest on the Christian faith in redemption; that had been either renounced or explained away into a mere figurative way of describing the influence of moral teaching or example of virtue: if there was any intellectual basis for the optimism of the age, it must rest on some theory of nature, not on any belief of divine grace. So the optimism of Leibnitz rested on his theory of a pre-established harmony between nature and grace, the kingdom of efficient and that of final causes.[1] Leibnitz assumes this harmony on the ground of Theism, and adopts the theory that this is the best of all possible worlds, simply as a hypothesis which he does not attempt to prove from facts. His only reason for the assertion is, that it is in the actual world, which has been called into existence by the infinitely wise and good God, and therefore must be the best possible. He does indeed prove that the best possible world may include evil in it; but he does not attempt to show that it must include just the amount of evil that exists; and while his theology is that of Lutheran orthodoxy, his belief that in the end good will infinitely overbalance

Theodicée, §§ 18, 247.

evil, rests not upon the love of God revealed in Christ, but simply on the general truth of God's power, wisdom, and goodness. Yet this final issue he calls the City of God;[1] and he gives Christ as the God-man a place in the best possible universe, as the chief reason of its being chosen of God, and the head of all the Church by whom the whole creation is to be liberated from the bondage of corruption.[2] But while recognising the special doctrines of Christianity, Leibnitz puts them, as it were, into a framework of natural metaphysics and theology; and practically his system tends to make the hopes of men rest, not on the salvation that God has wrought in Christ, but on the general principles of his universal government, as necessarily leading to the production of the best possible world. This tendency was more fully manifest in the Wolffian system that succeeded that of Leibnitz, and formed the philosophical basis of rationalism in Germany, whether in its earlier supernaturalistic or in its later naturalistic form.

In the philosophy of Kant there is the same reliance on the natural and absence of recognition of the supernatural as in the earlier systems of the century, though there is far less confidence in the power of human nature either to know what is true, or to do what is morally good. There is a deeper perception of the real difficulty of the problem, both intellectual and moral, and consequently little or nothing of that light-hearted optimism that marked the age of enlightenment in its earlier stages.

In the *Groundwork of the Metaphysic of Ethic*, Kant

[1] *Causa Dei asserta*, § 144; *Theodicée*, § 19.   [2] *Causa Dei*, § 49.

acknowledges not only the speculative impossibility of explaining the postulate of freedom implied in the categorical imperative, but also the practical impossibility of seeing how the maxims of pure reason can be a spring of action ; and on the latter point can only say, that the idea of a pure cogitable world, or universal kingdom of ends in themselves, could not fail to excite in man a lively interest in the moral law, and is a legitimate idea for a reasonable faith, though all knowledge falls short of it.[1] In his treatise on *Religion within the Bounds of Pure Reason*, he deals not with the abstract problems of ethics, but with those presented by the actual facts of human nature and life : the question here is not how the conception of duty in the abstract can influence the will, but how mankind as they are may be brought to the performance of duty. At the outset of that work, he questions the current opinion that the world is advancing to a state of perfection in virtue of the inherent goodness of human nature,' and he finds in man a bias to evil antecedent to all empirical acts of will, which he calls the radical evil. This bias, whose origin is utterly inexplicable, may however be overcome. How this can be, is indeed equally inexplicable ; but the principle, " I can because I ought," is for Kant a proof that an evil will may become good. Our own endeavour, however, may be insufficient for this, and may only make us susceptible of a higher aid. Man's endeavour is necessary, and only when he puts it forth may he hope that what he cannot do himself will be supplied from above. But it is not necessary that he should know wherein this help

[1] Kant's *Metaphysic of Ethic*, Semple's translation, p. 82, 83.

consists, but only what he has himself to do in order to obtain it. This help is set forth in Christianity, but it is there clothed in the form of a history; and what really is the salvation of mankind is, not the historical facts, which are the garb, but the ideal truth that is clothed in that garb, and that is the idea of the ethic good in its entire purity going hand in hand with the conscious conviction that such ideal really belongs to the internal predisposition of our humanity. This is practical faith in the Son of God as incarnate, expressed in terms of pure reason (*Religion, etc.*, § 79).

It is not my purpose here to criticise, but only to state, the views of Kant; but one can hardly help asking, What after all is the help from above that man is to receive? Is it merely that the fact that the ideal of goodness is in some way his has been clothed for his easier apprehension in a historic garb? If so, it seems a help as unsubstantial as it is unnecessary. Kant finds something more real when he comes to that part of religion that has to do with the Church, or kingdom of God. Even a morally well-disposed man, he says, must strive for his freedom from temptation, to which he is exposed from his contact and relation with other men. Therefore the good principle cannot conquer unless there be a union of men according to the laws of virtue, a moral community, or ethical state. Now a commonwealth not merely civil but ethical, must not only give law to itself, but be ruled by a Being, in relation to whom all moral duties are laws, *i.e.* it must be a people of God, a Church. The ideal or invisible Church corresponds to the kingdom of ends of which he spoke in his *Ethics;* but in its practical realization there are always two elements in its creed, the pure rational moral truth, and a historical embodiment of it, which is necessary in order to lead the mass of mankind to the pure ethical truth. " The historical element of the sacred writings is in itself indifferent. The riper reason becomes, the more it is capable of being satisfied with the exclusive moral interpretation, the less indispensable become the statutory dogmas of the creed. The transition of the creed into a purely rational faith is the coming of the kingdom of God, towards which, however, we can draw near only in an infinite progress. The actual realization of the kingdom of God is the end of the world, the close of history."[1]

In an essay on Perpetual Peace,[2] Kant discusses the more terrene conditions of the perfect moral commonwealth, and from it we may perceive the relation of his philosophy to other forms of thought and action. He accepts Hobbes' theory that the natural state of mankind is one of war, and he desiderates as the ultimate end a peace that shall contain in it no seeds of war, and so bring to end not only actual war, but even the possibility of it. As preliminaries to this he indicates certain negative conditions, the removal of the chief sources of war. There must be no inheritance of States, no standing armies, no national debts, no barbarous hostilities. Then as definitive articles he lays it down, that such State shall be republican, *i.e.*, as he explains it, constitutional, in its government; that there should be a federation of States, and a universal hospitality among their members. Then he indicates what he

---

[1] Schwegler, *History of Philosophy*, English translation, p. 240.
[2] *Zum ewigen Frieden*, Kant's *Werke*, Band VI.

considers to be the guarantee that such a state of things is possible, and may in the end be attained. Nature, *i.e.*, from his Theistic point of view, Providence, scatters men over all the earth ; leads them to form civil society, so as to rise above the state of universal war ; divides nations from each other by the physical features of the earth, and by speech, manners, and religion ; but unites them by mutual interests, each country being dependent on others for many of the comforts or even necessaries of civilized life, and each in turn supplying some wants of others. Hence the spirit of trade thus called forth knits different nations together, as each needing the other, and so tends to promote the idea of all being members of one great whole.

Thus on this side of it Kant's philosophy was in contact with those discoveries in political economy which are perhaps the most useful achievement of the eighteenth century, and show the way in which we may really to a certain extent look to natural law for the social amelioration and perfection of mankind. The optimistic theories of the *Aufklärung* as to the upward tendency of human nature have proved unfounded and false, as no one saw more clearly than Kant; but this at least has been found to be true, that the disposition of nature in reference to the production of wealth, dictates and suggests to mankind mutual and friendly intercourse, instead of isolation and war. The whole policy of the political economists, from Adam Smith onwards, is based on the belief that there are natural principles and tendencies at work leading to mutual friendship and the general good, if only they are not checked and interfered with by unwise laws and governments. Kant held this view of what civil government can do towards the moral progress of mankind. He thought that its functions should be as much as possible negative, consisting in the removal of barriers and hindrances to the operation of those causes that in their own nature are working for good. This is the line in which an influential class of politicians have been working for a long time now, and to a certain extent their labours have been productive of great good. Since the publication of Adam Smith's *Wealth of Nations*, it has been more and more recognised that the restrictions on manufacture and trade, that were thought necessary under the old commercial system, are needless and harmful, and that the wealth and prosperity of nations are far better promoted by free trade. Cobden and the other leaders of that movement also expected much from it in the way of promoting peace and good-will between different nations. As the material benefits of free trade arise from the fact that the interests of different countries are not conflicting but identical, inasmuch as their productions mutually supply each other's wants; so it was anticipated that the belief and practical experience of this would draw them towards one another, and their intercourse in common would make them more friendly, and less apt to quarrel or think they would gain by the calamities of their neighbours.

To a considerable degree these anticipations have been realized, but not nearly to the full extent to which they were entertained. At the time of the International Exhibition of 1851, such hopes were at their highest. When products of the industry and art of all nations were gathered together, and people too from all countries flocked to the sight with mutual interest and admiration for each other's achievements, it seemed a wonderful triumph of peace, as if art and commerce had brought about an era when war was to be no more, and the nations were to be united in one great alliance by the ties of mutual intercourse and common interests. These anticipations, however, have not been realized. Since that time there have been more great wars carried on by the most civilized nations of the world than in the forty years before; the passions and ambitions of men have proved too strong to be held in control merely by a regard to their interests. We may thankfully recognise that political economy has done much to promote not only the material wellbeing, but the peace and amity of nations; and in so far as this has been done by removing artificial trammels, and giving free scope to the industries and exchanges that the nature of the world dictates, we may recognise in this that even the physical laws and conformation of the earth have been so ordered as to work in the direction of a universal society of peace and friendship. But we cannot believe that these causes alone will certainly produce such a perfect society. Though the arrangements of nature, in the instincts that lead to family life and civil society, and in the economic relations that bind nations together, point the way and impel men towards a perfect society, there is a disorder in the moral condition of man that hinders and baffles all these tendencies. The philosophical theories that assert a gradual process of evolution and advance from less to more and more perfect forms of civilization, can give no guarantee of the certainty of such progress.

III. In contrast to such secular efforts and hopes to realize the perfect state, either by human power in the direction of socialism, or by giving free play to the laws of nature in political economy, the Christian belief of the kingdom of God trusts to divine grace for the accomplishment of the end. But, as we have seen, there have been various views among Christians in former times as to the form which the kingdom of God is to take; some of these survive and some new ideas have appeared in the present day.

1. There is still held, by the Roman Catholic Church, the medieval theory that the outwardly organized Church, the hierarchy of bishops, priests, and deacons, is the kingdom of God; that the divine grace, by which the ideal society is to be established, comes through that hierarchy as its channel; and that the end will be realized when all human relations and conduct are ordered and guided by that hierarchy. This is asserted, in its highest ultramontane form, in the dogmatic decrees of the Vatican Council (1870), and its opposition to all modern liberalism is brought out in the Papal Syllabus of Errors (1864).

2. There is the view that the kingdom of God is the whole body of Christians, which in one point of view is the Church, and in another the Christian State, but is the same body, and has for its function to carry out the will of God in all departments of social life. This was the system established by Zwingli at Zurich; it was also that of Cromwell and his supporters in the English Commonwealth, and of the Puritans of New England; and in modern times it found an earnest advocate in Dr. Arnold of Rugby. The power of rule

in the Christian community, according to this view, is in the hands of the civil magistrate; he is bound to exercise this according to the mind of God, as revealed by Christ; and any ecclesiastical government or discipline can only be a department of the functions of the Christian State, and subordinate to its supreme authority. This view, when held in any earnestly Christian spirit, implies that the body politic must consist entirely of Christians, at least as much so as any visible Church can. In its earlier forms, it required that all citizens must be members of the one ecclesiastical body regarded as the true Church, and implied the death or banishment of all who dissented from it. As held by Cromwell and the Puritans, it was not so exclusive, but admitted all who agreed on fundamentals, though they might belong to different organizations of Church government; but it required that all entrusted with public office be godly men. In Dr. Arnold's idea, the Church is still more comprehensive, including all Christians, Roman Catholics as well as Protestants; but all others, such as Jews and unbelievers, must be excluded from political power, though fully tolerated. He did not accept the modern idea, that all the inhabitants of a country have a right to a share in its government; but held, that what the payment of taxes gave to all is a right to protection of life and property, while the right of government belonged to those who are full citizens, and in a Christian country ought to be limited to Christians. Consequently he opposed the admission of Jews to Parliament, and held that if they were admitted the nation would cease to be Christian, and would be no longer co-extensive with the Church. Non-Christians, in a Christian State, he regarded as aliens, who ought to be kept in the position of the μέτοικοι in the ancient Greek commonwealths, enjoying protection but having no share in the government. If they have such a share, the State is no longer Christian, and the members of the Christian Church in turn are placed in the position of μέτοικοι, as they were in the pagan Roman Empire. Such a State is not their πόλις, and they ought not to recognise it as such.

Modern political opinion has decided against Arnold's distinction, and made citizenship, with all its privileges, co-extensive with the inhabitants of the country; and consequently since non-Christians have been admitted to political power, Great Britain is no longer a Christian State in the sense in which it might be called so in Arnold's time, and in which he wished to keep it so. It can no longer, therefore, be said that the kingdom of God, as he understood it, is a reality, in this or in any land. This doubtless is no argument in theory against Arnold's view of what ought to be, any more than the failure of the Puritans in the Commonwealth proves their ideal to have been wrong. But both naturally suggest a doubt, whether any such ideal can be attempted in the present mixed state of society without grave evils. That can hardly be regarded as a sound or stable political system which would require the exclusion from political power of all non-Christians as long as they are so numerous and so influential in thought and society as they are at present; and, on the other hand, to connect political power with the profession of Christianity would either set a premium on hypocrisy, if the test were strict, as in the Commonwealth, or admit many merely nominal Christians into the Church; and in either case there would be great danger that the administration of the State, though professedly Christian, would not be really Christian in spirit.

But even if it be admitted that such a Christian State is impracticable at present, it may be held that it is the ultimate ideal that is to be one day realized when the kingdoms of this world shall become the kingdom of our God and of his Christ. This is the view of Rothe, and in this Arnold agreed with him, though differing from his further position that the Church in the sense of a priestly government was instituted by the apostles.[1] Rothe's views are very fully developed in his *Theologische Ethik* under the head of the moral community (*die moralische Gemeinschaft*). Moral society is of various kinds in the circles of art, science, social life, and civic life. In all these natural differences separate men; but such separation is to be removed by moral progress. Besides these circles, there is the original natural relation from which they all spring, the family, and the circle of purely religious action, the Church, which is not affected by the natural differences among men.[2] He contends against the view that the State has only to do with outward acts, or that it is essentially an institution for maintaining rights (*Rechtsinstitut*), according to which the State only exists on the supposition of moral abnormity, and so must tend to disappear. It is in his view a divine institution as the essential

---

[1] Arnold's *Life and Correspondence*, by A. P. Stanley, p. 436.
[2] *Theol. Ethik*, § 280–8.

means and sum of all means for reaching the divine end of the world, and so has divine right. The State includes in itself the family, art, science, society, and civic life; but not the Church, which, as purely religious, knows no national limits. As long as the State has not reached perfect development, the Church continues separate in each particular State, and as a universal society forms the bond of union among them.[1] But when the perfect moral community has assimilated and included in its organism all the other circles, the need of a purely religious one disappears, and the Church is merged in the perfect State, or rather organism of States, which is the kingdom of God. For the ultimate ideal of the State is not a universal State, but a world-wide alliance of States (*Weltstaatenbund*). With the realization of this the human race is completed and generation ceases. Mankind has become a race of angels.[2]

In regard to this view it may be observed, that in a state of absolute Christian perfection many of the functions both of the Church and of the State would be unnecessary. If all the members of the community were perfect in moral character, admonition, discipline, and warning against sin would be needless; and so also would be criminal judgments, police, and punishments. The form of such a society would be different alike from the State and from the Church as they are now; and it does not seem to be any more proper to describe it as a perfect State than as a perfect Church. We may say that this ultimate kingdom of God is the perfection of all the divinely ordained forms of human

---

[1] *Theol. Ethik*, § 424–39.   [2] *Ib.* § 444–8.

society here, the family, the State, the friendly circle, the Church, and that each of them are merged in it; but it is to be remembered that neither the family, nor the State, nor the friendly association, can by themselves bring about the ideal. These are natural ordinances of God pointing towards the ideal of his kingdom, and affording a foundation for it, but having no power to realize it; the Church, on the other hand, is an institution of redeeming grace, and is the manifestation and working of that divine grace which really accomplishes the ideal. Least of all, therefore, can it be regarded as a mere temporary help to be superseded and set aside in the end.

More particularly we find in the New Testament that Christ and his apostles enjoin a method of dealing with offences by way of fraternal discipline, which is quite different from the procedure of civil government. Repentance is to be accepted as meeting the ends of discipline, and in the event of obstinate disobedience, the utmost judgment to be passed is one of exclusion from the Christian society. There are to be no bodily or external inflictions; the only weapon used is to be the sword of the Spirit, which is the word of God. This is a kind of government fitted to be effective with those who are earnestly seeking after holiness though liable to fall through weakness or temptation, such as Christians are presumed to be; but it would not suffice to restrain the passions of reckless, self-seeking, ungodly men. A state of things might be conceived in which the civil sword could be dispensed with, and Christian discipline suffice for the regulation of a society whose members, with whatever imperfections, all desire to obey God's law. But if a state be supposed in which even Christian discipline was needless, much more would penal laws be superfluous in such a society. If the gradual progress of the community in virtue would in the end render both unnecessary; yet surely civil government could sooner be dispensed with than the discipline appointed by Christ for his disciples; that is, the State would sooner be merged in the Church than the Church in the State.

This theory confuses the two kinds of government; and assumes that when the State becomes Christian, the government of the civil magistrate suffices for the discipline of the Church, and that in such a case Christian magistrates are the governments and rulers spoken of in the New Testament. But the directions given for the exercise of Church government and discipline clearly show, that it is quite different from magistratical power, and that the persons who exercise it are not civil magistrates as such. To suppose that they are really takes away the power of discipline from the Church, and only leaves to it that of preaching the Word and conducting public worship. Either there is no discipline at all, or it is exercised, at least directed, by the civil magistrate.

3. The view that the kingdom of God is to be realized in an alliance of Church and State, each in its own province independent of the other, and each carrying out the will of God on its own responsibility, which was that of Calvin and of the Scottish Covenanters, has only survived to the present day in a considerably modified form. As held in the sixteenth and seventeenth centuries, it implied, quite as much

as the Puritan ideal, that the State should be really Christian, and that it should not merely provide endowments for the Church, but aid and support her discipline, when necessary, by civil penalties and pains. It was also assumed that the Church included within its pale all the Christians of the nation; and if allowance had to be made for some who, while professing Christianity, could not fall in with the order established in the Church, these were regarded as exceptional cases, which it was hoped would be few. This scheme was thus tainted with that vice of intolerance that was common to almost all the political and ecclesiastical systems of those times; and when at a later period its adherents worked themselves free of that fatal error, the system of an allied Church and State assumed a somewhat different aspect. The State had no longer a truly Christian character; and though it continued to maintain some Christian ordinances, such as the Sabbath, the marriage laws, and the like, this came to be done, not so much out of regard for their divine institution, as for political or social reasons. Practically the duty of the State towards religion came to be regarded as consisting mainly, if not exclusively, in endowing the Church. This became more glaringly inadequate when the Church thus endowed was not a communion embracing nearly all the orthodox Christians in the country, but only one out of a number differing only in matters of order and government. The old Covenanters would not recognise the modern State Church system as at all an adequate realization of their ideal, nor has the alteration been in all respects for the better. In some ways the modern scheme of Church and State alliance is an improvement on the old covenanting system, as in getting rid of the taint of intolerance; but in other ways it is a degeneracy, in so far as it substitutes a very partial and formal patronage of religion by the State for the hearty, vigorous support which, on the old view, the civil ruler owed to the cause of God. The old system, by its use of the solemn form of a covenant, brought the alliance of Church and State under an express religious sanction, and made it an act of homage to God, and the fulfilment of its duties a continual course of obedience to him; whereas, according to the practice of modern times, it is often really a compromise between Christ and the world, the State compounding, as it were, by formal favours to an established Church, for an entire neglect of the law of Christ in all other things.

It may be questioned, indeed, whether the solemn act of covenant with God has sufficient warrant, apart from such a special divine government as Israel was under. Every covenant between God and man must come from God, and not from man. We are not entitled on every occasion or for every end, even of a good kind, to take up the position of covenanting with God. The Covenanters fully recognised this; and they believed that in the circumstances in which they were placed there was a warrant and call to them, from the Word and providence of God, to enter into such a covenant; but it is a fair question whether this was indeed the case. In the beginning of the Solemn League and Covenant itself, it is declared that "the glory of God and the advancement of the kingdom of our Lord and Saviour Jesus Christ" was the first object the Covenanters had before their eyes; and this may indicate that the idea of the kingdom of God is the more general one, of which that of a nation in covenant with God is only a particular and occasional form. If such a solemn covenant was only to be justified by the peculiar emergency and special circumstances in the course of providence, it cannot be held to be the normal and necessary way in which the kingdom of God is to be realized. The more general expression of the ideal is that both Church and State, each acting in its own province, should do the will of God under the power of Christian motives and influences, so that not in one exclusively, but in both together, the kingdom of God may be found. This was not sufficiently recognised by the Reformers and Covenanters, who were still to some extent under the influence of Augustine's mistake of identifying the Church with the kingdom of God, and the State with the world. This led to some confusion in their doctrine, as well as to errors in their practical policy.[1]

4. Still another theory of the way in which the kingdom of God is to be realized arose in the eighteenth century. By that time the Christian character of Protestant States was becoming practically very faint, and they were becoming very much indifferent in matters of religion. Then the theory arose that civil government has only to do with external things, such as the protection of life and property, and that religion lies beyond its province altogether. As the doctrine of the divine right of kings was exploded, the theory

[1] See Appendix, Note W.

arose that civil government owes its authority entirely to the consent of the people, in the form of a real or imaginary social contract, and that it has no legitimate power beyond what is tacitly or expressly given by that contract, or is necessary for the attainment of the ends of it. As great evils had been felt to arise from the excessive and oppressive interference of governments in the affairs of the subjects, the tendency in the eighteenth century was to limit the functions of the State to the mere preservation of order, which was Kant's idea, as well as that of many others. When the English colonies in North America asserted their independence, the individualistic philosophy of the *Aufklärung* was the prevalent one, and the United States were constituted on the basis of a social contract merely for secular purposes, tolerating and protecting all religions, but professing and favouring none. Then many Nonconformists in Britain, disapproving of the conditions of alliance between Church and State, and influenced by the prevailing political theory, adopted the opinion that there should be no such alliance, and that the best or only security against persecution and civil control of the Church is that the State should not attempt to support religion, but confine itself purely to secular affairs. This is the doctrine usually known among us as Voluntaryism, and called by some German writers Free Churchism,[1] though neither name is very appropriate, and it might more characteristically be called Individualism.[2] It is defended elaborately from the point of view of the rights and duties of

---

[1] See Krauss, *Das Protestantische Dogma von der Unsichtbaren Kirche.*
[2] See Cunningham, *Historical Theology,* ii. p. 560.

individual conviction by Vinet.[1] In this country it has been mostly confined to those who advocate a popular government in Church as well as in State; but in America it is held by some in connection with Episcopalian views of Church order. Dr. Samuel Smith Harris, bishop of Michigan, in a series of lectures on *The Relation of Christianity to Civil Society*, makes the distinction between the two as broad as possible. The State derives its authority from beneath, from the consent of the people; it is democratic and secular. The Church is from above; it derives its authority from Christ; it is theocratic, being the kingdom of God which Christ established. The only point at which the two societies touch each other is the individual. The Church can only influence the State by influencing the several individuals of which the State is composed, and the State can only aid the Church by its several individual members doing so each for himself. He holds that the relation between the Church and civil society that exists in the United States of America is the ideal one that was present to the thought of Jesus, and that all Christian history has been leading up to the possibility of this relation being brought about.[2] This seems far too optimistic a view of the present to be well founded. There is a great deal to be said in favour of the opinion that as long as nations on the one hand, and Churches on the other, are in their present condition, it is best that there should be no alliance between Church and State. The civil power is now exercised not exclusively by Christians, but by

---

[1] *Essai sur la manifestation des convictions religieuses.* Paris 1842.
[2] *The Bohlen Lectures*, 1882, p. 107. London 1883.

men of any or of no religion; and the Christian community is divided into a number of sects with widely different opinions and aims. In such circumstances the State cannot be really Christian; nor can any one Church represent the Christian religion as such, and hence no practicable alliance of Church and State would be a real and adequate homage to Christianity. But to say that this state of separation is not only the best for the present necessity, but the best absolutely, the ideal that Christ contemplated, is a different thing. Dr. Harris reaches this conclusion by inferences drawn entirely from our Lord's sayings in reference to the Roman Empire, which declare the relation of his kingdom to it as distinct and independent, yet having a province of its own, and therefore not interfering with civil government. It may be doubted, however, whether from these sayings alone we can deduce what are the duties of a Christian State, or what is the ideal relation of Church and State, when both are really and earnestly willing to do the will of Christ. Dr. Harris at once and without discussion identifies the Church with the kingdom of Christ, and regards civil society as the world. This is just a repetition of Augustine's view, and the danger is at hand of its leading in practical application to consequences similar to those which that had in the Papacy. If the State be the world, and the Church exclusively the kingdom of God, then it would follow that the only way in which the State could serve that kingdom would be by being wholly subject to the Church to obey all its dictates.

The theory that identifies Church and State we saw to be only suitable for a condition of things in which all members of society should be truly Christians, and not for any mixed society: of the theory that goes to the opposite extreme, and denies that they can have any alliance, we may say that it is only suited to the circumstances of a mixed state of society. It may be, probably it is, true, that as long as the State is but imperfectly Christian, a position of separation and non-alliance is the safest and best for both parties; but if this be the absolute ideal, it is difficult to see how it can be continued after Christianity has fully leavened the whole body politic. Must the State even then continue to be purely secular in its aims and actings? This is not very easy to believe. Or is it to be supposed, that in the event of the whole community being christianized, the need of civil government would cease, and the State thereupon disappear, leaving only a Church as the perfect kingdom of God? This is the theory of those who think that the necessity of civil government arises only from sin, and that in a sinless world there would be no such thing. But as long as mankind lives upon the earth, and is not raised above liability to mistake and difference of view about earthly things, some civil government seems necessary.[1] Or, again, is it held that there is to be no perfection in the present order of things, but that the ideal kingdom of God is to be ushered in by a supernatural divine interposition? This is the view which was very prevalent in the times when the Church was opposed by a heathen and persecuting State, and to which these are inevitably drawn who regard the State as still essentially secular and unchristian.

[1] See Rothe, *Theologische Ethik*, § 424.

5. We may reckon this another form of opinion, Chiliasm or Millennialism, which looks for the establishment of the perfect kingdom of God on this earth to the second advent of Christ in person, and the judgments he is to execute on the ungodly and antichristian powers of the world. This view is based upon the descriptions of the Messianic kingdom in the Old Testament, which are all painted in earthly colours, and contain features that are inconsistent with the New Testament teaching as to the nature of the spiritual bodies of the glorified saints. It is clearly the teaching of our Lord and his apostles, that the final and eternal state of the saved is to be one in which they neither marry nor are given in marriage (Matt. xxii. 30 and parallels), but have glorified spiritual bodies (1 Cor. xv. 44-54), in a world in which all things are made new, a new earth with new heavens. That is the state which we commonly call heaven, though it is often represented in Scripture as having its seat on this earth renewed and glorified. Whether its locality is in this or in another sphere, is a matter of no importance; since, if it is to be on this earth, it must clearly be under totally different conditions from those of its present state. The question of the millennium is whether, besides and before this final state, there is to be an absolutely perfect realization of the kingdom of God on this earth as it now is, brought about by the second coming of Christ in visible glory to execute terrible judgments on his enemies, to raise from the dead his saints and martyrs, and to reign with them in person for a thousand years. In this period pre-millennialists look for the fulfilment of the Old

Testament prophecies that speak of an earthly reign of God or of the Messiah. The grossly carnal and worldly conceptions of this reign, that were held by many in primitive times, are indeed repudiated by all the more reasonable adherents of the theory; but the very assertion of a personal reign of the glorified Saviour with glorified saints on the earth as it now is, implies a mixture of earthly and heavenly things, and to some extent worldly conceptions of the state of glory. It also implies, that the perfect state of the kingdom of God on earth is to be attained, not by means of the agencies and influences now at work, but by a sudden supernatural interposition that ushers in a new dispensation, and breaks all continuity between the present and the millennial age. The practical tendency of this is to lessen the motives and encouragements to work for the kingdom of God. Since it is not to be brought to its success and triumph by the loving efforts of Christians, and the blessing of God upon these, but by the second coming of Christ, Christian labour has not the encouragement of hope, without which it can hardly be very strenuous and persistent; and since everything is expected from that miraculous appearance of Christ, there is apt to be less concern for the evils of the present. Things are not to be expected to improve, but to grow worse and worse, till at last Christ comes again in visible majesty to restore all things. But, as we have seen, one of the chief points in the teaching of Jesus about the kingdom of God is its continuity, as a living principle, from its beginning inwardly and secretly without observation, till its complete development and perfection in openly manifested glory. The New Testament knows of one decisive break in the continuity of the future course of the kingdom of God, when the dead shall be raised, the living changed, and all appear before the judgment-seat of Christ; and it is careful to show that the life beyond the resurrection is not a resumption of this earthly one, but life in a spiritual body, on a changed earth. Nay, it asserts the continuity of spiritual life even through this great physical change (John xi. 25); and describes the day of judgment as only the manifestation of a righteous judgment that is always going on (Rom. ii. 5).

Whether the kingdom of God is to have a perfect realization in this world before the cosmical change that must usher in the new heavens and new earth, or whether its only complete realization is to be in that future world, is not quite clear; as the Biblical representations of the future of the kingdom are various, and some of them seem to point to the one alternative and some to the other.

The Old Testament pictures of earthly bliss in the Messianic times cannot be regarded as deciding anything either way; for these were the only colours in which the blessings to come could be depicted in those days, and are not to be pressed literally. But in the New Testament we find some passages that seem to describe a gradual progress of the cause of Christ onwards to universal and complete triumph in the end, as in Christ's parables of the Mustard Seed and the Leaven, and Paul's statements in Rom. xi. 25–32; and other passages that foretell a portentous growth and progress of evil, opposing the kingdom of God, over which it can only gain the victory by terrible conflicts. Such are the parables of the Tares and the Draw-Net, Paul's representations in 2 Thess. iv. 3–12 and 1 Tim. iv. 1–3; and the images of the powers of evil in the Apocalypse. There, however, we have also the description of the reign of Christ and his saints for a thousand years, during which Satan is bound; but at the end of that time he is said to be loosed again, and to gather the nations of Gog and Magog for a last assault against the people of God.

We seem to be warranted in believing that Christianity is yet to spread over all the earth, and bring all nations under its influence; but at the same time we are warned not to regard this state, for which we hope, as one of absolute perfection; else there would be no possibility of a final rebellion and assault of evil. The wheat and tares are to grow together till the harvest in the end of the world; and it may be that the loosing of Satan again is the means by which the tares shall be finally gathered out. When the Church and kingdom of God shall be thus perfect and pure, then shall come the new heavens and new earth, and all the saints shall be raised and made perfect in glory. The millennium described in Rev. xx. 1–6 must be regarded as belonging to the world as it now is, before the cosmical changes afterwards spoken of (chap. xxi. 1), and this makes it pretty certain that whatever it may denote, it is to be brought about by the spiritual agencies by which God's kingdom is advanced now, and not by a supernatural interposition, ushering in a new dispensation. We cannot, therefore, find refuge from the difficulties of realizing the kingdom of God here by postponing its establishment till the second advent of Christ.

6. What then are we to regard as the true ideal of the kingdom of God in this world? If the realization of it is not to be postponed to a future state, but to be aimed at in the present order of things; and if the former attempts to realize it have all more or less conspicuously failed: is it possible to point out any way in which a better result may be looked for? We may be helped to an answer to this question, if we observe, that in each of the ways in which it has been attempted to set up the kingdom, something has been done towards the advancement of Christianity and the attainment of the ideal society; and that they have failed in so far as they acted in a one-sided way, or assumed prematurely that the task was accomplished, when no more than one department of human life, if even that, had been Christianized. The medieval and Roman Catholic theory identified the kingdom of God with the Church, and held that it was realized when the Church directed and ruled the world, and that was a great and pernicious mistake; but in so far as the Church was doing its proper work, evangelizing the barbarous nations and ameliorating the laws and usages of society, it was really building up the kingdom of God. Those who made the kingdom of God consist in a Christian State, which should also be the Church, did important service in guiding public policy in accordance with righteousness and the interests of Christianity; but they unduly repressed many of the elements of national life, and allowed no free independent action to the Church; and those who sought the ideal in an

alliance of Church and State did noble and lasting work, though they assumed too readily that the motives and purposes of that alliance were truly Christian. Each of these efforts did good in some way; but the good was marred by one-sidedness, or defeated by grasping prematurely at an ideal for which the times were not ripe.

May not this indicate that the way to the realization of the ideal is in the line of a more cautious and deliberate working out of all the different activities whose one-sided pursuit has led to disastrous consequences, and caused the failure of less comprehensive plans? The Church is not to undertake alone to do the work of the kingdom of God; for if so, it must either assume a control over civil government, as the Church of Rome did in the Middle Ages, or leave the State to be guided by merely worldly motives and considerations, as is the tendency of extreme voluntaryism. Nor, on the other hand, can any civil government do the work of the kingdom of God to the exclusion of the Church; and any attempt at a civil theocracy, as that of the Puritans, hinders and hampers the Church in its free and full activity. Nor is it to be supposed that a legal alliance between Church and State, however ratified by solemn religious covenant, will of itself secure the realization of the kingdom of God. But if Christians would earnestly labour, in all departments of social life, to promote the doing of God's will by themselves and others, using in each department its appropriate means and methods,—in the Church, the ordinances of worship and edification; in the State, the constitutional ways of influencing public opinion and action; and in general social life, the opportunities of Christian influence,—would not that lead in the direction of the realization of the ideal? That ideal would be a state of things in which the Church should be actually fulfilling her mission of making disciples of all nations, teaching and training up the successive generations of mankind to healthy and vigorous Christian life, in which the nations thus Christianized should direct their public action and government to the ordering of all their secular affairs in a Christian spirit, not either receiving dictation from the Church or giving it to her; but each in its own province seeking to carry out the will of God; the teachers of the Church reading that will in Scripture, and using that as the sword of the Spirit, and the rulers of the State seeing God's will also in the laws of nature and the natural relations of peoples, and so ordering home and foreign policy as to give to the world the blessings of a true and lasting peace.

What precise form the kingdom of God would assume in its perfect state it may not be possible to say. The Bible was not given to enable us to forecast the detailed arrangements of a state of things that is not yet; it is enough that it affords principles to guide us as to present duty, and promises that give us assurance of the final pefection of God's kingdom. The Christian ideal differs from most other social ideals in not including any particular forms of organization; because its power lies not in these but in an inward vital influence. The idea of a perfect State, as conceived by philosophers from Plato downwards, has generally consisted of arrangements as to its constitution, form of government, and the like; it was hoped by means of these to secure the best state of human society; and if that could have been realized in any such way, it would have been possible to indicate beforehand the form that society would assume in its perfect state. But Christ's ideal of the kingdom of God was to be realized by the vital power of God's redeeming love; and therefore the agency that he set on foot for its accomplishment did not necessarily imply that the final form of it must be known before it appeared. In the New Testament the advance of the kingdom of God is compared both to the erection of a building and to the growth of a tree; but the latter image is the more adequate. A building is erected according to a definite plan; and those who are engaged in the work must know the plan, and what the result is to be. But the growth of a tree, though not less really according to a divine idea, does not make its plan manifest; and those who tend and help it by their husbandry may in its early stages have no conception of the form of beauty and majesty it is one day to assume. Their labour to promote its life and health is helping on that consummation, even though they have not a plan or pattern to guide them. So we are called to be fellow-workers with God towards his kingdom, doing what in us lies to promote the growth of that true spiritual life which is the secret and guarantee of its ultimate perfection; and we know that in working for this we are advancing the kingdom of God, even though we can lay down no exact programme of what it is to be. It is enough that we have the assurance that such labour is not in vain; and that the kingdom of God shall not remain for ever a mere ideal, but be one day a reality in the form of a perfect human society, in which all shall in love serve one another, and so serve and glorify God. The assurance of this is given, as in many words of Jesus, so specially in the apocalyptic visions, one great purpose of which seems to have been to show that the end of God's work of salvation is to be not only the perfection of individual men, but the city of God, and the certainty of that is grounded on the redeeming work of Christ:[1] it is the Lamb that was slain who overcomes all the powers of evil, and reigns with God for ever. To this end, too, we may believe that both human effort and natural laws co-operate, though they are unable apart from divine grace to reach the end. Men are called to be fellow-workers with God; and nature also and its laws are the work of God, and do his will, working together for his great end. We have always to remember that still as of old the kingdom of God is within you: what the precise form of its perfect realization is doth not yet appear, but it shall be the completion and manifestation of that kingdom that cannot be moved, which we receive even now.

[1] See Bernard, *Progress of Doctrine in the New Testament*, Lect. VIII.

APPENDIX.

APPENDIX.

Note A, p. 5.—The Kingdom of God in recent Theological Literature.

The comparatively recent introduction of the purely historical method in Biblical theology is illustrated by Weiss' sketch of the rise and progress of that science (*Die Biblische Theologie des neuen Testaments*, § 5–7). He says: "The first step by which the contents of Scripture began to be separated from dogmatic was an independent collection and exegetico-dogmatic discussion of the so-called *dicta probantia* which had hitherto been attached for support to the individual *loci* within Dogmatic itself. The exposition of the doctrinal contents of the Bible is here only a means, not an end; the exegesis of the individual passages torn from their connection has a quite dogmatic stamp." He goes on to observe how even under the influence of rationalism the attempts at Biblical theology still retained this dogmatic stamp, and he ascribes to Neander the merit of having given a fresh impulse to the deeper study and more thoroughly historical treatment of the science. His account of the way in which the teaching of Jesus has been exhibited by successive writers (§ 12) shows that in proportion as Biblical theology has assumed a more truly historical character, the notion of the kingdom of God has come to occupy a more prominent and commanding position. The same thing may be observed in reference to Old Testament theology, as appears in such works as Ewald's *History of Israel*, Oehler's *Biblical Theology of the Old Testament*, Riehm's *Messianic Prophecy*, and others.

Of the growing sense of the importance and value of

the idea of the kingdom of God, not only in a historical but in a directly theological and religious point of view, one of the earliest indications was F. D. Maurice's work, *The Kingdom of Christ* (2nd edition, 1842). This book is not a mere treatise on the Church, but deals with the subject as a fundamental one that underlies the whole of Christianity, and determines its character. Julius Hare refers to it as an illustration of Neander's saying, that "throughout the history of the Church we see how Christianity is the leaven that is destined to pervade the whole lump of human nature;" and calls it "one of the wisest and noblest works that our Church has produced since the *Ecclesiastical Polity*." It may be well, however, to bear in mind a remark he makes in the same connection: "It has been seen too often, both in philosophy and elsewhere, that when people have fancied that the world was becoming Christian, Christianity was in fact becoming worldly" (*Guesses at Truth*, p. 313, ed. 1871). Archbishop Whately's two essays, *The Kingdom of Christ Delineated*, have reference to the nature and relations of the Church, but do not deal with the deeper questions raised by Maurice.

The work entitled *Ecce Homo* makes large and good use of the notion of the kingdom of God as explaining the teaching of Jesus and the society that he founded. With all its deficiency and one-sidedness, this work has the great merit of dealing with the things it treats of as realities, not as mere notions or doctrines; and so it is full of suggestiveness, and lays down positions which necessarily lead to higher views of Christ and his work than the author himself expresses. A series of articles, entitled *The Kingdom of Christ on Earth*, in the *Bibliotheca Sacra* (April 1871 and subsequent numbers), by Samuel Harris, D.D., President of Bowdoin College, gives a very clear outline of the scriptural notion of the kingdom, and brings out its connection with the redemption of Christ and the work of the Holy Spirit. *The Republic of God*, by Elisha Mulford, LL.D., professes to traverse the whole ground of theology, and occupies very much the position of Maurice, whose sermons are frequently quoted. *The Manifesto of the King*, by Dr. J. Oswald Dykes, expounds the Sermon on the Mount in such a way as to bring out very clearly and beautifully as its great subject the kingdom of heaven, its nature, laws, and relations. *The City of God*, by A. M. Fairbairn, D.D., Principal of Airedale College, contains a series of thoughtful and suggestive discussions, mainly of an apologetic character. The longings of the world for the kingdom forms the subject of one of Archbishop Trench's Hulsean Lectures, *On the Unconscious Prophecies of Heathendom*; and that this forms the completion of the Christian revelation is strikingly shown in the last of Bernard's Bampton Lectures, *On the Progress of Doctrine in the New Testament*. These works show how in various schools of religious thought among English writers this subject has of late attracted an amount of attention that was not given to it formerly.

In Germany a similar tendency may be seen. Rothe's *Theologische Ethik* is largely occupied with our subject. The section of that work which treats of the moral society is occupied with showing how a perfect moral organization of mankind, which is the primary and all-comprehending moral demand, is realized by a gradual progress, from the family, through the State, to the kingdom of God. Ritschl makes important use of the notion of the kingdom of God in his theological system, as discussed scientifically in his work, *die Christliche Lehre von der Rechtfertigung und Versöhnung*, both in its Biblical and in its dogmatic part; and he makes it the starting-point of his *Unterricht in der Christlichen Religion*, in which he expounds the principles of Christianity in a more elementary way. Oosterzee, in his Christian Dogmatic, makes the kingdom of God the general subject of the whole science, and the basis of its divisions; but he does not justify this plan by an investigation of what the kingdom of God really is. Schweizer's *Glaubenslehre*, and Lipsius' *Evangelisch-Protestantische Dogmatik*, discuss the subject at considerable length in connection with the doctrine of the Church; and in a treatise, entitled *das Protestantische Dogma von der unsichtbaren Kirche*, by Prof. Alfred Krauss, of Strassburg, there is a very able and careful investigation of the notion of the kingdom of God in the New Testament, in relation to that of the Church. More purely exegetical is the treatment of the subject in *die Idee des Reiches Gottes*, by Carl Wittichen. The subject is also discussed more or less fully in most of the many works on the life of Jesus, the theology of the New Testament, and the exposition of the Gospels. A consideration of the subject in a popular and practical way in a series of discourses on the principal passages about it in the New Testament is given in a work, entitled *Vom Reiche Gottes*, by Dr. J. H. B. Dräseke, 3 vols., 1850.

These references are not made with the view of giving an adequate account of the literature of the subject, which I do not feel able to give, but merely to show its prominence in recent thought, and to indicate some books that I have found in various ways useful and suggestive.

NOTE B, p. 21.—THEOCRATIC IDEAS IN THE ANCIENT EASTERN EMPIRES.

The statements in the text may be illustrated by some quotations from the inscriptions of which translations are given in the collection entitled *Records of the Past*. The very first of these begins thus: "The palace of Rimmon-Nirari, the great king, the powerful king, the mighty king, king of the land of Assyria, whom as his own son Assur, king of the gods of heaven has favoured, and with the kingdom of the world has filled his hand. . . . Rimmon-Nirari, the glorious prince to whose help the gods Assur, Sammas (the sun), Rimmon, and Merodach have gone, and have enlarged his country" (vol. i. p. 3). Similarly Khammurabi says: "The favour of god and Bel the people of Sumir and Accad gave unto my government. Their celestial weapons unto my hand they gave" (*ib.* p. 7). Similar expressions occur in inscriptions of Sennacherib (*ib.* p. 25) and of Shalmaneser (vol. iii. p. 83). Specially emphatic is the following: "I am Assurbanipal, the progeny of Assur and Beltis, son of the great king of Riduti, whom Assur and Sin the lord of crowns from days remote, prophesying his name, have raised to the kingdom: and in the womb of his mother have created him to rule Assyria" (vol. i. p. 59). In a subsequent part of the same inscription he describes the gods as fighting for him (*ib.* p. 101); as also does Sennacherib (*ib.* p. 50, 51). Assurbanipal also describes his kingdom as established by the will of the gods; and declares that he caused worship to be offered to them (*ib.* 59, 60); while after quelling a revolt he says: "The yoke of Assur, which they had thrown off, I fixed on them; prefects and rulers appointed by my hand I established over them. The institutions and high ordinances of Assur and Beltis and the gods of Assyria I fixed upon them" (*ib.* p. 81). Tiglath Pileser I., in narrating his successive conquests of different tribes, says of each: "The heavy yoke of my empire I imposed on them. I attached them to the worship of Ashur my lord" (vol. v. 14, 15, 17); and summing up all his victories, declares: "I brought them under one government; I placed them under the Magian religion, and I imposed on them tribute and offerings" (*ib.* p. 20). Shalmaneser represents himself as enforcing the decrees of heaven along with his own laws. "An image of my person I made. The decrees of Assur, the lord of princes, my lord, and my collected laws, upon it I wrote" (vol. iii. p. 86). But with all these claims of divine authority there is no profession that it is right and justice that is so enforced; and it is significant that the first approach to this seems to be made in the Behistun inscription of Darius. "Says Darius the king: Within these countries, whoever was good, him have I cherished and protected; whoever was evil, him have I utterly destroyed. By the grace of Ormazd these countries have obeyed my laws" (vol. i. p. 114).

NOTE C, p. 31.—PLATO'S RELATION TO THE ATHENIAN DEMOCRACY.

The view given in the text, that Plato's *Republic* was a reaction against the principles of the Athenian democracy, and presents an essentially different type from it, may seem to be contradicted by the following statements of Schwegler: "The Platonic State is the Greek idea of a State in general presented in the form of a narrative. . . . It is Greek political life raised into the idea that constitutes the genuine burthen of the Platonic *Republic*. In it Plato has exhibited Grecian morality on its substantial side (side of instinctive observance). If the Platonic Republic appeared mainly as an ideal, irreconcilable with empirical reality, it is not the ideality, but rather a defectiveness in ancient political life that is to blame for this. It is the restrictedness of personal subjective freedom that, before the Greek States began to break up in licence, constituted the characteristic of the Hellenic political view" (*History of Philosophy*, p. 89). But a little farther on he states that Plato had grown up in aversion to the extravagances of the Athenian democracy (p. 91); and Zeller shows that Socrates, whom Plato followed in this, was in some respects widely estranged from the Grecian view of the State, and advocated a principle which brought him not only into collision with the Athenian democracy, but with all the political notions of the Greeks (*Socrates and the Socratic Schools*, p. 136-8). Hegel does more justice than most modern writers to the Athenian polity, and remarks with truth that "if we would have the verdict of the ancients on the political life of Athens, we must turn not to Xenophon, nor even to Plato, but to those who had a thorough acquaintance with the State in its full vigour, who managed its affairs, and have been esteemed its greatest leaders, *i.e.*, to its statesmen" (*Philosophy of History*, p. 271, 2); and then he quotes the oration of Pericles referred to in the text. It is, I think, important to recognise in the picture of the

Athenian State there given an ideal different from that of Socrates and Plato, and in some respects opposed to it. For this ideal is in substance just that of modern liberal culture, to which some would look as a substitute for Christianity for securing the moral progress and perfection of mankind. It should not be forgotten that this has been tried, under favourable circumstances, in an age of which we have clear historical knowledge; and the causes of its failure should be studied by those who rest their hopes on it. In regard to these the judgment of Thucydides (ii. 65) is, that Pericles was quite right in thinking that the Athenians were well able to overcome the Peloponnesians, had they but been animated by patriotism and public spirit such as his. The chief improvement of modern times in the way of making democracy more stable, and applicable to large nations and not merely to single cities, is the principle of representation, the effect of which in extending political organization is well shown by Professor Seeley in his work, *The Expansion of England*. Doubtless, had that principle been introduced in the relations of Athens to her subject States, the Athenian Empire might have been more durable; but it is impossible to avoid seeing that there were deeper causes of its degeneracy and failure than any mere political arrangement could obviate.

NOTE D, p. 36.—PHILOSOPHICAL BASIS OF ROMAN LAW.

The distinctive character of the Roman Empire, as one that imposed law on the subjects, and the connection of that law with the philosophy of the Socratic and Stoic schools, have been recognised by the best modern writers on the subject. Thus Sir Henry Maine, in his *Early History of Institutions*, explaining how the ancient patriarchal system has disappeared in most parts of Europe, says: "So far as regards the Roman institutions, we know that among the most powerful solvent influences were certain philosophical theories of Greek origin, which had deep effect on the minds of the jurists who guided the development of the law. The law thus transformed by a doctrine which had its most distinct expression in the famous proposition, 'all men are equal,' was spread over much of the world by Roman legislation. The empire of the Romans, for one reason alone, must be placed in a totally different class from the Oriental despotisms, ancient and modern, and even from the famous Athenian Empire. All these were tax-taking empires, which exercise little or no interference in the customs of village communities or tribes. But the Roman Empire, while it was a tax-taking, was also a legislating empire" (p. 329, 330). The connection of Roman law with Greek philosophy is more fully stated by Professor Lorimer: "The foundations of the Roman law were laid deep in the study of nature, both in its subjective and objective manifestations. Like the Christian Apologists and Fathers, the Roman jurists accepted the Socratic ethics chiefly in the form in which the Stoical doctors presented them. . . . It must ever redound to the glory of the Stoics, that they were the first explicitly to proclaim the unity of the human race, whilst they avoided the sin and folly of claiming an equality which God has denied. . . . The advantages of the rational and philosophical conception which the Romans formed of the source of jurisprudence were not confined to the development of a municipal system, which after the lapse of ages still illuminates the path of modern legislation. The idea of the *persona* was felt to contain the germs of that cosmopolitan system, the realization of which the ancient world was not privileged to behold, and which we ourselves even now have seen but in part. The sentiment of a brotherhood of mankind is one of those innate conceptions which belong to humanity as such. . . . Like all that was true in Stoicism, moreover, it had its roots in the more catholic creed of Socrates. Still in this direction especially the Stoics surpassed their master. It is impossible not to see in Zeno's universal State, and in the cosmopolitan notions of the Stoics as a school, a clearer presentiment than any their greater predecessors possessed of the possibility of a system of international law; and as regards the Roman jurists, it is instructive to remember that it was through them, as apostles of the doctrine of personality, that the seed which the Stoics had sown ultimately germinated" (*Institutes of Law*, 2nd ed., p. 156–9). See also Bryce, *The Holy Roman Empire*, chap. ii.

NOTE E, p. 42.—NATURALISM AND PESSIMISM.

A remarkable acknowledgment of the uncertainty of the hopes that mere naturalism affords, is made in the work entitled *Natural Religion* by the author of *Ecce Homo*. Its aim is to show that the modern school of science that discards the supernatural is not atheistic, but is really a religion as truly as Christianity is, and that it is not a mere theory, but has, like Christianity, a church and a mission, in so far as it is the function of the civilised nations to spread their civilisation to others who are still destitute of it, and also in so far as the tendencies to Atheism, Nihilism, and Anarchy must be stemmed by the religion of culture and science. But in his *Recapitulation* at the end of his essay, the author admits that it is doubtful whether mere natural religion can succeed in this mission: "When the supernatural does not come in to overwhelm the natural, and turn life upside down; when it is admitted that religion deals in the first instance with the known and the natural: then we may well begin to doubt whether the known and the natural can suffice for human life. No sooner do we try to think so, than pessimism raises its head" (p. 261). The author here recurs to a possibility, that he had suggested before when describing the various forms of religion suited to the childhood, youth, and manhood of humanity, the possibility that in the race, as in the individual, manhood is to be succeeded by old age, and that in turn by death. In that previous passage he indicated somewhat distinctly the condition on which alone pessimism can be avoided (p. 156). "It need not be so if, as was said above, the service of Necessity may become freedom instead of bondage; if the Power above us, which so often checks our impatience and pours contempt on our enthusiasms, can be conceived as not necessarily giving less than we hope for, because it does not give precisely *what* we hope for, but perhaps even as giving infinitely more." True; but then in the end he frankly acknowledges that the science of nature can give us no certainty of this. It may form the basis of a culture, an enthusiasm, or even a religion; it may lift men above earthliness and secularity; it may form the basis of a cosmopolitan society: but this city is not one that hath foundations, unless the builder and maker of it be recognised as God, the God revealed by Christ. There is no certainty that it shall not fall into hopeless ruin, if we know nothing of God but what Nature teaches. This final admission of our author is strikingly confirmed by a historical instance suggested by his own essay. The idea of the brotherhood of man and of a universal society of the human race, such as Jesus proclaimed in his kingdom of God, was reached independently by the Stoic philosophers, if not even by earlier thinkers. But it is not to Stoicism but to Christianity that the world owes the realization of such universal philanthropy, because the Stoics had no guarantee that their ideal was possible. Just in proportion to the loftiness of their ideal was the difficulty of believing it to be attainable. "There is, as it were," says our author, "a suicide mark below which our philosophy is always liable to sink. If we came to think life irreconcilably opposed to our ideals, and at the same time were enthusiastically devoted to them, life would become intolerable to us. . . . Something of the kind happened with the Stoics of the Imperial period. Their philosophy was only just above suicide mark, and was continually dropping below it" (p. 61). Now, can our author's natural religion secure us from such a danger? By his own admission it cannot. All that he can say in the end is, that if religion fails us, it is only when human life itself is proved to be worthless (p. 262). This is but cold comfort; it makes the possible ruin the more terrible; and the last word of this natural religion is an *if*. "Supernatural religion met this want by connecting Love and Righteousness with eternity." That is most true of Christianity, and is any other way of supplying the want possible? If the infinite and eternal power revealed in nature is indeed possessed of love and righteousness, then, and then only, are we assured that our ideals, be they as high as they may, shall not be disappointed, that we shall not receive less good than we ask for, though we may not receive the very thing we ask for, but may receive something very different, that may seem evil though indeed it is a higher good. That is the Christian belief, and that gives inextinguishable courage and hope to Christians aiming at the improvement of the world in all ways, material, moral, and religious. But can this belief be maintained in an age of science, which demands real and solid evidence for everything it accepts as true; is it a survival of that devotion to the good, that marked the youth of humanity into its manhood, where the true alone can continue to be relied on? The Christian faith is admitted to be good, more hopeful and comforting than that of natural religion; but is it true? Can we any longer, in an age of science, believe a revelation that is beyond the range of what science deals with, and differs from all that science finds in her field of labour? This is the vital question for Christianity, and we must not shrink from it, though the answer can only be indicated here, that if the kingdom of God proclaimed by Jesus is a reality, the Christian hope is true and sure.

NOTE F, p. 51.—ON THE PHRASE "KINGDOM OF PRIESTS."

On the exact meaning of the expression מַמְלֶכֶת כֹּהֲנִים (Ex. xix. 6) there has been some discussion among interpreters. The LXX. render it βασίλειον ἱεράτευμα, a royal priesthood, a phrase which is used also in 1 Pet. ii. 9; the Vulgate has, in Exodus, *regnum sacerdotale;* in 1 Peter, *regale sacerdotium.* Keil contends strongly for the LXX. rendering, holding that מַמְלָכָה must mean kingship, and that the expression denotes, not merely a nation of priests, under God as their king, but a body of kings who are to reign for God over other nations. So much stress does he lay on this idea, that he maintains that this clause does not describe what was involved in the theocracy as established by the covenant of Sinai, but a great and glorious promise to the fulfilment of which the theocracy was but a means, the universal sway over the nations foretold by Balaam in Num. xxiv. 8, 17 foll., by Moses in Deut. xxxiii. 29, and still more distinctly in Dan. vii. 27. That the translation which he advocates is a possible one, seems to be proved by the ancient versions which he cites, conveying the idea of the Israelites being kings as well as priests; but that the other rendering, which takes "kingdom" in the passive sense, is inadmissible here, does not seem to be made out. The parallel of "a holy nation" in the next clause seems to tell in its favour; for elsewhere, when "kingdom" and "nation" are mentioned together, the former is used in the passive sense (1 Kings xviii. 10; Jer. xviii. 7). Anyhow, this clause is decisive against the idea that a royal priesthood denotes, not the privilege of the theocracy then to be set up, but a promise only to be accomplished through and after that. For it is undoubted, that to be a holy nation was a privilege that belonged to Israel then in virtue of the covenant (Lev. xix. 1; Deut. xiv. 2); and it is impossible to suppose that the two clauses so closely conjoined refer to two widely different things, so that it would mean, "Ye shall be ultimately, when the kingdom of God is completed, a royal priesthood, and even now a holy nation." This is a meaning that could never naturally be drawn from the words as they stand; and it is safe, therefore, to reject a view that requires it to be put upon them. The two expressions, "kingdom of priests" (or "royal priesthood") and "holy nation," are evidently parallel; and there is not such a wide difference between the two renderings of the former as Keil thinks. According to the ideas of ancient times, and indeed of despotic government in all times, kings as well as priests stand in a peculiarly close relation to God. They have absolute authority over their subjects, and they themselves are subject to heaven alone. So in Ps. lxxxii. they are called gods and sons of the Highest; so Horace says, "*Regum timendorum in proprios greges, Reges in ipsos imperium est Jovis;*" and so Shakespeare puts into the mouth of Richard II. the maxim of divine right: "The breath of worldly men cannot depose The deputy appointed by the Lord." A people, therefore, who are all directly under God as their king, are in the position in which kings alone stand in nations under despotic government; and as kingship in this view has a sacred character, it is closely associated with priesthood. The Hebrew idea of priests was that they were the Lord's, that they were holy, that they drew near to the Lord (Num. xvi. 6); and all these are implied in what is said of Israel as a whole here; hence they are priests, standing in direct relation to God, and so enjoying royal privileges and dignity. Kingship is also associated in ancient ideas with freedom; for under an absolute government the king was the only man who was really free. Hence the Stoics' assertion, that the wise man is free, was completed by the more paradoxical statement, that he is a king; and so in Scripture the assertions that the children of God reign as kings, possess all things, and the like, are simply strong and emphatic assertions of their freedom. The Christian view of freedom indeed, and of the way in which it is obtained, differs widely from that of the Stoics; and hence we do not find that the people of God individually are called in Scripture kings, though the name is given to them collectively, and they are said to reign with Christ. The representation of Israel being a royal priesthood, then, would seem to be the same as that of their being the kingdom of Jehovah, and simply brings out, in more emphatic form, the freedom, and holiness, and direct access to God that belonged to them as such. Another view of this passage that also dissociates these titles from the actual state of Israel under the law is that of Kurtz, who holds that when the people desired that God would not speak with them directly, but that Moses might speak to them for him, they withdrew from the privileges that God had offered to them of being a kingdom of priests, and that thenceforth only the house of Aaron enjoyed that privilege. But this is an unfounded and unnatural supposition. The narrative, in its plain and obvious sense, suggests that the covenant which God offers to make with Israel in Ex. xix. 3–9 is the same as that whose solemn ratification is described in chap. xxiv. The special consecration of the tribe of Levi and house of Aaron was not inconsistent with the whole nation being a kingdom of priests: in early times, as in the days of the judges, priestly functions were not confined to them; and if afterwards it became necessary to give them, and the central national worship conducted by them, more exclusive rights, this was just parallel to the institution of the human kingship, and proved that the ideal of a pure theocracy could not be realized in Israel.

NOTE G, p. 57.—ON THE EARLY RELIGION OF ISRAEL.

How far the religion of Israel in early times really was the worship of one only God standing in a moral relation to his people, is indeed a question, the great question of Old Testament history. That such was the religion of the great prophets of the eighth century B.C. is undoubted; but that they had to contend against a very different set of ideas in the mass of the people is equally undeniable. The contemporaries of Amos, Hosea, and Isaiah conceived Jehovah as a merely national God, standing in a natural and necessary relation to Israel, and to be served by outward gifts and sacrifices. As against these notions, the prophets proclaimed that what Jehovah required of them was, not such material offerings, but holiness, love, righteousness; and that for the absence or violation of these he would judge them and all nations. Now, was this a new conception of religion, introduced then for the first time? So say those who would trace the religion of Israel to a purely human origin and development; and, no doubt, as the mass of the people were strangers to the prophetic ideas in the eighth century, it may be presumed that they were so also in earlier times. But this does not prove that these ideas were absolutely new then; and if we consider how slowly such a spiritual conception of religion would penetrate a rude and early people, and how apt it would be to be corrupted, we can well believe that it had been taught before, though all along it had to struggle in the minds of the people with the lower ideas of the heathen around. Whatever uncertainty there may be as to the dates and mutual relations in point of time of the different laws and records of Hebrew antiquity, the Decalogue and the Book of the Covenant (Ex. xxi.-xxiii.) are generally recognised as the oldest; and it is noteworthy that in them we have almost exclusively moral precepts, and comparatively few that relate to religious worship or observances. The ideal presented to us in these laws is not that of a people reverencing a national God by external acts of worship, and looking to him for help and blessing, no matter what their moral conduct might be: rather they are called to recognise their God as maker of heaven and earth, and to show their loyalty to him by observing his ordinances of justice, as well as by offering him gifts and sacrifices. Whatever may have been the ideas of the mass of the people, there is no reason to doubt that such men as David, Samuel, and Moses himself viewed Israel's relation to Jehovah in the same way as Amos and Isaiah did. We may therefore quite legitimately take this as the true idea of the theocracy or kingdom of God in Israel. Even Kuenen, who endeavours to explain the religion of Israel in an entirely naturalistic way, virtually admits this when he says: "Moses may have owed his ideal of morality to his intercourse with the Egyptians, but he could not regard its realization otherwise than as the will of the God of his fathers; the inaccessible, pure, austere God of light was predestined, as it were, to proclaim and maintain that ideal. The great merit of Moses lies in the fact that he thus connected the religious idea with the moral life. Jahveh comes before his people with moral demands and commandments; this is the starting-point of Israel's rich religious development, the germ of those glorious truths which were to ripen in the course of centuries" (*Religion of Israel*, Eng. tr. i. p. 282). See also W. Robertson Smith, *The Prophets of Israel*, Lect. ii.; and Fairbairn, *The City of God*, p. 134-41.

NOTE H, p. 61.—VIEWS OF THE KINGDOM OF GOD IN THE PSALMS.

If we examine the Psalter, as a representation of the religious ideas of Israel, we find that a kingdom of God is spoken of, more or less explicitly, or God invoked or described as king in twenty-seven psalms. In many of them there is simply the invocation "my King" addressed to God (Ps. v. 2, xliv. 4, lxviii. 24, lxxiv. 12, lxxxiv. 3, cxlv. 1), a title of the Deity which is naturally suggested by religious feeling, and customary in most nations (*Moloch, Baal,* Ζεῦ βασιλεῦ, etc.); though in several of these psalms it is connected with the peculiar ideas of the theistic and ethical religion of Israel. In others, again, these Israelitic ideas come out more distinctly in their moral or prophetic forms. Sometimes we find expressed the view, of which the prophet Amos is the most prominent teacher, that God, the King of Israel, is not connected with his people by a mere natural tie, but governs them and all nations in righteousness, according to their moral conduct. This comes out most emphatically in the earlier psalms, as ix. 4, 7, x. 16, xi. 4, xlvii. 2, 6-9. At other times, the prophetic vision of a restored theocracy, or reign of God over Israel and ultimately over all nations, which Isaiah most fully depicts, is in the psalmist's eye; and this is especially in the later psalms, as lxxxix. 18, xcvi. 10, xcvii. 1, xcviii. 6, xcix. 1. Closely connected with this class of psalms are those poems that refer to a human king (Ps. ii., xx., xxi., xlv., lxxii., cx.), which all came in time to be applied to the expected Messiah, while it is a disputed question whether they had an original reference to one or other of the historical kings of Israel or Judah, and if so, to which of them.

In such psalms the reign of God in Israel is represented as carried on by means of the human king, who rules in his name, and the hope and promise is expressed of a more perfect realization of the righteousness and peace that are the ends of the kingly government than had ever yet been seen. But there are other psalms in which a different view is taken, and God is represented as reigning without any reference to the earthly king. Such are the 9th, 10th, 11th, 47th, 48th Psalms, which cannot be supposed to be either earlier than the beginning, or later than the end, of royal government in Israel. Neither is it satisfactory to say, that the divine reign spoken of in such psalms is something different from the theocratic kingship, as for instance God's providential government of the universe, as distinct from his moral government of his people. The distinctions of God's kingdom of nature, of grace, and of glory, current in later dogmatics, are foreign to the simple and concrete thought of those early times. The end of the kingdom is the same, whether it be the direct work of God, or of a king ruling in his name, to crush wickedness and to save and protect the poor and humble. This appears if we compare Ps. ix. 8–12 with lxxii. 4–7. In the former, God himself is represented as doing what, according to the latter, the king is to do. The king, to whom Jehovah gives his judgments and his righteousness, is to save the poor and needy, and to break in pieces the oppressor; but this does not to the Israelite eclipse the truth, that God himself reigns for the same ends, or prevent the recognition of this reign of God as manifest when his judgments do really humble the proud and save the lowly. God is still Israel's king dwelling in Zion, even though there is an earthly king sitting at his right hand, whose throne is the throne of God; and to the eye of faith it makes no difference whether he executes his judgment directly or through the human sovereign. So in the prayer for the king in Ps. xx. we read, ver. 6: "Now know I that the Lord saveth his anointed: he will hear him from his holy heaven with the saving strength of his right hand." But this trust in the Lord's protection of the king is equivalent to direct confidence in the Lord himself; ver. 7: "Some trust in chariots, and some in horses: but we will remember the name of the Lord our God." Whatever blessings Israel enjoyed under the reign of godly kings, the pious Israelite traced up to God the true king of his people. He gave the king his judgments and his spirit, that he might judge righteously; he saved him, and made him victorious in battle; so that Jehovah was still reigning over his people. In any striking events by which the ungodly were overthrown and the humble saved, they recognised the Lord himself acting as king, sitting on the throne judging right. Not only swarms of locusts (Joel ii. 11), but the hosts of the Medes (Isa. xiii. 3, 4, 17), are Jehovah's armies. Nay, even in the phenomena of nature, the thunderstorm and the tempest, they saw and acknowledged the Lord sitting as king (Ps. xxix., xciii.).

These views of God's reign, as seen in his works of nature and of providence, formed a natural means of leading on devout and enlightened Israelites to the recognition of the kingdom of God as universal, embracing not Israel alone, but all nations. For when God saves his people by executing judgment on hostile nations that attack and oppress them, he shows his superiority over these nations too, and displays such mighty power as may and must attract the admiration and awe of all nations. It is not that the earthly king is made a sovereign of all nations, or the people of Israel made mistress of a universal empire; but the divine king, who is ruling and training them just by making himself known to them, is by his judgments and his blessings to them making himself equally known to all nations. This comes out especially in Ps. xlvii., where, along with the special relation of God to Israel ("our king," ver. 6), it is also said, "Jehovah is a great king over all the nations" (ver. 2); "God is king of all the earth" (ver. 7); "God reigneth over the heathen" (ver. 8). It is also to be observed, that in the Old Testament generally the heathen are not described as exposed to God's wrath as such, but on account of their sins.[1] If heathen nations are said in one place (Isa. xliii. 3) to be given as a ransom for Israel, this may be understood in the sense in which it is said elsewhere, that the wicked is a ransom for the just, *i.e.* comes to suffer while the just is delivered (Prov. xi. 8, xxi. 18). When judgments are denounced on heathen nations, it is always for special sins of a moral kind (Amos i., ii.; Jer. x. 25; Ps. lxxxix. 6 foll.; Mal. i. 2, 4); and in other places God's forbearance towards the heathen is described, as in the Book of Jonah.

NOTE I, p. 78.—THE DOCTRINE OF A SUFFERING MESSIAH IN THE OLD TESTAMENT.

That the Old Testament contains the doctrine of a suffering and atoning Messiah must, I think, be maintained, notwithstanding the objections of the rationalists, and the things that seem to give weight to these objections. The chief of these is, that in the time of our Lord the idea that the Messiah should be crucified and rise again was strange and offensive, not only to the mass of the Jews, but even to Jesus' own disciples. This seems to show that the notion of a Saviour who should die to atone for his people's sins, could not be clearly and obviously found in the Old Testament, but must have been imported into its

---

[1] See Oehler, *Old Testament Theology*, § 219.

sayings, by some arbitrary allegorical or typical interpretation, after the death and resurrection of Jesus. It is undeniable that some of the applications of the Old Testament by the apostles in proof of Christian doctrine are of a typical character, such as could not have been perceived beforehand; and even if all those referring to the suffering of Messiah were of that nature, there would be nothing inconsistent with the truth and authority of Jesus. But that in point of fact there was a more definite and obvious prediction of one who was to save his people by dying for their sins, is shown by several considerations.

1. The legitimate and natural interpretation of several passages, especially Isa. lii. 13–liii. 12, and Zech. xii. 10–xiii. 1, xiii. 7, points to this.

2. The words of Simeon (Luke ii. 34, 35) and of the Baptist (John i. 29) show that this idea was not strange to some at least in our Lord's time.

3. The notion of a suffering and atoning Messiah is found in the Talmud and Cabalistic writings of the Jews; and it is very hard to suppose that it was adopted by them from the Christians, or came from any other source than the representations of the Old Testament.[1]

The fact is, that what proved a stumbling-block to the Jews in our Lord's work was not merely the sufferings he had to undergo, but more especially his condemnation by the Sanhedrin and death on the cross. They were offended, in the first place, during his ministry, because while claiming to be the Messiah, he seemed only to perform the part of a teacher, and refused to head a movement for deliverance from the Roman yoke. Had he set on foot such an attempt, even though he had been opposed by many of the people, and had suffered defeat and ill-treatment in the war, yet the mass of the people might have clung to him, hoping that through suffering he would at last make his way to victory. But that the Messiah should not only suffer but die, and above all that he should be

---

[1] See Hengstenberg, *Christology of the Old Testament*, iv. 332-64.

condemned by the supreme and sacred Court of Israel, and die the death of a malefactor, they were not prepared for; and even Jesus' disciples did not expect that his sufferings would go so far; and had their hopes dashed to pieces by his crucifixion. Their hopes were, indeed, revived by his resurrection; but that resurrection, not to an earthly life, but to life in a glorified spiritual body, could restore hope only to those who had learned to welcome Jesus' salvation as a spiritual kingdom of God, not an external one of this world. Hence the ultimate cause of offence to the Pharisees and Sadducees was, that the disciples of Jesus proclaimed the Messianic kingdom, with all its blessings, to be already come by the exaltation of Jesus. This manifestly implied that the kingdom was not the mere reign of the hierarchy, as the Sadducees thought, nor the supernatural earthly theocracy for which the Pharisees looked; but a spiritual one. Hence it was, that as soon as Saul of Tarsus was convinced of the resurrection of Jesus, his whole religious ideas were at once changed, and that he was no longer looking and working for a salvation to come, but by faith rejoicing in one already come. The notion of a suffering Messiah in some form could be made to harmonize with that of his kingdom being a merely secular one; but as held by Christians it was inconsistent with any such idea, for it represented his triumph as consisting in a resurrection and ascension to heaven, manifested by a sending forth of the Holy Spirit for the teaching of the world : it was not merely that " the Messiah is subject to suffering," but also that he first by the resurrection of the dead " should proclaim light both to the people and to the Gentiles" (Acts xxvi. 23), implying, as Alford says (*in loc.*), " That this light, to be preached to the Jews and Gentiles, must arise *from the resurrection of the dead*, and that Christ, *the first* ἐξ ἀναστάσεως, was to announce it." So, in Justin's *Dialogue* with Trypho, the Jew is represented as acknowledging it as proved from the Scriptures that the Messiah was to suffer, but still thinking of an earthly reign, and counting it madness to speak of Jesus as reigning through the gifts of the Spirit (c. 36, 39).

NOTE J, p. 117.—THE TEACHING OF JOHN THE BAPTIST ON THE KINGDOM OF GOD.

In the New Testament the kingdom of God is first brought under our notice in the preaching of John the Baptist, and that gives a sort of rough outline in a few lines, which is afterwards filled in by the much fuller and more varied teaching of Jesus to a complete picture. As the ministry of the Baptist prepared the way for that of Christ, so a study of what he proclaimed about the kingdom may help us better to understand our Lord's work and teaching in regard to it.

1. John's primary announcement was, that the reign of heaven, or of God, was at hand, *i.e.* that the time was near at hand when the promises given by the prophets of a new and better kingdom of God, and the hopes and longings of God's people after that blessed state, would be realized. In this announcement by itself there would be nothing unintelligible or startling to any of the Jews. It was just what they all were looking for, and there seems to have been a pretty general opinion that the time had nearly come for the fulfilment of the promises. There was, indeed, great difference of view as to the way in which the reign of God was to come, and probably also as to the nature of it; but that God was to establish once more a kingdom over his people on the earth, they all believed; and all might rejoice to hear that he was soon to do so. John referred to the prophecies as explaining his own ministry, and so also the kingdom that he announced; and one incidental expression seems to show that his thoughts about it went back to the very beginnings of God's promises to his people. When he says (Matt. iii. 9): "God is able of these stones to raise up children to Abraham," he indicates that he regarded the kingdom that he proclaimed as the fulfilment of God's ancient promise to Abraham. This seems to show that John regarded

the establishment of the kingdom of God as a matter of grace, not as the Pharisees thought, to be merited by obedience to the law, but bestowed by God in pursuance of his free promise to Abraham. The expression is in the line of such passages as Deut. ix. 4, 5, Ps. cv. 8-12, 42-45, and points towards Paul's argument against the legalists, in which he goes back from the law given at Sinai to the free promise to Abraham four hundred years before (Gal. iii. 15-18).

2. But an equally prominent point in the Baptist's preaching was, that the people need to be prepared for the approaching reign of God by repentance, *i.e.* change of mind and conduct. The call to such a change was the burden of his preaching, and from the account that Luke gives of his specific instructions to various classes of the community we learn, that the reformation which he urged consisted essentially in a return to the duties of justice, humanity, and contentment (Luke iii. 11-14), in other words, that it is a moral change, and a recognition and fulfilment of the great moral duties incumbent on men in their several relations. In this John followed in the steps of the prophets of Israel, who were ever preachers of righteousness, and rose above the conceptions of the priests of that day, who only insisted on the fulfilment of the law as an outward positive rule. The change he called for was an entire change; and it was symbolized by the rite of baptism which he administered to those who confessed their sins, and showed themselves willing for the new life. It was an emblem of their being cleansed from sin, and so made ready for the reign of God which was at hand.

3. A third important element in the Baptist's message was the announcement of an impending judgment, which he describes as "the wrath to come," and declares is to be executed by the Messiah who is to come after him. The Messiah is depicted as a husbandman, cutting down the trees that bear no good fruit, and winnowing the wheat from the chaff in his thrashing-floor. This description

just follows out that line of prophetic announcements, according to which Israel is to be restored by a process of sifting judgment, by which the wicked should be destroyed from among the people of God. At the same time, John joins with this a word that goes back to that other series of prophetic utterances which speak of the conversion and renewal of Israel by God's pouring out his Spirit on them; for he says that the Messiah shall baptize, not merely with water as he did, but with holy spirit, *i.e.* with pure and purifying influence from God.[1] This spiritual baptism must have been conceived as securing the reality of that repentance, and those fruits of repentance, which the baptism of water represented. On this account he recognised the coming Messiah as greatly his superior, more above him than a master is above a domestic slave. Still the predominant view of the Messiah's work in John's description is that of sifting by judgment, so much so, that he adds to the announcement of the baptism with the Holy Spirit, "and with fire," referring most probably to the same fire that is to burn up the chaff.[2] Messiah is to purify the penitent with the Holy Spirit, and to execute destructive judgment on the impenitent. Such was the way, it would seem, in which John expected the kingdom of God to be established. Accordingly, when Jesus appeared to be following a course different from this, receiving publicans and sinners, and eating with them, living no ascetic life, but freely partaking of the good things of this world, and not enjoining on his disciples the duty of fasting, but rather calling them to happiness and joy; John was perplexed at a line of conduct so different from what he thought Messiah

---

[1] Πνεύματι ἁγίῳ is indefinite in all the Gospels; and as used by the Baptist, we are hardly warranted in giving it the distinct Trinitarian meaning which it has later.

[2] Καὶ πυρί (Matt. iii. 11; Luke iii. 16) has indeed been understood by many good interpreters as a synonym of the Holy Spirit; but the view that refers it to the fire of judgment seems more agreeable to the context. The omission of the words in Mark i. 8 and Acts i. 5, where the severer side of John's preaching is also omitted, seems to favour this; and the objection, that the single object ὑμᾶς unites both ideas, and so proves them to be one, is not conclusive, for ὑμᾶς is collective.

would pursue, and for a time was in doubt if Jesus were really the Messiah.[1]

4. Another feature in John's ministry is noteworthy, though it is only indicated by Luke. From the circumstance that when asked by publicans and soldiers, who must have been in the service of the Roman Empire, what they should do, he did not call on them to renounce that service, but only to perform its duties with honesty, justice, and humanity, it seems fair to conclude that John did not regard the kingdom whose approach he proclaimed as a worldly one, but as one to which men might belong even though they were servants of an earthly kingdom. His views certainly differed in this respect from those of the Zealots or of the high priests and rulers, as on the other hand they differed from the Pharisees in taking a deeper view of the preparation necessary for the kingdom of God.

NOTE K, p. 122.—ON THE PHRASE "KINGDOM OF HEAVEN."

The phrase βασιλεία τῶν οὐρανῶν is peculiar in the New Testament to Matthew's Gospel, in which it occurs in the received text thirty-two, in that of modern editions thirty-three times; βασιλεία τοῦ θεοῦ occurs only four times, but equivalent phrases are used in three other places. In Mark and Luke the former expression no longer appears, but βασιλεία τοῦ θεοῦ is uniformly employed, even in places that are in other respects exactly parallel to Matthew's text. In endeavouring to explain these phenomena, scholars are divided in opinion as to whether there is any difference of meaning between the two phrases, or merely one of expression.

[1] That John's message (Matt. xi. 2; Luke vii. 19) expressed a real doubt in his own mind, and was not merely a device to instruct his disciples, may be regarded as certain; and that the doubt arose from the free and gracious character of Jesus' ministry, so different from his own, is made highly probable by the facts that it was in regard to this that a question had been raised by John's disciples (Matt. ix. 14-17; Luke v. 33-39), and that our Lord refers to this difference in his discourse after that message (Matt. xi. 16-19; Luke vii. 31-35). John had recognised Jesus as the Messiah by his personal character and by divine signs; but when he seemed not to be doing the work of Messiah his conviction was shaken.

The older writers generally took the latter view, that the terms are synonymous, explaining them by the use of "heaven" as meaning God. This is held by Grotius, Lightfoot,[1] Wolf,[2] Campbell,[3] and Storr.[4] Some more recent scholars still maintain the same opinion, such as Robinson,[5] Tholuck, Alford, Lipsius, Schürer. Bengel finds a certain shade of difference between the two expressions, inasmuch as he thinks that when God is designated "heaven," the spiritual nature of his kingdom as distinguished from those of the earth is meant to be emphasized; and this view is held also by Stier. Other modern writers go farther, and make a still wider distinction between the two phrases. Meyer and Cremer[6] take τῶν οὐρανῶν as indicating the place of the kingdom = ἐπουράνιος, 2 Tim. iv. 18, as a kingdom whose blessings are now in heaven, and are to come to the earth at the last day. Following this interpretation, Weiss[7] thinks that the phrase was not originally used by Jesus, but was introduced by Matthew, after the destruction of Jerusalem had disappointed the hopes of an earthly kingdom, to make it plain that the kingdom proclaimed by Jesus was not of this world.

Notwithstanding these diverging views, the old opinion that the two phrases are synonymous seems to be well-founded, for the following reasons:—

1. The use of "heaven," or "the heavens," for God among the Jews is undoubted. Not to speak of the examples from the Talmud, of which Lightfoot and others have collected many, and in view of which Weber[8] gives "heaven" as one of the characteristic Jewish names of God, the same usage is found both in the Old

---

[1] *Horæ Hebraicæ et Talmudicæ* on Matt. iii. 2.
[2] *Curæ Philologicæ et Criticæ in N. T.*
[3] *On the Gospels.* Dissertation V.
[4] *Dissertation on the Meaning of "the Kingdom of Heaven" in the New Testament,* translated from the Latin. Biblical Cabinet, vol. ix.
[5] *Lexicon of N. T. Greek.*
[6] *Biblico-Theological Lexicon of N. T. Greek.*
[7] *Lehrbuch der Biblischen Theologie des N. T.* §138; *Leben Jesu,* i. p. 444.
[8] *System der altsynagogalen palaestinischen Theologie,* p. 145.

Testament (Dan. iv. 36; Ps. lxxiii. 9), the Apocrypha (1 Macc. iii. 60, iv. 10, 24), and the New Testament (Matt. xxi. 25; Luke xv. 18, 21). There can be no doubt, therefore, that the construction of the phrase βασιλεία τῶν οὐρανῶν as "kingdom of (the God of) heaven," meaning the same as "kingdom of God," is quite possible consistently with grammar and usage, and as it seems to be used interchangeably, there is a presumption that this is its meaning.

2. The very phrase "kingdom of the heavens," מַלְכוּת הַשָּׁמַיִם, was used by the Jews, in the sense of the dominion of God, sometimes viewed in its moral and sometimes in its Messianic aspect. This too is an undoubted fact; and it does not make much difference whether, as is generally thought, this use of the phrase was older and independent of the Christian revelation, or, as Stier[1] thinks, was of later origin, and began with John the Baptist, and thence passed into the later Rabbinical writers. This seems very improbable, for the use of "heaven" for "God" was undoubtedly earlier, and it is unlikely that the Jews would adopt so largely a phrase of Christian origin. But whether of earlier or later origin, the Rabbinical usage of the phrase shows how it would be most likely to be understood, and so confirms the presumption that it meant the same as "kingdom of God."

3. It is to be observed that the Greek word βασιλεία, like the Hebrew מלכות, ממלכה and the Latin *regnum*, has a wider significance than the English "kingdom," and much obscurity is caused by its being uniformly rendered by that word in our Bibles. It denotes not only the realm of a king, but also his reign or royalty; and in some places it must be understood in one or other of these latter senses. So it must be taken when it is used with verbs of motion, as when it is said to be at hand, to come, to come nigh, etc. We cannot speak of a realm coming; but the coming or approach of a reign is a most natural and intelligible expression. So, too, the phrases κηρύσσειν βασιλείαν, εὐαγγέλιον τῆς

[1] *Words of Jesus*, vol. i. p. 82.

βασιλείας must mean to proclaim a reign, the glad tidings of the reign, not the realm. Now in many places where the context shows that βασιλεία must mean "reign," and not "realm," we find it combined in Matthew with τῶν οὐρανῶν, as in the very first announcement of the Baptist, ἤγγικεν ἡ βασιλεία τῶν οὐρανῶν, Matt. iii. 2. Where βασιλεία means realm, the genitive after it may be that of place; but where it means reign, that is impossible, and it must denote the subject, *i.e.* him who reigns, unless it be explained as merely equivalent to an adjective. If we take "the heavens" as meaning God, which as we have seen it may do, then the construction is simple and natural, "the reign of the heavens is at hand;" otherwise we have either the anomaly of speaking of the realm of the heavens approaching, or else we must understand by "the reign of the heavens" the "heavenly reign," which is grammatically very harsh, and in meaning very vague.

4. This view of the identity of the two expressions gives a simple and natural explanation of the variation in usage between Matthew and the other evangelists. The use of "the heavens" for "God" is a specially Hebraistic one, the Greeks did not use οὐρανός in that way; and so we can easily understand why Matthew on the one hand, writing mainly for Jews, retained the expression which probably our Lord used often, if not always; while the other evangelists, writing for Gentiles, who would not be familiar with the Hebrew idiom, and to whom it might be puzzling, substituted for it an equivalent but more intelligible Greek phrase. This might be, even if, as Bengel and Stier think, the phrase "kingdom of heaven" was chosen by the Baptist and Jesus to express the spiritual nature of the kingdom; for in that case the later evangelists have simply left that shade of meaning unexpressed, because they needed to paraphrase the Hebraistic language of Matthew. The view of Weiss, that the expression βασιλεία τῶν οὐρανῶν indicates that the completed kingdom of God realizes itself first in heaven, does not seem at all a natural

one. What sense can be given to the statement "the kingdom of heaven has come near" on that view of the meaning of the expression, is very hard to see. That and other statements must refer to a kingdom that is to be set up, or is set up, on earth; and though the epithet "of heaven" may denote that it is, as Jesus said to Pilate, not of this world, there is no positive evidence to show that the epithet was introduced by Matthew, and not rather used by our Lord himself. Also the assumption, that the Gospel of Matthew was written after the fall of Jerusalem had removed the hope of an earthly fulfilment of the theocracy in Israel, is very precarious. The form of the discourse in Matt. xxiv. proves that it cannot have been so long after the destruction of Jerusalem as to preclude the expectation of an immediate personal return of Christ, and the parenthetic note to the reader in chap. xxiv. 15 makes it highly probable that the Gospel was not written after the fall of the city at all, but before that event. Anyhow, it is not easy to believe that a writer who left Jesus' prophetic discourse in the form which it has in Matt. xxiv. would make a systematic change in the leading term of his whole teaching, in order to show its harmony with the events of history. It is generally thought, and with more reason, that the form in which Luke has recorded Christ's prophetic discourse shows that he wrote after the fulfilment of the prediction of the fall of Jerusalem; but that Matthew's report indicates the reverse in his case. Further, there is every reason to think, that of the two expressions for the kingdom, $\beta a\sigma\iota\lambda\epsilon ia$ $\tau\hat{\omega}\nu$ $o\dot{\upsilon}\rho a\nu\hat{\omega}\nu$ is the older, which gave place, especially in Gentile circles, to $\beta a\sigma\iota\lambda\epsilon ia$ $\tau\hat{\omega}\nu$ $\theta\epsilon o\hat{\upsilon}$; and the opinion of an opposite relation is very improbable. If the phrase kingdom of heaven was introduced to emphasize the spiritual nature of the kingdom, it is curious that it is never used by any of the later writers of the New Testament.

NOTE L, p. 127.—THE KINGDOM IN JESUS' TEACHING
A PRESENT REALITY.

The view given in the text of the meaning of the kingdom of God in Jesus' teaching, as denoting what was already a present reality, requires elucidation and support; because it is held by many, and among others by so high an exegetical authority as Meyer, that the phrase refers to a thing of the future. Meyer says (on Matt. iii. 2): "In the teaching of Christ and in the apostolic writings, the kingdom of the Messiah is the actual consummation of the prophetic idea of the rule of God; and as it is unaccompanied by millenarian ideas (which exist only in the non-apostolic Apocalypse), so also is it without any national limitation, so that participation therein rests only on faith in Jesus Christ and on the moral renewal which is conditioned by the same, and 'God all in all' is the last and highest aim, without the thought of the world-rule, and the expectation of the renewal of the world, of the resurrection, of the judgment, and also of the external glory, losing their positive validity and necessity,—thoughts which rather form the subject of living Christian hope amidst all the struggles and oppressions of the world. Moreover, those expressions $\beta a\sigma\iota\lambda\epsilon\iota a\ \tau\hat{\omega}\nu\ o\mathrm{\dot{\nu}}\rho a\nu\hat{\omega}\nu,\ \kappa\tau\lambda.$, never signify anything else than the *kingdom of the Messiah*, even in those passages where they *appear* to denote the (invisible) Church, the moral kingdom of the Christian religion, and such like, or to express some modern abstraction of the concrete conception which is one given in the history,—an appearance which is eliminated by observing that the manner of expression is frequently *proleptic*, and which has its historical basis in the idea of the nearness of the kingdom, and in the moral development which necessarily precedes its manifestation." Meyer here protests against two views of what Jesus meant by the kingdom of God, one identifying it with the Church, and the other resolving it into some modern abstract notion, which he holds to be inconsistent with the concrete meaning it must historically have had. The former of these views is a mistake that has had serious consequences in the Church's history; but in regard to the latter it must be remembered that though an abstract notion, such as we may draw from it now, could not be present to the minds of our Lord's hearers, it may yet be the most exact expression of the essential idea of his teaching. It is for this reason that I have treated in separate lectures the historical teaching of Jesus and the doctrinal idea of the kingdom of God that may be gathered from it. In the same way, in such terms as *covenant, sacrifice, priest*, we must distinguish the concrete historical sense from the essential ideas that theology recognises in them, which we moderns must express in modern forms of thought. In his anxiety to be true to the historical meaning, Meyer is led to maintain that the kingdom of God in Jesus' mouth always means the future reign of the Messiah, and that where it seems to be described as present, this is done only by way of anticipation. But this requires a very forced and unnatural interpretation of a number of passages. The opening announcement of our Lord's ministry, "the reign of God is at hand," must be held to imply an expectation of the nearness of the second advent that has been entirely falsified by history. This is conceivable in the case of John the Baptist, but not so in that of Jesus himself. Again, the saying in Matt. xi. 12, "The kingdom of heaven suffereth violence," is explained as describing "that eager, irresistible striving and struggling after the approaching Messianic kingdom which has prevailed since the Baptist began to preach; it is as though it were taken by storm." But the text says nothing of the kingdom approaching, but rather, especially when compared with Luke xvi. 16, implies that it is already present: "every man entereth violently into it." Still more decisive is Matt. xii. 28, on which Meyer says: "The reasoning is founded on the axiom, that such deeds, wrought as they are by the power of God's Spirit, prove that he who performs them is no other than he who brings in the kingdom, the Messiah. Where the Messiah is present and working, there too is the kingdom; not yet, indeed, as completely established, but preparing to become so through its preliminary development in the world." But this seems to substitute for our Lord's direct argument from his casting out demons by the Spirit of God to the fact of the reign of God having already come, an indirect one, through the unexpressed premise that he is the Messiah. Besides, if the reign of God has come where the Messiah is present and working, must it not be already established? If the work of Christ on the earth was merely a preliminary preparation for the reign of God to be established in the future, then our Lord's argument loses all its force and truth; and to convey Meyer's idea would need to have been expressed quite differently. It is true Meyer also speaks of the kingdom as in development as well as in preparation now, and waiting only complete establishment in the future; but that only shows that we must recognise here the idea of inward life, which Meyer seemed at first to reject as an unhistorical modern abstraction. The same difficulties apply to Meyer's explanation of Luke xvii. 21, "The kingdom of God is within you," or "among you;" which is an equally strong assertion of its being even then a present reality. On Matt. xiii. 24, where Jesus introduces the parable of the Tares by saying "the kingdom of heaven has become like a man that sowed good seed," Meyer says: "The aorist is to be explained from the fact that the Messiah has already appeared, and is now carrying on his work in connection with his kingdom." This is a vague and ambiguous expression. If it means merely preparing for his kingdom, it affords no explanation of the text; if it means actually reigning or acting as king, it makes the kingdom not merely future, but present. Again, on ver. 38 Meyer writes: "The good seed represents the sons of the kingdom, the (future) subjects, citizens, of the Messianic kingdom, who are established as such by the Messiah in their spiritual nature which is adapted thereto." Here the qualifying adjective "future" is inserted without necessity or warrant, for the reference to chap. viii. 12 does not seem sufficient to justify it.

These passages seem clearly to show that Jesus, on various occasions, spoke in such a way as to imply that the kingdom of God which he founded was not entirely a thing of the future, but a present reality even then. This is confirmed by the general impression produced by his statements about his kingship before Pilate. These suggest that his claim was, not that he ought to be a king, but that he actually was a king, having a kingdom not of this world, established not by force, but by bearing witness to the truth. Meyer himself rightly holds that these words are a description, not, as Hengstenberg held, only of his prophetic, but really of his kingly office.

There are indeed, on the other hand, many sayings of our Lord in which the kingdom of God is spoken of in the future; and it is these that give the chief support to the view of Meyer. Some of them, however, are spoken of individuals entering or not entering the kingdom; and as the entrance of individuals might be doubtful or future, these sayings decide nothing as to whether the kingdom itself was already present or not. Such are Matt. v. 20, vii. 21, etc. There are some, however, which speak of the kingdom absolutely in the future, and certainly show that in some sense it is a thing not yet realized. Such are the petition in the Lord's prayer: "Thy kingdom come;" the saying in Matt. viii. 11; and the parable of the nobleman who went away to receive a kingdom (Luke xix. 11–15). In regard to these, however, it is to be observed that the expressions, the kingdom of God coming, the kingdom of God coming with power, the Son of man coming, the Son of man coming in his kingdom, the Son of man coming in glory, the kingdom of God appearing, seem to be used synonymously in the Gospels; so that sometimes when the simple phrase "coming" is used, it means the glorious or powerful manifestation of the kingdom, and does not necessarily exclude the idea of its being already present. So in Luke xix. 11, the parable of the nobleman going to receive the kingdom is said to have been spoken, because they thought that the kingdom of God was immediately to appear. In Matt. viii. 11 and Luke xiii. 28, the reference seems to be to Abraham, Isaac, and Jacob as raised from the dead in the future kingdom; but the saying is one of those in which Jesus makes most distinct use of external images such as were current among the Jews, and it cannot be pressed in its literality as against the sayings above adduced, speaking of a present spiritual kingdom. The idea suggested in the seed-parables of a vital growth and development of the kingdom of God, seems to harmonize those different representations of it, showing not that the word is used in different senses, but that the thing denoted by it has different forms and stages of existence, as seed, blade, ear, and full corn in the ear.

NOTE M, p. 138.—JESUS' LAST CONTROVERSY WITH THE JEWS.

The reality of the kingdom of God as proclaimed by Jesus, and its difference from the ideas of the Jews, come out very strikingly in his last great controversy with the ecclesiastical authorities, in the temple before his last Passover (Matt. xxi., xxii., xxiii.). Jesus had entered Jerusalem in a humble yet significant triumph, riding on an ass' colt, hailed by the people as the Messiah. Now at last he had openly accepted such homage, because now there was no longer any danger of its being made a political movement; he can unmistakably declare his real meaning; and the time has come when he must do so, and bring matters to a crisis. Therefore he no longer refuses to be publicly announced as the son of David coming in the name of the Lord (xxi. 9–17). Thereafter the priests and elders come and ask him by what authority he does these things (xxi. 23), meaning by that, not exclusively any one part of his proceedings, such as the casting out of the traffickers from the temple, but the whole of his conduct since his coming up to Jerusalem. Jesus answers by a counter-question about the baptism of John (ver. 24). This is not a mere evasion, but a direct and sufficient reply to their demand so far as it was legitimate. John had borne witness to Jesus, and his baptism had pointed to one to come who would baptize with the Holy Spirit; if John's baptism were from heaven, it testified the Messianic authority of Jesus; he asks, therefore, what they say of it. They feel the force of this, and are sensible that if they admit John's baptism to be of God, Jesus will have a conclusive answer to their question (ver. 25). They really do not believe John's divine mission; but they are afraid openly to call it in question, and so are shut up to the humiliating acknowledgment that they cannot decide the point. Jesus then proceeds (vers. 28-32) to illustrate their position in reference to the mission of John by the parable of the two sons, the first of whom represents them, and the second the publican and harlots[1] who had repented at the preaching of the Baptist. Before that, it is implied, the people as a whole had failed to do the will of God, the religious leaders and their disciples professing to do so, but not really doing it, and the ungodly openly disregarding it. Many of the latter had been moved to repentance by John, and so entered the kingdom of God; but those who were now questioning Jesus had not even afterwards repented. In the next parable, which he adds immediately (vers. 33-40), the figure of the vineyard again appears, and this time it is described with such circumstances of detail as to recall the prophetic pictures of Israel as the kingdom of God (Isa. v. 1-7), and the complaints made of old of the absence of fruit such as God looked for. Even when Israel was most diligent and zealous in outward worship and offerings, the prophets had declared it to be unfruitful in true righteousness, and called for that,

[1] I follow the reading of Westcott and Hort, which seems on the whole the most probable.

as the Baptist also had done; but for that they had been opposed, and persecuted, and slain by the rulers of the people. At last the husbandman sends his son; but they treat him in the same way, and even hope, by getting rid of him, the heir, to secure the vineyard to themselves. Even such was the conduct of the priests and elders. They resented Jesus' claim to exercise authority in his Father's house, and desired to have it for their own; " our place and our nation," they say (John xi. 48). By a judgment extorted from their own mouth (Matt. xxi. 41), the kingdom of heaven is to be taken from them and given to a nation producing its fruits. This can denote no others but those who, like the publicans and harlots, repented at the preaching of John, or of Jesus himself. He reminds them, by a quotation from a psalm (ver. 42), that it has happened before that one rejected and despised by the authorities has become the head of God's house: so the son in the parable, though cast out and killed, may yet be exalted to reign.

But Jesus goes on to give yet another parable (xxii. 1-14) to show that in rejecting the Baptist and himself, they are not only refusing to do the work to which God calls them, but, turning away from the great blessing that he is offering, the very kingdom for which they profess to have been looking. The kingdom is now represented as the marriage feast of the king's son, and the guests seem to be pictured as refusing, because they do not believe it is ready, but at bottom because they do not care for it. Could anything be a truer or more seasonable picture of the Jews' conduct? They would not believe that the long-expected reign of God was come, because they saw no outward signs of it; because, being carnal, they could not see that kingdom which is righteousness, and peace, and joy in the Holy Spirit. Some of them simply disbelieved, and went on with their worldly occupations; some seized and killed those who persisted in saying that the kingdom was come. They are justly destroyed, and others brought in to the supper. No question will be raised as to their previous character or origin; only they must come in wedding garments, *i.e.* appreciating the feast and honouring the king's son.

Thus all these parables, rising naturally one from the other, bring out Jesus' claim, and virtually appeal to all the prophets as well as to John. They show, in a way the hearers could not mistake, that he declared that the reign of God was come, and men called to enjoy its blessings and to obey its laws. To this point, too, the next question of the Pharisees and Herodians is directed (vers. 15-17). They will not believe that this can be the reign of God, and therefore they do not scruple to take advantage of Jesus' open declaration to ensnare him in a statement which the jealous Roman procurator must resent as treasonable. "If the reign of God is come, can it be right to pay tribute to Cæsar?" But this only gives Jesus the opportunity of showing by another touch how far the reign of God is from being an earthly one, such as they looked for. The duty of rendering to God the things that are God's, the work and fruits of the vineyard that he looks for, does not exclude, but includes that of rendering to all their due, and therefore to Cæsar the things that are Cæsar's (vers. 18-22).

The question of the Sadducees which followed (vers. 23-28) had also a bearing on the matter in hand, the nature of the kingdom of God. For the Pharisees expected a resurrection of the just at the beginning of the Messianic kingdom; and the Sadducees may have thought that as Jesus opposed the Pharisees' idea of the kingdom in other points, so he would in this also. They accordingly laid before him their argument, to show that the earthly relations of life could not be reconstituted by a resurrection. Jesus' reply (vers. 29-33), affirming the resurrection, and grounding it on Scripture, at the same time showed that it was to be to a heavenly life, in which the conditions of earthly existence would not be reproduced, so that they need not look for a kingdom in this world, either with or without a resurrection. The essential blessing of the kingdom is to have Jehovah as their God; and that implies eternal life, not the restoration of earthly relationships, but life to God. Jesus thus virtually condemned the worldly views of the future blessedness as held by both Pharisees and Sadducees.

Even the following question of the lawyer about the greatest commandment (vers. 34–36) was not so remote as it might seem from the subject of this great controversy. The charge that Jesus had brought so pointedly against the Pharisees, of not rendering to God the obedience for which he looked, while yet their great concern was to observe the law, showed that there must be some radical difference between him and them in their view of the law. Naturally, therefore, one of them might raise the question, what is the great commandment in the law, and he seems to have asked it in a candid, though yet doubting spirit; and on hearing Jesus' answer he frankly recognised its truth, and gave his own consent to the preference of love to God and man above all offerings (Matt. xii. 32, 33). Most appropriately then Jesus said, "Thou art not far from the kingdom of God;" for the recognition of what the law really required would show him the truth of Jesus' representation of the Pharisees, with all their zeal for the law, as disobedient and unfruitful, and so would lead him to repentance.

Jesus then becomes himself the questioner, and shows them, by their inability to reconcile the saying in Ps. cx. 1 with their notions of the Messiah as a mere son and successor of David, that the true founder of God's kingdom is far other and greater than they expect (Matt. xxii. 41–46). Then, having thus in the course of this long controversy fully brought out the points of difference between him and the scribes and Pharisees, he turned to the people and his disciples, and solemnly warned them against their example and spirit, and uttered his sevenfold woe against their hypocrisy (xxiii. 1–36). The head and front of their offence is, that they will not enter the kingdom of heaven, nor suffer others to enter. This they have done by their perversion of the law and preference of its outward ritual parts to the inward and spiritual. They are, indeed, extremely active and zealous in making proselytes, but they lead them astray by their perverted morality when they have gained them over, and being blind leaders of the blind, both fall into the ditch. From such teachers men can learn only to save outward appearances, but nought of that purity of heart without which none can see God. They profess, indeed, to honour the prophets whom their fathers slew; but really they are acting in the very way and spirit of those who killed the prophets, and soon they shall actually be doing like deeds. They are filling up the measure of their fathers' guilt, and soon the inevitable retribution for all the righteous blood shed on the earth shall come on them. The stern denunciation passes into the tender and touching lamentation, which is a last appeal to Jerusalem, and which, in finally leaving them, still gives some hope of their yet becoming willing to welcome him as coming in the name of the Lord (xxiii. 37–39).

Note N, p. 165.—Jesus' Teaching as to His Coming Again.

It seems evident from the Gospels that Jesus spoke of his coming again in two different ways, sometimes as a spiritual manifestation of his power as the founder of the kingdom of God, and sometimes as a visible appearance in person to judge the world. The former is more spoken of in the discourses contained in the fourth Gospel, and the latter in those reported by the Synoptists; but this distinction is not absolute. John's Gospel contains sayings of Jesus pointing to a personal advent at the last day (vi. 39, 40, xiv. 3, xxi. 22, 23), though there are more frequent and fuller statements about his coming by the Spirit, the Comforter, to manifest himself to his disciples. In the synoptic Gospels, on the other hand, while the advent of which Jesus speaks is generally the personal coming in glory, yet in some places, such as Matt. xxvi. 64, he refers to the establishment of his kingdom by the power of his spirit. There seems therefore no reason to doubt that Jesus spoke both of a spiritual coming that was to be immediate, and of a personal appearing at the end of the world. It is not always easy to determine which is meant in particular sayings; and it is not impossible that the evangelists in reporting our Lord's discourses may have sometimes failed to observe the distinction, and made some of his words about his coming by the spirit appear as if they referred to his personal appearance in glory, which was more thought of in that age. This at least seems the least violent solution of the difficulty presented by our Lord's prophetic discourse in Matt. xxiv., in which his advent to judgment seems to be predicted as immediately to follow the fall of Jerusalem, and to occur within the lifetime of that generation. All attempts to make the words as they stand consistent with the lapse of ages before the latter event do violence to εὐθέως, ver. 29, and give an unnatural meaning to γενεά or to γένηται, ver. 34. Nor is it possible to separate the two events spoken of in the discourse so as to make the saying, "This generation shall not pass away till all these things be accomplished" (ver. 34), apply only to the destruction of Jerusalem (vers. 15–28), and not to the coming of the Son of man (vers. 29–31). On the other hand, although it is noticeable that nearly all the images in these verses (29–31) are taken directly from Old Testament passages which do not refer to a personal coming of Messiah or literal convulsions of nature,[1] yet an interpretation which regards all these things here as figurative descriptions of the triumph of the gospel, cannot be held to be fair or satisfactory. The attempt to explain the apparent juxtaposition of events widely distant in time on the principle of what has been called the perspective of prophecy, does not succeed in giving a very clear or intelligible explanation of the discourse, or in accounting for the very definite and precise words in which the nearness of the

---

[1] See Isa. xiii. 10; Joel ii. 30, 31; Dan. vii. 13; Isa. xxvii. 13.

coming of Christ is announced. Neander says with reason: "If Christ had been but a prophet, we might indeed suppose that the image of the glorious future which unveiled itself to his seeing glance in moments of inspiration, was involuntarily blended in his mind with the realities of the present; and that events, separated by long intervals of time, presented themselves as closely joined together. . . . In Christ, however, we can recognise no blending of truth with error, no alloy of the truth as it appeared to his own mind. . . . But it is easy to explain how points of time which he kept apart, although he presented them as counterparts of each other, without assigning any express duration to either, were blended together in the apprehension of his hearers, or in their subsequent repetitions of his language."[1] Substantially the same is Meyer's view;[2] and though not at all free from difficulties, yet on the whole it seems the least objectionable explanation of a very difficult passage. The same principle may be applicable also to Matt. x. 23 and xvi. 28; but it does not seem impossible to understand the latter of these passages just as it stands of the spiritual coming of Christ. Weiss indeed holds that the sayings that indicate a near advent must be regarded as genuine utterances of Jesus, and endeavours to explain the fact that this has not taken place by means of the special character and limitations of prophetic revelation.[3] Now Jesus indeed expressly said, in that very discourse, that the day and hour of his second coming were known to the Father alone, and not to the angels, nor even to himself, the Son. We accept these words in their natural sense, as expressing a real limitation of his knowledge during his state of humiliation; but to suppose that while fully conscious of his ignorance he made a positive statement as to the time of his coming, which proved to be entirely wrong, is hardly consistent with his perfect truthfulness and moral purity.

[1] *Life of Christ*, p. 407. [2] On Matt. xxiv. note 3.
[3] *Leben Jesu*, ii. 480—4.

Note O, p. 188.—The Notion of the City of God.

The final consummation is depicted in the Apocalypse under the image of the city of God, the new Jerusalem. This idea of the city of God seems to have arisen after the return of the Jews from the Babylonian captivity, when under the Persian Empire Israel was no longer an independent nation or kingdom of God, but Jerusalem as a city had a municipal government by its own law and its own officials. Even earlier, indeed, the hopes of deliverance are specially centred in Zion, as the dwelling-place of God, in the prophecies of Isaiah, and the psalms composed after the deliverance from Sennacherib (xlvi.-xlviii., etc.); and the post-exilian people were not so much attached to the land of Israel as to the city of Jerusalem: it was the peace of Jerusalem for which they prayed, the good of Jerusalem they desired to see; and so the hopes of the future assumed the form of a city of God instead of or along with the older form of the kingdom of God.

As a form of society, a city differs from a country or kingdom in this, that it is a closer association, since its members live near each other, have habitual daily intercourse, and a more manifest unity of interests than those who only form a nation inhabiting a wide region of varying character. Hence political institutions, as the very term indicates, first grew up in cities, and in the ancient world always reached their fullest development there. On the other hand, the social community in a city must be smaller than in a kingdom or empire; and where, as in the case of Athens and other Greek cities, the importance of the city greatly preponderated over that of the land, those dwelling beyond its walls could only partially share in the privileges of citizens. Still, in the Athenian hegemony, and still more in the Roman Empire, the idea was introduced of a city being a common home and fatherland for a people much larger than its walls could contain. So the Jerusalem of the second temple was the capital not only of Judea, which was but a tributary province of the Persian Empire, but of all Israel dispersed through that empire, but still subject in religious matters, and in many secular things as well, to the Jewish authorities at Jerusalem. Hence in many of the later prophecies, the exaltation of Jerusalem over all rival and opposing powers is presented as the great object of faith and hope. Clearly the danger in the substitution of the city for the kingdom of God is that it might lead to the idea of exclusive privileges for a few, who should rule over the others, as Athens did over her allied States; and the prophetic pictures of the glories of the city of God counteract this by dwelling on the equal rights and blessings of all nations as citizens of Zion (Ps. lxxxvii.).

Our Lord recognises the peculiar position that Jerusalem had come to hold when he calls it "the city of the great king" (Matt. v. 35), and speaks of all Israelites as its children (Matt. xxiii. 37); but while he foretells the desolation of the earthly Jerusalem and the coming of the kingdom of God with power, he speaks of the final blessedness of his people, not under the image of a new city of God, but under the still more gracious and endearing one of the house of his Father.

Paul, however, has the idea of the upper (*i.e.* heavenly) Jerusalem as the city to which Christians belong, in contrast with the earthly Jerusalem which is in bondage with her children, the Jews who will still remain under law (Gal. iv. 26-31); and writing to Philippi, a Roman colony, he makes use of the same idea (Phil. i. 27, iii. 20). The idea of the city of God is largely used also in the Epistle to the Hebrews, and there the meaning of its being described as "above" or "heavenly" more clearly appears. The heavenly things are the true or real (ἀληθινά), as distinguished from the figures or shadows of them on the earth (Heb. viii. 1, x. 23, 24). They are not made with hand, *i.e.* not of this creation, but ideal and eternal. To these spiritual realities belongs the city of God, which is to come, *i.e.* to be enjoyed by us in the future, when all earthly things shall have passed away. This truth is pictorially represented in the closing chapters of Revelation. The descent of the new Jerusalem from heaven is contemporaneous with the passing away of the heaven and earth, and all things being made new; and it indicates that what had hitherto been an ideal, laid up in heaven and looked for by the faith of God's people, is at last to become real. The picture of a city gives a more concrete exhibition of the blessedness of the saints than a kingdom could afford. They are described as having direct and blessed fellowship with God amid all the elements of happiness, and the idea of limitation connected with the notion of a city is as far as possible removed by the vast size ascribed to the new Jerusalem, and by its blessings being extended to the nations without.

NOTE P, p. 196.—ON LUKE XVII. 21.

There is a question among interpreters, whether the words ἐντὸς ὑμῶν should be rendered "within you" or "among you." The former view is that of the Vulgate, Chrysostom, Erasmus, Luther, Calvin, Campbell, Olshausen; the latter is preferred by Beza, Grotius, Wolf, Bengel, Meyer, Alford, and others; while Stier and Lange combine both meanings. Though the preponderance of authority of modern scholars is in favour of the rendering "among you," yet the arguments in favour of the other rendering seem to be decidedly the stronger. These are: (1) "Within" is the proper meaning of ἐντός; while it is very doubtful whether it is ever used in the sense of among. Meyer refers to several passages of classical writers; but of these, two at least are not instances in point. Thuc. vii. 5. 3: ἐντὸς τῶν τειχῶν; Plato, *Leg.* 789 A: ἐντὸς τῶν αὐτῶν μητέρων, in both which it clearly means "within," not "among." A better instance is Xenophon, *Anab.* i. 10. 3: ὅσα ἐντὸς αὐτῶν καὶ χρήματα καὶ ἄνθρωποι ἐγένοντο πάντα ἔσωσαν; but even this is doubtful, for there is a possible construction on which it would retain its proper meaning "within" even here. But even if there is some warrant in classical Greek for the rendering "within," and that at best is slight and dubious, it is a strong presumption against it that the word is never so used in Biblical Greek, either elsewhere in the New Testament or in the LXX. The usage of language, therefore, is decidedly against this rendering. (2) The connection of the clause with what goes before points in the same direction. The statement, "Behold, the kingdom of God is among you," affords no contrast to what had been denied in the previous verse, that the kingdom of God cometh with observation. The whole force of the contrast must, on that view, rest on the present tense; but that is not made in the least emphatic, as it might have been by saying, "is already among you," if that were the point of the words. Nor, again, does the rendering "among you" enable us to do justice to the "for" with which the clause is introduced. That the kingdom of God was among our Lord's hearers, gives no direct proof that it cometh not with observation; whereas the assertion, that it is within man, affords a plain and obvious proof that its coming and progress are not to be observed by outward marks and signs.

Probably these linguistic and exegetical considerations would have been held decisive in favour of the rendering "within you," were it not for the difficulty, on the other side, that the words were addressed to the Pharisees who had not inwardly received the kingdom which Jesus proclaimed. This is thought by many to make it impossible to suppose that Jesus said "the kingdom of God is within you." But this does not neutralize the evidence from the words themselves, that this is what he did say; nor does the difficulty seem an insurmountable one. We need not suppose, as Calvin does, that "you" refers to the disciples; but we may compare it with other sayings of Christ to unbelievers: "The kingdom of God is come nigh unto you" (Luke x. 9-11); "The kingdom of God is come upon you" (Matt. xii. 18; Luke xi. 20). The kingdom of God was offered to them, and in so far as their consciences and hearts were in any degree touched by Jesus' words, it might be said to be within them; while in the case of some of his hearers, it was in them in the fuller sense. A parallel to this occurs in Deut. xxx. 14: "The word is very nigh unto thee, even in thy mouth and in thy heart," quoted in Rom. x. 8, and spoken in both cases to hearers of the word indiscriminately. Our Lord is explaining how it is that the coming of the reign of God is not discerned by outward signs, and he says it is inward, when it comes at all it is within you. Had he said "within my disciples," it would have seemed to exclude others, and to represent it as the privilege only of a select few, with which others had nothing to do. But he so speaks as to make it plain, that though not marked by outward signs, it is near and free to all.

There is another interpretation of this passage given by Elliott (*Horæ Apocalypticæ*, iv. 223, 224) which makes the whole clause not a part of Christ's words to the Pharisees and bystanders, but part of what is supposed to be said of the kingdom connected with "Lo there:" neither shall they say "Lo here" or "Lo there; for lo, the kingdom of God is within you," *i.e.* within your city or district. This is so unnatural, and produces such an ill-balanced and incomplete sentence, that it cannot be regarded as correct; and the meaning that it gives to "within you" is not clearly supported by the authorities which Elliott adduces, and even if sometimes admissible, would not be at all obvious here.

Note Q, p. 197.—Definitions of the Kingdom of God.

It may be well to consider the more outstanding definitions that have been already given of the kingdom of God, so as to justify the attempt to frame a new one; and we may begin with those of the Reformation. Luther says in his Larger Catechism: "What is the kingdom of God? Nothing else than what we learned in the Creed, that God sent his Son Jesus Christ our Lord into the world to redeem and deliver us from the power of the devil, and to bring us to himself, and to govern us as a king of righteousness, life, and salvation, against sin, death, and an evil conscience. And besides, he has given us his Holy Spirit, to apply the same to us by his holy Word, and to illumine and strengthen us, by his power, in the faith." In Calvin's Catechism it is asked, "How dost thou pray that this kingdom may come? That God would daily increase the number of believers, that he would enrich them continually with new gifts of his Spirit till he have entirely filled them; further, that he would make his truth more clear and bright for dispelling the darkness of Satan, and by advancing his righteousness abolish all iniquity. Are not all these things daily done? They are in such sort that the reign of God may be said to be begun; we pray, therefore, that it may continually grow and advance, till it shall reach its highest point, which we hope shall be at the last day, when God alone, all creatures being brought into order, shall be exalted and glorified, and so shall be all in all." The Heidelberg Catechism says: "Thy kingdom come, that is, so govern us by thy word and Spirit that we may submit ourselves unto thee always more and more, preserve and increase the Church, destroy the works of the devil, every power that exalteth itself against thee, and all wicked devices formed against thy holy Word, until the full coming of thy kingdom, when thou shalt be all in all."

The definition in the Roman Catechism includes something similar to these, though it is complicated by giving a variety of senses to the kingdom of God, and by identifying it with the external Church. It describes it as meaning, 1*st*, his general providence by which he rules and governs all things; 2*nd*, The special and particular kind of providence by which he defends and cares for godly and holy men, under which head comes the kingdom of Christ, who reigns in us through the inward virtues of faith, hope, and love, by which we are made as it were parts of the kingdom, and being in a special way subject to God, are consecrated to his worship and adoration; *3rd*, The kingdom of glory, which is simply grace perfected and completed. Then the kingdom of Christ is identified with the Church visible, and its coming includes the extension of the Church, its purification, and its final victory (*Cat. Conc. Trid.* p. iv. c. xi. § 14–23).

In the Larger Catechism of the Eastern Church it is asked, "What is the kingdom of God spoken of in the second petition of the Lord's prayer? The kingdom of grace, which, as St. Paul says, is righteousness, and peace, and joy in the Holy Ghost. Is not this kingdom come already? To some it has not yet come in its full sense; while to others it has not yet come at all, inasmuch as sin still reigns in their mortal bodies that they should obey it in the lusts thereof. How does it come? Secretly and inwardly. The kingdom of God cometh not with observation; for, behold, the kingdom of God is within you. May not the Christian ask for something further under the name of God's kingdom? He may ask for the kingdom of glory, that is, for the perfect bliss of the faithful" (Schaff, *Creeds of the Greek and Latin Churches*, p. 509).

It may be useful to compare some of the definitions of the kingdom of God given by modern writers who have made much use of the idea. This is what Maurice says in his work on the *Kingdom of Christ*: "He certainly died who, as we believed, was the Son of God and the King of Israel; he actually rose with his body, and came among us who knew him, and spake and ate with us; this is the accomplishment of the union between heaven and earth; it is no longer a word, it is a fact. And of that fact the risen Lord tells his apostles they are to go into the world and testify, nor merely to testify of it, but to adopt men into a society grounded on the accomplishment of it. In connection with that command, and as the ultimate basis of the universal society, a NAME is proclaimed in which the name that had been revealed to Abraham, and that more awful one which Moses heard in the bush, are combined and reconciled. This society is the Church, which is further described as a universal and spiritual kingdom, that kingdom which God had ever intended for men, and of which the universal kingdom then existing in the world was the formal opposite" (vol. i. p. 369, 370). But then he goes on to say, that "while this universal society, according to the historical conception of it, grew out of the Jewish family and nation, it is, according to the theological conception of it, the root of both." . . . "The gospel is the revelation or unveiling of a mystery, and that mystery is the true constitution of humanity in Christ, so that a man believes and acts a lie who does not claim for himself union with Christ" (*ib.* p. 372, 373).

The following may be gathered from *Ecce Homo:* "Christ's kingdom is a true brotherhood founded on devotion and self-sacrifice" (p. 118), and he claimed "the character first of Founder, next of Legislator, thirdly in a certain high and peculiar sense of Judge, of a new divine society" (p. 38). Much more abstract are the German definitions. Ritschl says: "The kingdom of God is the highest good guaranteed by God to the Church (*Gemeinde*) founded through his revelation in Christ; but it is meant as the highest good, only inasmuch as it at the same time stands fast as the moral ideal, to whose realization the members of the Church bind themselves one to another, through a determinate mutual mode of action" (*Unterricht in der Christlichen Religion*, § 5). This is rather a proposition about the kingdom of God than a definition; and a subsequent statement is more analogous to other descriptions, "the totality of subjects of God's kingly rule who are bound together through righteous acting" (*ib.* § 7), "from the motive of love" (§ 8). Lipsius defines it as, according to its essence, "the universal human community removing all external distinctions of men as unimportant for their religious and moral destination, which, founded in God's fatherly love, and animated by God's will of love, is to embrace all mankind, and penetrate all departments of human life" (*Evangelisch-*

Protestantische Dogmatik, § 911). Kahnis says: "By it we understand the fellowship of salvation which God has founded in the old covenant, fulfilled in the new covenant, in order to perfect it in the future world" (*Lutherische Dogmatik*, p. 406).

Dr. Harris, in the series of articles in the *Bibliotheca Sacra*, above referred to (p. 348), lays down the following propositions on the subject:—1. "The divine agency is historical. 2. God's action in redemption involves the miraculous. 3. It constitutes a revelation. 4. The knowledge of God revealed through his action in redemption is a moral power in the establishment and administration of his kingdom. 5. God's action in the establishment and administration of his kingdom is continued through all generations in the Holy Spirit." The practical result to which he is led by this line of thought is expressed in the following passage: "The kingdom of heaven is organizing rather than organized. It creates for itself an organization; yet the kingdom of heaven is not the organization, but rather the life which produces it. The life which creates the organization penetrates and purifies also the family and the State, renovates individuals, and blooms and fructifies in Christian civilisations; and these also are its historical manifestations. Always the kingdom of heaven is within you. In the variously organized Churches of history, without doubt, the life has been revealed and organized. But no one has been the only and complete outgrowth and manifestation of the life. The kingdom of Christ is neither identical nor co-extensive with them." This, though not very precise as a definition, gives, I think, a more correct and scriptural conception than any of the others.

NOTE R, p. 201.—DIFFERENT VIEWS OF THE RELATION OF THE CHURCH TO THE KINGDOM OF GOD.

On the relation between the Church of Christ and the kingdom of God, very various views have been held at different times, and are entertained yet by different parties. The view which separates them most widely is one which is expressed by many of the early Fathers, and is maintained by some in the present day, the chiliastic or millenarian doctrine. According to this view, the kingdom of God is entirely a thing of the future, the theocracy to be established after the kingdoms of this world are destroyed, when Christ shall come again; while the Church is a thing of the present, and is merely the intermediate form of the community of God's people in this age before the kingdom of God has come. Baumgarten in his exposition of the Book of Acts lays great stress on this distinction. In reference to the question of the disciples in Acts i. 7, he says that it is not, as generally thought, a sign of their misunderstanding, but rather of their right understanding of our Lord's words; that they knew nothing of the arts of modern exegesis, by which the promises of the kingdom and the people are resolved into a realm of the spirit and a congregation of saints; and that Jesus virtually confirmed the assumption that an outward kingdom was to be restored to Israel (*Apostelgeschichte*, i. p. 16, 17). The kingdom of God is the outward manifestation of his sovereignty over a holy people on earth; it can only be erected by Christ himself in Israel as the chosen and prepared people; during the time of Israel's unbelief, the divine community assumes a form that has no appearance of a kingdom; and the Church is this domestic or patriarchal form which it bears, till a complete form of it, embracing national and civil society, is established (*ib.* iii. p. 75–83). So also Auberlen, in his work on Daniel and Revelation, contends that the Messianic kingdom, predicted in Dan. ii. and vii., is not that which Christ set up at his first coming, but that which is to be set up at his second advent, when the kingdoms of the world are to be destroyed, and Christ's kingdom is to be no longer one not of this world, but external and visible. Views more or less similar to this are also expressed by Delitzsch, Kurtz, Hofmann, and in general that school of modern German students of prophecy who have followed Bengel, and regard him as having done great service to the Church by freeing Chiliasm from the stigma of heterodoxy formerly attached to it.[1] Similar are the opinions of English pre-millennialists, who hold that the kingdom of Christ is a thing of the future, to be established at his second coming.

This view of the kingdom of God is indeed consistent with some of the passages that speak of it, as, for instance, those that speak of men entering, or inheriting, or obtaining the kingdom. Many of these are interpreted by Meyer as referring to the coming of Christ in glory. But the only passage that seems directly to suggest it is the parable of the Pounds (Luke xix. 11-17), which the Lord is declared to have spoken to remove the idea that the kingdom of God should immediately appear, and in which the household left by the nobleman to use the pounds given them, seems to be distinguished from the kingdom which he has received on his return. But it is to be observed that the evangelist expressly describes the error that the parable was designed to meet as having reference not to the existence, but to the appearance of the kingdom of God; and that the parable cannot be pressed beyond this, appears from the many places in which Jesus declared that in his ministry the kingdom of God was at hand, was come upon them, was being violently seized, was within or among them; and from the repeated and explicit declarations of the apostles, that in the exaltation of Jesus God had made him king. For the rest, the view of the kingdom as purely future and millennial rests on a too literal interpretation of certain Old Testament prophecies, and fails to recognise that the kingdom of God foretold by the prophets was fulfilled when Christ came in the flesh. That there is to be a manifestation of it in outward power and open dominion in all the spheres of human life which will be very different from anything as yet seen, is highly probable; but that even its highest perfection stands

---

[1] See Auberlen, *Daniel and Revelation*, p. 216-239, 373, 374.

in organic connection with its present power, seems clearly taught by the parables of the Mustard Seed and Leaven, and is the only thing that can reconcile the various sayings of Jesus.

Diametrically opposed to this view, which entirely disjoins the Church and the kingdom of God, is that which identifies them. This has been very frequently held, and indeed is often tacitly assumed as a matter of course. This identification, however, takes different forms, according to the different views held as to what the Church is. To the Roman Catholic, the Church which he makes the kingdom of God is the external society organized under the government of the hierarchy, and the kingdom of God is therefore in his view a corporate body, as easily discernible as any earthly State, only differing from them in not being limited to any country, and having for its functions certain religious exercises. In this society the will of God is infallibly made known through its officers, and enforced by its discipline; and the blessings of forgiveness, peace, joy, and hope are bestowed through its ordinances. Now, about the kingdom of God there is in Scripture hardly any statement that even seems to point to any such conception; and it rests almost entirely on the identification of the Church with the kingdom. There are, indeed, many places in which the Church is spoken of as an external society; but if it were not identified with the kingdom of God, few if any of these would even appear to ascribe to it the power of bestowing or possessing all saving blessings, as the Roman Catholic doctrine holds.

The Reformers, following those who in earlier times had protested against the external view of the kingdom of God, met it by the distinction between the Church invisible and visible. They did not question the identification of the Church with the kingdom; only they said we must distinguish between the real and the seeming. The true Church, or body of Christ, or kingdom of God, is the company of believers, who are known only to God, and cannot be certainly distinguished by men, and therefore is called invisible: those who profess and seem to be believers constitute the Church, or body of Christ, or kingdom of God, as it appears to men, and is therefore called visible. Thus the Church is still identified with the kingdom of God, only both are now viewed in a twofold aspect, as in one respect visible, in another invisible. Now, it is undoubtedly true that this distinction between real and seeming does apply to both the Church and the kingdom of God, as indeed it does to many other things. For, as Jonathan Edwards[1] clearly points out, there is the same twofold way of using all the names by which the followers of Christ are described, believers, saints, disciples, Christians. But it does not follow that all these are exactly synonymous, that faith is the same thing as holiness, or constitutes the whole of Christianity. All these, indeed, characterize the same persons, but not necessarily in the same respect or at the same time. So those who are members of Christ's Church are also members of the kingdom of God; but that does not imply that the two notions are exactly the same, or describe them in the same respect. The very fact of the two names being both used in Scripture, and used in very different ways, seems to show that they are not exactly the same, or to be so readily substituted for one another as has been commonly done. Hence the most accurate modern theologians recognise that they ought to be distinguished, though they are not at one as to the precise way in which this is to be done.

Some think that the notion of the invisible Church, as held by Protestant theologians, does not correspond to the language of Scripture; that the Church spoken of by Christ and his apostles is always a recognisable community of men, and what Protestants mean by the Church invisible is what in the New Testament is called the kingdom of God. This view is distinctly expressed by Ebrard and Lipsius. The former says: "The *multitudo electorum* forms no *cœtus*, no *ecclesia*,

[1] *Qualifications for Communion*, Part II. § 1.

for an unconnected multitude of individuals that are indeed inwardly each for himself united to Christ, but can mutually recognise each other as truly believers only in the smallest part and only occasionally, and even then not with absolute certainty, are no קהל, no *ecclesia*, no organized gathering fellowship, nor gathered community.... An invisible Church is even in itself a *contradictio in adjecto*.... We must therefore reject this use of *eccles. invis.* What is meant to be designated by it is no Church, but the kingdom of God as yet invisible, but in future to be visibly erected."[1] This reasoning assumes that it is an essential element in the idea of the Church of Christ that it be an organized body. Its organization does not, in Ebrard's view, require a hierarchical system, as the Church of Rome holds, but is of the most elementary kind, a distinction between some as ministers from the others to whom they minister. But is organization, even in this elementary form, an essential attribute of the Church spoken of by Christ and his disciples? It is not involved in the name; it is not laid down as a fundamental principle; and if it be said that it is implied in the description of the Church as a body having many members, it is to be observed that the body is described as made one by the working of the Spirit (1 Cor. xii. 2, 12, 13; Eph. iv. 4, 16), so that the organization symbolized by these images belongs to the body of true believers, and not merely to the outward community of professing believers. It is not so impossible for true Christians to recognise one another as Ebrard seems to think. They are commanded to do so by their profession of faith in the observance of the ordinances of Christian worship; and though the community of those who do so is not co-extensive with the body of true believers in Christ, yet it is not to be separated from that as a different body under a different name. It does not therefore seem either necessary or possible to reject the distinction of the Church invisible

---

[1] *Christliche Dogmatik*, § 481; cf. Lipsius, *Evangelisch Prot. Dogmatik*, § 880–2.

and visible. Unless we go back to the Roman Catholic idea that Christ instituted an organized hierarchy, beginning with the apostles and forming the groundwork of an external society, we must hold that he instituted his Church simply by commanding his disciples to gather together in his name. But he never commanded hypocrites and unbelievers to join with them, though he did not give men power to prevent them doing so. Thus he did not institute a Church of mere professors, but a Church of believers, really though imperfectly represented by the visible Church of professors. If the visible Church does not rest on a hierarchical organization, it must rest on the true Church, which is invisible, and to which Christ's commands are really addressed. It may be, and probably is true, that Protestants have often been led, by their antagonism to the external and sacerdotal doctrines of the Church of Rome to give too exclusive prominence to the Church invisible, and attach too little importance to the Church visible, and lower their ideas of the unity, purity, and catholicity that should belong to it; but this is not to be remedied by giving up the idea of the Church invisible. Nay, it is just by emphasizing the truth that the visible Church is not a separate and independent body, but the manifestation of the invisible, that we shall best enforce the duty of using every effort to make the real conform to the ideal of the Church which is Christ's body.

More scriptural than any of the distinctions between the Church and the kingdom of God yet mentioned, is that which regards the Church as the preparation and auxiliary to the kingdom. So Dräseke[1] describes the Church, which he understands in the sense of the Augsburg Confession, as the workshop of the kingdom of God; and he unfolds what he means by this in four particulars. The Church testifies of the kingdom, dispenses its blessings, collects its members, and represents (*veranschaulicht*) its heavenly form. These are the functions of Christ's professing followers, in the use of

[1] *Vom Reiche Gottes*, ii. 323 foll.

the means of grace, the preaching of the word and observance of the sacraments; and in these ways it may be said that the Church works at the realization of the kingdom of God. Oosterzee[1] takes a similar view, but takes into account the twofold aspect of the Church. The Church visible is the training school of the kingdom, while the Church invisible is the germ of the kingdom. This seems to be in accordance with the representations of our Lord; and it brings the two ideas into more close and living connection with each other. Meyer[2] thinks that in Matt. xvi. 18, 19 the relation indicated between the two is that the Church is a preparatory institution, which is to be transformed into the kingdom of heaven at Christ's second coming; but he interprets most of our Lord's sayings about the kingdom in the millenarian sense of its being future. Weiss[3] recognises in the teaching of Jesus the announcement that the kingdom of God was already present, not only in his person as the king, but in his disciples. The society into which Christ formed them was designed to be a preparation for the future perfection of the kingdom, but it is never itself called the kingdom.

The distinction indicated by these writers seems to be true and well founded, but we can hardly rest satisfied without going somewhat deeper. If the Church be merely distinguished as the preparation or training school for the kingdom of God, and placed in no other connection with it, then we should be led to regard the kingdom as to be established suddenly by some supernatural process, and so brought back to the chiliastic view of the relation. Somewhat akin to this is the view of Kahnis,[4] that the Church is an æon of the kingdom of God, that which extends from the ascension of Christ to his second advent. Oosterzee avoids this by saying that the Church is the germ of the kingdom; but that is a figurative expression, and we must seek to understand what it signifies. There must be some difference beyond the mere temporal or relative

---

[1] *Christian Dogmatics,* § cxxix.
[2] *Com. in loc.*
[3] *Bibl. Theol.* § 14.
[4] *Lutherische Dogmatik.*

one, a difference in the functions or exercises of the Church and the kingdom of God; for so far as they are viewed spiritually, there is no difference in the persons of whom they are composed. The members of the Church invisible are believers in Jesus; and they form the kingdom of God, and enjoy its blessings. But there is a difference in the kind of society which they form, when viewed as the Church and as the kingdom of God. This difference is described by Ritschl[1] as consisting in this, that the Church is a religious idea, and the kingdom of God a moral one. The Church is a society in which believers in Jesus are called to unite for the purpose of common worship of God in his name; but the kingdom of God has for its end the fulfilment of his will in the moral law, which embraces not only the religious functions of worship, but all the duties of man in all his relations. The same distinction in substance is made by Julius Müller, when he says that "the State, science, art belong to the kingdom of God, but do not fall within the limits of the Church, which is an organized community for the manifestation and culture of religious life."[2] This may seem to be a narrow conception of the Church, but when we look at the matter carefully it is that to which we are led by the representations of the New Testament, and which is really implied in all the Protestant descriptions of it.

The most generally accepted Protestant definitions of the Church imply this as its essential character. The Lutheran and Anglican Churches define it as a company of faithful men in which the gospel is preached and the sacraments administered, thus describing it by functions that are properly acts of religious worship. So the Westminster Standards define the visible Church as consisting of all those that profess the true religion, and that profession is made in acts of religious worship. This is distinctly brought out by Amesius, who says that the acts of profession by which the visible Church is distinguished are those in which its members present

---

[1] *Unterricht in der Christlichen Religion*, § 9.
[2] *Dogmatische Abhandlungen*, p. 309, 310.

themselves to God to receive spiritual blessings in Christ, and to give glory to him.[1] In like manner Owen[2] makes the visible Church to be essentially an assembly for common worship.

The duties which Jesus enjoined on his disciples, and for which he bade them unite in a social body, were religious in their nature, proclaiming the glad tidings about him, baptizing, teaching, praying together, observing the Lord's Supper. Their duties as members of the kingdom of God were more comprehensive, and were to be discharged by them individually as each directly responsible to his master. They were united as a company for common worship and what pertained to that. Their worship, however, was to be a moral and spiritual service, including the presenting of their bodies as a living sacrifice, and doing good and communicating, as well as the sacrifice of praise; hence their Church activity included the care for the poor and the admonishing of moral offenders.

NOTE S, p. 230.—THE DOCTRINE OF THE ATONEMENT IMPLIED IN THE KINGDOM OF GOD.

While I have argued that Ritschl's doctrine of Christ's work as founding the Church, which is the religious community aiming at the realization of the kingdom of God, implies, if thoroughly carried out, the essential point in the Catholic doctrine of the atonement, I do not mean to assert that it would lead him to the exact position of Lutheran and Reformed orthodoxy, as maintaining the theory of satisfaction to divine justice strictly so called. He would only be in the position of Hofmann, with whom, even as it is, he expresses much sympathy. But though his orthodox opponents did not think so, I believe that Hofmann maintained in substance the essential truth of Christ being our substitute and representative, while he denied, as Ritschl also does, the judicial character of God's

---

[1] *Theologiæ Medulla*, Lib. I. c. xxxi. § 29.
[2] *On Evangelical Churches.*

dealings with him and with mankind in general. I may be permitted to refer here to two articles in the *British and Foreign Evangelical Review* (Jan. and April 1865), in which I gave reasons for this view of Hofmann's position.

We must distinguish the Catholic faith on this subject, *i.e.* what has been held by the great mass of Christians in all ages, from the more precise theories that have been adopted by various theologians, such as the juridical, the governmental, the mystical, the sympathetic, with their various modifications and combinations. Many who deny that juridical theory, which seems to me as it did to the Reformers and the Protestant Churches the most adequate and scriptural, do not deny what alone can be called the Catholic faith of the Church of Christ, that the sufferings and death of Christ are the objective ground of our forgiveness and salvation. Even in regard to the more articulate doctrine of satisfaction to divine justice, a better understanding than has generally prevailed would not perhaps be unattainable if men had clear notions of each other's meaning, and would not take up extreme positions. But it is only the general doctrine of redemption by Christ, as distinct from mere teaching, example, and suasion, that 1 contend to be implied in the Christian idea of the kingdom of God.

NOTE T, p. 236.—THE KINGDOM OF GOD IN THE EARLY FATHERS.

In post-apostolic times the idea of the kingdom of God continues to find a prominent place in the thoughts of Christians; and as already in the apostolic Epistles, it is chiefly viewed as a thing of the future. One of the earliest witnesses to this is Hegesippus, who, in his account of the martyrdom of James (Eus. *H. E.* ii. 23), describes him as testifying of Jesus as the Son of man sitting in heaven on the right hand of the great power, and about to come in the clouds of heaven. He also relates that the grandsons of Judas the Lord's brother were brought before Domitian as being descendants of David, and interrogated about Christ and his kingdom, of what sort it was, and when and where to appear; whereupon they replied, that it is not worldly nor on the earth, but heavenly and angelic, to be at the end of the age, when coming in glory he shall judge the quick and the dead, and render to each according to their deeds (Eus. *H. E.* iii. 20).

In Clement's 1st Epistle to the Corinthians the kingdom of God or of Christ is spoken of as future (c. 42, 50); but at the same time the Christian community on earth is described as a πολιτεία (c. 2), and the conduct of Christians in it as πολιτεύεσθαι (c. 3, 20); and along with this Pauline expression he also uses the figure of the body and its various members, as the basis of his exhortations to unity and peace. Here, therefore, we see that the expectation of the kingdom of God in the future was not entirely disjoined from the present privileges and blessings of believers.

In the so-called 2nd Epistle of Clement the kingdom of God is more frequently spoken of, and always as future (c. 5, 6, 9, 12); and in the last of these places the time of its appearance is described by a mystical saying ascribed to Christ, pointing apparently to the consummation of all things.

In the Epistle of Barnabas the view of the kingdom of God as future appears in connection with that of the millennium as the world's Sabbath (c. 7, 15, 11), which, however, he does not conceive in any gross or carnal way, as was done by Papias and others, who spoke of outward and earthly enjoyments in the thousand years' reign of Christ and his saints on earth.

In Polycarp's Epistle to the Philippians there occurs a passage where, with an allusion to Paul's Epistles to the Philippians and to Timothy, both the present situation of Christians is described as a commonwealth, and the future reign is referred to; c. v.: "If we are pleasing to the Lord in this world, we shall receive also the world to come, as he has promised to raise us from the dead; and if we behave as citizens worthily of him, we shall also reign with him." Then follows a quotation from 1 Cor. vi. 9, 10, mentioning the kingdom of God. In the account of the martyrdom of Polycarp, his noble saying is recorded when asked to revile Christ: "Eighty and six years have I served him, and he has not injured me at all, and how can I revile my king, who saved me?"

In the Ignatian Epistles the kingdom of God is twice mentioned, both times as future, the apostolic warning, "they shall not inherit the kingdom of God," being applied to teachers of false doctrine (*ad Eph.* xvi.) and to those who cause divisions in the unity of the Church (*ad Philad.* iii.).

In the *Shepherd* of Hermas there is frequent mention of the kingdom of God, especially in the 9th Similitude, and there it seems to be identified with the Church, which is represented as a tower built up upon a great white rock, which is the Son of God. This rock is ancient, indicating the eternal pre-existence of the Son of God; but it has a door newly cut in it, which symbolizes the incarnation, and through this door all the stones are brought in that are to be built up on the rock. Their being brought in thus is spoken of as entering in to God, and entering into the kingdom of God, as if these expressions were synonymous; and that is said to be effected by a new birth, which is connected with baptism, in which they die to their old life, and begin to live anew to God. In the imagery of the tower, which is represented somewhat differently in this parable and in an earlier vision (*Vis.* iii.), there appears a consciousness of the distinction between the ideal and the empirical, the invisible and the visible Church, though it is but obscure and somewhat confused. In its ultimate form the Church is described as a tower so perfectly built together, that no joinings of the stones can be seen, but all seem to be of one piece with one another and with the rock on which they are built. This is explained as meaning that they who believe in the Lord through his Son, and put on the spirits of the Christian virtues, are one spirit and one body, and have one colour of their garments (*Sim.* vii. 13). It is this Church that is identified with the kingdom of God, and thus we find here a recognition, not only of that kingdom as the final and future realization of Christ's work of salvation, but also as in a true sense already present in its vital principle and power. Certainly the Church, of which Hermas has so much to say, is not the hierarchical organism of bishops, priests, and deacons, against which he makes an earnest protest, but the company of believers in Christ, which he desires to see purified from worldly conformity, timidity, selfishness, and faction, even more earnestly than from false doctrine.

NOTE U, p. 246.—AUGUSTINE ON THE CITY OF GOD.

Augustine's great work, *de Civitate Dei*, is designed to defend Christianity against the pagans who preferred their false gods to the true, and ascribed the calamities that had come on the empire, and especially the recent capture and sack of Rome by the Goths under Alaric, to the disuse of sacrifices since the establishment of Christianity. He begins by pointing out how the barbarians, contrary to all former usages of war, had spared Christian sanctuaries and those who took refuge in them, many of whom were heathens, and he explains how both the sufferings and the alleviations of the troublous time came alike on the evil and the good (*Lib.* i.). Then he enters on his main argument, and proceeds to show, as the first part of it, how many and great evils the Romans suffered before Christianity appeared, and while the pagan gods were alone worshipped. In the 2nd book he exhibits the moral evils that prevailed, and were fostered by the supposed requirements of the gods and their worship; and in the 3rd, of the natural evils and calamities of those times. Then, in book iv., he inquires whether the wide extent and long duration of the Roman Empire is to be ascribed to the pagan gods, first raising the question whether a great empire is really a good, and showing that without justice it is nothing but a successful robbery, and then proving, from the multiplicity of the Pagan deities, and the subdivision of the offices ascribed to them, that the Roman Empire could not be due to them. In the next book he refutes the view that attributed the rise of that empire to fate; and concludes that it must be ascribed to the one true God, who is supreme over all. He then inquires, for what reason God gave such success and power to the Romans; and he answers this question by referring to the testimonies of Sallust and other writers of the virtues of the Romans in early times, their love of their country, of liberty, and of honour. These he regards as both the natural and moral causes of their greatness. He brings out, especially by quotations from Virgil and other writers, that these were their highest motives; and argues, that though the love of praise is not a virtue, but rather a sin, yet it tends to restrain vices, and so produce a certain kind of morality. This is the ground of his well-known maxim, that the virtues of the heathen are but fair sins, because they proceed from no higher motive than love of praise, and are not done out of love to God and desire of his approval. They cannot therefore obtain the kingdom of heaven. But God is not unjust to forget them, and he rewards them with the kingdom of this world; hence it was that the power of the Romans grew in consequence of their virtues, and fell when they became degenerate.

The next five books are occupied with a discussion against those, chiefly the philosophers, who held that the heathen gods should be worshipped, not for earthly blessings, but for heavenly. These books do not contain anything that bears on his view of the city of God, but in book xi. he comes to the 2nd part of his work, the description of the origin and progress of the two cities, the earthly and the heavenly. In his account of them we may trace the effect of the view he gave before of the Roman Empire as gaining its power and prosperity by virtue prompted by love of praise. This he traces up to self-love, and so he says that two different kinds of love produced the two cities; self-love, rising to contempt of God, produced the earthly; and love of God, rising to contempt of self, the heavenly city (xiv. 28). This is the contrast between the children of God and the world; and he goes on to illustrate it by the opposition of Cain and Abel, of Ishmael and Isaac; those after the flesh and those after the spirit. But having argued that the rule over the world exercised by the Romans was a reward for virtues that were only fair sins, he is led to include in what has only a sinful origin the whole system of civil government, and in a word, to identify the State with the world as opposed to the city of God. The city of God he defines as consisting of those who live according to God, and these are they who are renewed by his Spirit and his grace (xiv. 4). This seems to be quite in agreement with the scriptural conception. Then he distinguishes two conditions of the city of God. It is a stranger in this world, not founding a State here, though it brings forth citizens in this world; but it is to reign in heaven, when its citizens are to be raised from the dead, and gathered together to reign for ever with their king (xv. 1). This probably explains why Augustine takes as the title of his work *the City of God*, not the more common biblical term *the Kingdom of God*. He wishes to describe by it the persons composing the people of God, and he conceives them as having been living in all ages of human history; hence he traces the city of God down from the creation and the fall of man; but the kingdom is that condition of the city that is still future and heavenly. The kingdom of this world still belongs to those who live not for God but for man or self in some form or other; the kingdom of God or reign of the city of God is yet to come. So far does Augustine extend the limits of the earthly city, that even the Old Testament theocracy, according to him, does not belong to the city of God, but was only a part of the earthly city separated and moulded into an image of the heavenly (xv. 2). He takes Cicero's definition of a republic, in a body of people united by agreement in law and common interest,[1] and argues, that as by Cicero's own explanation law implies justice, and there can be no real justice without true religion; there never was a Roman republic according to that definition (xix. 21). But if a people be defined as a body of rational beings united by a harmonious communion of what it loves,[2] then the definition will be true of Rome, but not less so of all other nations (xix. 24). Thus by means of his fundamental position, that there can be no true virtue without religion and the grace of God, he repels the theory of the Roman lawyers and philosophers, that the system of Roman law, making all the members of the empire fellow-citizens and defining their rights and duties (civil law), was the ideal of a reign of righteousness and peace.

In all this depreciation of the State and civil government as belonging to the earthly city, or the world, as contrasted with the city of God, or the Church, we perceive a reproduction of the ideas of Tertullian, only with more depth and acuteness. But, on the other hand, Augustine combined with this, not the ultra-spiritual Montanistic ideas of Tertullian, but the ecclesiastical notions of Cyprian, whose polemic against the Novatians he continued against the Donatists. This comes out in his discussion of the millennial reign predicted in the Apocalypse. He applies that to the whole course of the Christian ages, from the first to the second advent of Christ. During that time there is a reign of God and his saints in the midst of their enemies, distinct from that future reign in which they have perfect and eternal peace. The devil is bound, according to Christ's parable, when his captives are taken from him, *i.e.* when men are converted to Christ; and those who sit on thrones, to whom judgment is given, are the prelates of the Churches, to whom is given the power of the keys to

---

[1] "Cœtus multitudinis juris consensu et utilitatis communione sociatus."
[2] Cœtus multitudinis rationalis rerum quas diligit concordi communione sociatus.

bind and loose (xx. 9). This last point is the ominous seed of error, and though it is not enlarged on, it cannot be regarded as a mere passing remark, for it is but a striking expression of the principle for which Augustine contended in the Donatist controversy, that outward organization is essential to the unity of the Church, and purity of life is to be subordinated to that.

Augustine's view of the millennium is not the same as that of Eusebius and others, who in their first joy and exultation at the Church's deliverance from persecution, and the establishment of Christianity by Constantine, regarded this as the fulfilment of the prophecies of Scripture about the reign of God and of Christ on the earth.[1] A similar view has been held in modern times by Hengstenberg, who made the millennial kingdom consist in the political ascendancy of Christianity, and dated it from Charlemagne's coronation in 800. Augustine's idea is much more spiritual, and attaches far less importance to earthly power and prosperity than those, though it laid the foundation in theory for a system that raised the external above the spiritual. His twofold principle, that, on the one hand, the civil government belongs to the world as distinguished from and opposed to the city of God; and, on the other hand, that the divine government of the city of God is exercised through the bishops of the churches and their ecclesiastical discipline, formed the groundwork of the theory of Church and State which was carried out in the Middle Ages as the way in which the kingdom of God was to be realized. In virtue of the former idea, as the State has only secular things to deal with, and selfish motives to work upon, it is necessarily inferior to the Church, which has to do with spiritual things, and has in it the motives and powers of divine grace. If the State as thus conceived is to be subservient to the cause of God and Christ at all, as Augustine firmly held it

[1] See the discourse at the opening of the Church at Tyre, Eus. *H. E.* x. 4.

should be, it could only be so by being guided and directed by the Church; thus the kingdom of the world would become the kingdom of God. Then, in virtue of the other principle, the organ of the kingdom of God is to be found in the episcopal government of the Church; and thus the submission of the State to the Church means its obedience, not to the spiritual influences of true Christians, acting on the understanding and conscience, but to the decisions and dictates of an ecclesiastical hierarchy.

It is also to be taken into account here, that Augustine in his later years, departing from his earlier and purer view, adopted the principle that physical constraint might and should be used against those who professed false religion. To this there was some practical provocation in the fact that forcible means were first employed by some of the Donatists, the fanatical zealots called *Circumcelliones*, who without any settled occupation went about among the peasants' huts, and employed the violence they had formerly used against heathen idols at the risk of their own life, now also against what they consider apostate Churches. This violence no doubt could only be repressed by the secular power; but it is greatly to be lamented that a man like Augustine gave his countenance to the error, that the civil power should not only repress such lawless force, but use the very same force, under sanction of law, to maintain the truth. He saw indeed clearly enough, with his spiritual discernment, that outward force never could produce real faith in Christ, or sincere belief of the gospel; and he was not the man to be satisfied with a mere forced or interested confession. But he observed that the chastisements of God's providence, though they could not really change the heart or effect true repentance, yet might and did prepare men for the reception of God's grace by humbling and emptying them of self-conceit; and so he inferred that penalties threatened and inflicted by human government might have the same effect, and so be means in a subordinate way of bringing men to faith in Christ. Then, from the general principle that civil rulers ought to care for the cause of Christ, and use their power for the advancement of his kingdom, he concluded that they ought to employ outward penalties, which might prepare men for true faith in Christ. But he never went so far as to approve of any one being put to death on account of religion, though when once the use of force is allowed in principle, it is practically impossible in the long run to stop short of the extremest measures if others are found to fail. Augustine supported his view of the lawfulness of using force on behalf of religion by a literal interpretation of the saying in one of our Lord's parables : " Compel them to come in" (Luke xiv. 23); and under the influence of it he was led to give a most unnatural and impossible explanation of our Lord's solemn disclaimer before Pilate of a kingdom of this world to be supported by force, holding it to refer only to the time then present, and not to that which was future.

NOTE V, p. 295.—TOLERATION IN CONNECTION WITH ATTEMPTS TO REALIZE THE KINGDOM OF GOD.

There has been a great deal of discussion in many quarters as to who or what body of men is entitled to the credit of having first expressed the truth now generally recognised, that no man should be persecuted or subjected to civil disability on account of religion ; and many inaccurate and unfair judgments on that point are current even in the works of good writers. Professor Masson complains that Hallam's account of the rise and progress of the toleration idea in England is very unsatisfactory, and that in making Jeremy Taylor's *Liberty of Prophesying* (1647) the first substantial assertion of liberty of conscience in England, he does injustice to a score or two of preceding champions of it, and to one or two entire corporate denominations.[1] The denominations he means are the

[1] *Life of Milton*, vol. iii. p. 109.

Independents and the Baptists, to the former of whom his own statement shows that this credit does not belong; and among the latter he finds the earliest utterance in a pamphlet by Leonard Busher in 1616. But he has himself done injustice by overlooking earlier statements, such as those of Bishop Hooper,[1] and others of the first generation of the Reformers. If the question is as to general statements against persecution, these may be traced back to the dawn of the Reformation. But while it was comparatively easy to make such assertions in general, especially for those who had not the responsibility of carrying them out in practice, the matter became complicated with a number of other considerations when the actual circumstances of the Church and of society had to be taken into account. What was to be done for the preservation of public order, or for preventing the liberty of one encroaching on the rights of another; was idolatry, or blasphemy, or sedition not to be punished; or were these to be sheltered by the plea of conscience? Thus in practice the question was a complicated one, and few of those who made or would have assented to the general statement, that religion was not to be propagated by the sword, or that conscience should be left free, carried out a complete toleration when they had the power and responsibility of government. Hence nearly all the Protestant Churches that have gained power or influence over the civil authorities have been guilty more or less of persecution. No important section of them is free from this charge; not the Lutherans, nor the Anglicans, nor the Socinians, nor the Independents, any more than the Presbyterians. These last have no peculiar guilt in this matter. Indeed, Professor Masson says: "The Church of England was more tolerant than the Church of Rome, and Scottish Presbyterianism or Scottish Puritanism was more tolerant (though the reverse is usually asserted) than the Church of England prior to 1640."[2] Probably

---

[1] See *The Westminster Assembly*, by A. F. Mitchell, D.D., p. 16.
[2] *Life of Milton*, vol. iii. p. 99.

the man who first practically carried out the principle of toleration was William the Silent; and the United Provinces of Holland was the country where full liberty of conscience was earliest enjoyed, a country where a Presbyterian Church was established. There the English Independents and Baptists found shelter, and from the divines of that Church the latter may have learned the principles which they published in England.[1]

Next to William of Orange, probably Roger Williams is entitled to the credit of having consistently carried out the principle of perfect religious liberty, not only by his work, *The Bloody Tenet of Persecution* (1644), but by his institutions for the government of his colony of Rhode Island. The Independents proper neither in Old nor New England are entitled to any praise in this respect. In New England they were led, in the attempt to set up a commonwealth in which Church and State should be co-extensive, to acts of the most unjustifiable and cruel intolerance; and in the old country though they united with more extreme men under the banner of Toleration against the Presbyterians, yet when they triumphed under Cromwell, the utmost length to which they went was the toleration of those who did not contradict any of the fundamental articles, a list of which, numbering sixteen, was drawn up by the Independent ministers at the request of the Parliament in 1654. Owen's *Treatise on Toleration*, appended to his sermon preached before the Commons the day after Charles I.'s execution, is one of the most judicious and moderate pleas for it of so early a date; but he expressly refuses toleration to Roman Catholics, and is somewhat indefinite as to those who differed on more than unessential points. But the more credit is due to him for his liberal sentiments so far as they went, because he was not indifferent to the claims of truth,

---

[1] See M'Crie's *Miscellaneous Works*, p. 474, in his review of Orme's *Life of Owen*, a work to which Hallam refers as an authority on the subject, but which M'Crie shows to be very inaccurate and misleading.

and the duty of a Christian ruler to acknowledge and protect the gospel of Christ and his religion. He owes to the true Christian religion, to take care that it be preached to his people, to protect it from violence, and allow public places for its preaching, to protect also Christian Churches or societies, and to provide for the maintenance of ministers, when the Churches are not able to do so. All these duties, however, he ought to perform, not only for those who agree in all points with what he holds to be the teaching of Scripture, but for all who hold the essentials of Christianity. He is not to judge on minor points of difference among Christians; but to countenance and defend the whole body of believers in Jesus, the common interest of Christ's people. This is brought out in a very striking way in Owen's sermon on Isa. xiv. 32, preached at the opening of Cromwell's Parliament in 1656; and the same sentiments are echoed in the Protector's speech on the following day, and the sermon and speech together give a vivid idea of how the Puritans conceived and sought to realize the kingdom of God. Owen goes back to that word of Isaiah which directs the hope of Israel away from foreign political combinations, to Zion as the Lord's foundation, and the security for the ultimate triumph of his people; and interpreting that in the light of the New Testament, he holds it to denote, not any one organized Church or orthodox faith, but the common interest of all Christ's people. This is that to which God has regard in all the dealings of his providence; this, as he applies it, is what has been God's aim in all his dealings with England; this is what the rulers of England must seek to promote, if they would prosper. He indicates the various other ideals of different parties, the Presbyterians, the extreme Sectaries, the Fifth Monarchy men, in contrast with his in the following passage (*Works*, viii. 418, 419): "What is the common interest of Zion that God takes care of, that he hath founded in the days wherein we live, in the great transactions of providence that have passed over us? Say some, that such a form of Church worship and discipline be established, such a rule of doctrine confirmed, and all men whatever compelled to submit unto them; herein lies that kingdom of Christ which he takes care of, this is that which God will have founded and established, and what this power, what this rule is, we are to declare. That that discipline be eradicated, the ministers' provision destroyed, and the men of such a persuasion enthroned to rule all the rest at their pleasure, seeing that notwithstanding all their pretended reformation they are yet antichristian, say others. Some say, that a kingdom and rule be set up in our hands, to be exercised in the name and authority of Jesus Christ, taking away all law and magistracy already established, to bring forth the law of righteousness conceived in our minds, and therein to be preserved,—all uniting only in this, that a sovereignty as unto administration of the things of God is to be theirs. Say others, lastly, that the people of God be delivered from the hands of their cruel enemies, that they may serve the Lord without fear all the days of their lives in righteousness and holiness,—that notwithstanding their present differences they may live peaceably one with, or at least one by another, enjoying rule and promotion as they are fitted for employments, and as he gives promotion in whose hand it is, that godliness and the love of the Lord Jesus Christ be preserved, protected, and secured from a return of the hand of violence upon it."

He extends his view, too, beyond the limits of his own country, and urges as the two ends that public men should aim at: "(1) To preserve peace, to compose differences, to make up breaches, to avoid all occasions of divisions at home; and (2) to make up, unite, gather into one common interest the Protestant nations abroad in the world" (*ib.* p. 424). Owen had no contracted ideas of the kingdom of Christ; he went beyond the narrowness of many of the defenders of national churches. He expresses himself in various places doubtfully as to the doctrine of an external kingdom and personal reign of Christ on earth; but he asserts confidently that if such a thing is to be, it can only be after the Jews are converted and Antichrist destroyed; and he ridicules the expectation of a millennial kingdom in any one country, "be it in Germany or in England," the "Jews not called, Antichrist not destroyed, the nations of the world generally wrapt up in idolatry and false worship, little dreaming of their deliverance—will the Lord Christ leave the world in this state, and set up his kingdom here on a molehill?" (*ib.* p. 376). Similar ideas are to be found also in Thomas Goodwin's sermons, and they were those that animated the government of Cromwell. He allowed, indeed, no independence of the Church in relation to the State; he forbade and prevented the meeting of any General Assembly of the Church of Scotland in his reign; and in England the parishes were filled partly with Presbyterians and partly with Independents, approved by the "Triers;" but there was no organized government. He would honour and employ all who were truly godly, however they might differ on minor points, and he endeavoured to extend toleration as far as possible.

NOTE W, p. 330.—ON THE SYSTEM OF ALLIANCE OF CHURCH AND STATE.

The system of the alliance of Church and State, each independent in its own province, but mutually aiding each other and working together for the cause of God, while more in agreement with Scripture than any that had been attempted before, is open to criticism, both on its theoretical and on its practical side; and the respect which we in Scotland owe to it because of what it has done, as maintained in the noble struggles of our fathers, for the religion of our land, should not prevent a fair consideration of such criticism. It is not entirely free from the effects of Augustine's identification of the Church with the kingdom of God, and of the State with the world; and this has led both to some doctrinal embarrassment and to some practical mistakes.

Doctrinally it seemed to follow from identifying the Church with the kingdom of God, that if the State is not, as on the papal theory, subject to the Church, but independent of it, it must be outside the kingdom of God in its Christian sense. But as the State was not to be condemned as antichristian, as it was by the Anabaptists, but held to be truly subject to God, and capable of serving him in alliance with the Church, it was necessary to maintain the doctrine of a twofold kingdom of God, of nature and of grace, or to distinguish the kingdom of God as Creator, under which the State is, from the kingdom of Christ as Mediator, which is the Church. This again led to a further distinction between the kingdom of Christ as he is God, and his mediatorial kingdom as the God-man. This distinction was used by Beza and by the Puritan and Scottish divines to meet the argument of the Erastians, that if the civil magistrate is under law to Christ, and bound to act in subservience to his cause, he is an officer in the Church, and entitled to exercise authority in spiritual things. Taken as a whole, their reply to this argument was satisfactory enough, but the use of this distinction laid them open to a charge of tending towards Nestorianism, by dividing the kingship of Christ. They did not really do so, but the distinction they made was not a very happy one, and the purpose of it might have been better served by the more scriptural distinction between the Church and the kingdom of God. Since the kingdom of God is an ethical and not a purely religious idea, it embraces all the activities of a Christian man; and as in the exercise of other lawful callings, so also in that of civil magistracy, or political power of any kind, the Christian may and should act as a member, not merely of a State which belongs to the world, but of the kingdom of God. A Christian magistrate may be said to have a function in that kingdom; but if the Church is distinguished from it as a society properly for worship, the magistrate has no office as such in it; and the Erastian argument can be met without asserting a twofold kingdom of God or of Christ, or identifying the State with the world.

The practical effect of the want of this distinction was that Churchmen as such were led to conceive it to be their duty to undertake the management or direction of all that belonged to the kingdom of God—that is, as they rightly saw, not merely religion, but all that is needed for the doing of the will of God in all departments of social life. That in so doing they were not only actuated by pure motives, but really accomplished much good, is true, and in Scotland at least, for ages after the Reformation, there was so little truly representative political life or expression of public opinion, that there was virtually a necessity for the Church courts, which were practically the best representation of the people, taking to do with matters not properly ecclesiastical. But whatever the necessity of the times may have required, and however such men as Knox, Melville, Henderson and others were actuated by pure patriotism as well as zeal for religion, that is not an ideal or even a healthy state of a community in which Church officers and Church courts have to do the work of statesmen. Least of all in the present day can this be looked for. The qualities that fit men for guiding the Church in its proper religious functions, and the reasons for which they are properly chosen to ecclesiastical office, are not the same as those that qualify them for managing secular affairs, or even advancing the kingdom of God in that department. To mention only one matter, a knowledge of political economy is not necessary for a useful pastor and teacher in the Church, but is indispensable for a Christian statesman. If the Churches would exercise their legitimate influence in public life, it is important that they should confine their action more strictly than they have sometimes done to what directly concerns religion, and at the same time recognise that the kingdom of God is a wider object than the Christian Church or religion, and for it they are to labour, not as Churchmen, but as citizens, along with their fellow-citizens, led not necessarily by those who are their true and fit leaders in religious concerns, but by those who have the gifts for leadership in other departments of social life.

www.ingramcontent.com/pod-product-compliance
Lightning Source LLC
Chambersburg PA
CBHW051738300426
44115CB00007B/615